Aliens R Us

The Other in Science Fiction Cinema

Edited by
Ziauddin Sardar and Sean Cubitt

Pluto Press

LONDON • STERLING, VIRGINIA

First published 2002 by Pluto Press
345 Archway Road, London N6 5AA
and 22883 Quicksilver Drive,
Sterling, VA 20166–2012, USA

www.plutobooks.com

British Library Cataloguing in Publication Data
A catalogue record for this book is available from the British Library

ISBN 0 7453 1544 5 hardback
ISBN 0 7453 1539 9 paperback

Library of Congress Cataloging in Publication Data
Aliens R Us : the other in science fiction cinema / edited by Ziauddin
Sardar and Sean Cubitt.
    p. cm.
  ISBN 0–7453–1544–5 — ISBN 0–7453–1539–9 (pbk.)
  1. Science fiction films—History and criticism. I. Sardar, Ziauddin.
II. Cubitt, Sean, 1953–
  PN1995.9.S26 A45 2002
  791.43'915—dc21
                                                              2001003316

10   9   8   7   6   5   4   3   2   1

Designed and produced for Pluto Press by
Chase Publishing Services, Fortescue, Sidmouth EX10 9QG
Typeset from disk by Stanford DTP Services, Towcester
Printed in the European Union by TJ International, Padstow, England

Contents

Introduction   1
Ziauddin Sardar

1. *Delicatessen*: Eco-Apocalypse in the New French Science
   Fiction Cinema   18
   Sean Cubitt

2. Rewriting the 'American Dream': Postmodernism and
   Otherness in *Independence Day*   34
   Jan Muir

3. Displacements of Gender and Race in *Space: Above
   and Beyond*   51
   Nickianne Moody

4. *Star Trek: First Contact*: The Hybrid, the Whore and
   the Machine   74
   Christine Wertheim

5. Japanimation: Techno-Orientalism, Media Tribes and
   Rave Culture   94
   Toshiya Ueno

6. Wicked Cities: The Other in Hong Kong Science Fiction   111
   Gregory B Lee and Sunny S K Lam

7. Saying 'Yours' and 'Mine' in *Deep Space Nine*   134
   Kirk W Junker and Robert Duffy

8. False and Double Consciousness: Race, Virtual Reality
   and the Assimilation of Hong Kong Action Cinema in
   The Matrix   149
   Peter X Feng

9. Global Visions and European Perspectives   164
   Dimitris Eleftheriotis

Notes on Contributors   181
Index   184

Introduction

Ziauddin Sardar

Science fiction explores space – 'in a galaxy far, far away', *The Outer Limits*, *Space: Above and Beyond*. It projects us into imagined futures – 'Beam me up, Scottie.' Yet as a genre the space that science fiction most intimately explores is interior and human; to tell future stories it recycles the structure and tropes of ancient narrative tradition and to devise dramatic tension it deploys issues and angst that are immediately present. The fiction in science fiction is the fiction of space, outer space, and time, future time. Far from being the essential object of its concern the devices of space and time are window dressing, landscape and backdrop. The 'science' offered by science fiction is populist dissection of the psyche of Western civilisation, its history, preoccupations and project of future domination – past, present and future. Science fiction is a time machine that goes nowhere, for wherever its goes it materialises the same conjunctions of the space-time continuum: the conundrums of Western civilisation. Science fiction shows us not the plasticity but the paucity of the human imagination that has become quagmired in the scientist industrial technological, culturo-socio-psycho babble of a single civilisational paradigm. Science fiction is the fiction of mortgaged futures. As a genre it makes it harder to imagine other futures, futures not beholden to the complexes, neuroses and reflexes of Western civilisation as we know it. 'Houston, we have a problem.'

THE DYNAMICS OF SPACE AND TIME

Space and time are dimensions that give perspective on our place in the order of the universe, our origins and ends. These themes have always fascinated the human imagination, they are present in the narrative tradition of all cultures and traditions of thought. They are the basis of religious teaching, the building blocks of epistemology and philosophy as well as science. The early myths and epic sagas of many narrative traditions relate stories about shifting, transcending or disrupting space and time. In mythic tradition such stories provide lessons in the proper order and meaning of space, time and the powers and forces of the universe. Myths and sagas popularise and disseminate epistemology as well as sophisticated contemporary knowledge about the world, they hone this material to their major purpose: providing basic moral and ethical precepts. Epistemology, philosophy and science begin, in all civilisations, with the same cultural perspective on the bounded sets of relationships between space and time as that found in the narrative tradition of myths and epic sagas. Just as there are many narrative traditions, there are many distinct traditions of science apart from the dominant Western tradition: Islamic science, Indian science, Chinese science, for example.[1] These sciences do not survive only in ancient treatises in archives and museums. Increasingly, they are revitalised in current academic thought, they are repositories for critiques of Western science, they are making a comeback as ingredients of other civilisational perspectives.[2]

So the basic ingredients out of which science fiction has been fashioned exist everywhere, in different civilisations and cultures, in the past and the present. Yet science fiction, the genre as we know it, does not. Science fiction is a very particular possession of just one tradition – Western civilisation. It does not exist in India, China (leaving out the special case of Hong Kong), Indonesia or Egypt – countries with flourishing and extensive film industries.[3] Moreover, only one kind of science provides the backdrop for science fiction, while its creators, contributors and in large part its audience are drawn from the West. This particularity is not accidental. An examination of the structure, themes and dramatic devices of science fiction provides an explanation for this particular and necessary relationship. What distinguishes science fiction is a particular view of science; a scientistic view of humanity and culture; the recycling of distinctive narrative tropes and conventions of storytelling. In each case science fiction employs the particular constellations of Western thought and history and projects these Western perspectives on a pan-galactic scale. Science fiction re-inscribes Earth history, as experienced and understood by the West, across space and time.

If science is essential to science fiction, a point for debate, then the science it uses is not only Western science, it is *the* Western science that has been used to define and distinguish the West from all other civilisations. The sociologist Max Weber, in common with Marx, posed the familiar foundational question of Western epistemology: why did the Industrial Revolution happen in the West and only in the West? What separates the West from the Rest is science and its instrumental rationality. The question and its answer were not products of nineteenth-century industrial transformation, however. They were a continuation, a reformulation, of a distinction that had been in existence since the expansion of Europe in the wake of Columbus, the era that saw the first stirrings of modernity, imperialism and modern science.

As the knowledge of the world was scrutinised in the excitement of first contact, European writers quickly came to an enduring conclusion. While they acknowledged the achievements of the ancient civilisations around the world, they found the contemporary descendants of these ancients guilty of intellectual atrophy, having degenerated from science into superstition. The West was scientific, rationalist, able to progress beyond the achievements of the ancients, the non-West lacked this capacity having turned its efforts to astrology, numerology and various other superstitious notions derived from its resolute adherence to non-Christian religions. The scientific imperatives out of which science fiction develops were an exclusive preserve and perspective that became intrinsic to the self-definition of the West. Science fiction as a distinct genre of literary and dramatic expression could only be the creation of a mass industrialised technological society founded on a particular view of science. To state that proposition leads to an inevitable conclusion, it places the genre in a process of historical transmission of ideas and narrative tradition that are particular to Western civilisation.

Science fiction has deep roots in the narrative tradition of Western civilisation, but its most immediate impetus is horror, fear, disquiet and disaffection at the power of the human intellect. It begins with Mary Shelley's *Frankenstein*, who is not the monster (though that is, interestingly, the predominant popular misconception) but the scientist creator of the nameless monster, Dr Frankenstein; and up the narrative thread where alchemists, magi, witches and wizards left off. Science fiction begins by viewing science as dabbling with dark arts and all their dangers. It begins as a nightmare Gothic horror story. Mary Shelley said she conceived the story in a nightmare, it was written as her contribution to a collective challenge issued to the guests at a weekend party to produce ghost stories. Science fiction in all its guises has never shed the essential characteristic of an air of menace. In some senses the essence of the science and the futures such fiction imagines is pervasive, potential doom. Science fiction, from the outset, has been the narrative of doomsday scenarios.

The pervasive doomsday theme makes it enticing to understand science fiction as a normative genre. In an increasingly secular age a genre devoted to the great secularising force, science, provides a medium for ethical and moral speculation and argument that science itself lacks. The most conventional moral in science fiction is a belief in humane principles, value-laden precepts that have no place in science. The answer to doomsday in the dramatic structure of science fiction storytelling is usually found in human values and human instincts that can counteract the rational abstract inhumanity of machines or scientific imperatives because they have not been included in their construction or operation. This is the constant plaint of the most popular pan-galactic franchise in all science fiction: *Star Trek*. Science fiction, in so many storylines, confronts the scientific spirit of unfettered inquiry, the 'to boldly go' principle, with the cautionary and dread laden speculation that 'they know not what they do'.

Frankenstein, the foundation classic of science fiction, was published in 1818, when technological industrialism was becoming apparent. In itself, *Frankenstein* was a reworking of the Faustus legend, itself popular at the time when the spirit of modern science first became apparent, the time of Christopher Marlowe's version, and again in the time of the Romantic reaction to pure rationalism, the Goethe version. The tragedy of Faustus is contained in the vital character flaw of the archetypal scientist: arrogance. The need to know, control and command the forces of the universe is what drives Faustus, a need founded on arrogant confidence in the capabilities of his own intellect. This leads inevitably to the Faustian bargain, the pact with the Devil that unlocks all the mysteries the scientist himself could not resolve. The inspiration for *Frankenstein* can be found in Milton's *Paradise Lost*. Lucifer's crime is also arrogance, the desire to command and control. To know is more important than to abide by ethical restraint, therefore science exists beyond the outer limits of ethical and moral propriety. Faustus is the morality tale of what you get when you venture beyond the space-time continuum of a circumscribed vision of human existence bounded by moral and ethical restraint. To see these principles prefigured in the fall of Lucifer and the temptation of humanity makes the moral cosmic and fundamental within the Western Christian worldview. Faustus is the prototype for all the mad scientists who inhabit the domain of science fiction. In which case, what science fiction is really telling us is that there is a deep tension within the formation of scientific, industrialised technological society, an unresolved disquiet about ends and means, an unending tussle over the formation of the project of science itself.

There is an argument in any analysis and critique of science fiction that concerns how important science actually is to the genre. A great deal of science fiction deals with the surface improbability drives of delight and fascination for the unlikely innovations science could some day, somewhere construct. Even when this fascination is both serious and thoughtful it is and is not to the point: it is indicative of and irrelevant to what makes science fiction work. The dramatic tension in science fiction is complex, more complex than the gadgetry it imagines. It is not a Luddites' fiction intent on demolishing the veneration of gadgetry, however apocalyptic its cautionary tales and morality plays.

Science fiction is both afraid of science and in love with science. It is precisely this duality that makes science fiction such an apposite genre for the literary and dramatic exploration of the Western psyche. At the end of the dramatic tale, doomsday is averted by rescuing both humanity and science to live and fight another day. What keeps science fiction alive as a genre is the impossibility of conceiving of any resolution of the tensions it exploits to fashion its stories. Science is the best of humanity's creations and can bring out the worst in us. Science fiction is a Manichean genre forever caught in the inescapable relation of the light and the dark and their dual necessity. It endlessly explores the idea of good science and bad scientists, the possibility of bad science in the hands of bad scientists against the backdrop of good science and good scientists working to create a future idyll for humanity. That good people make bad science is not its trope at all. Villainy and evil are not within, intrinsic in science, they are *dei ex machina*, external elements that enter to disturb the equilibrium, external elements that unlock doomsday and thereby permit the definition of the redemptive and normative view of science and humanity. And that's why science fiction needs aliens.

WHERE DO ALIENS COME FROM?

Alien presence is basic to science fiction. Yet, when science fiction makes the great leap of imagination and concludes we are not alone its speculation is mostly grounded in the present and past of Western civilisation. Outer space, distant galaxies, the whole universe is populated by fictional creatures intimately familiar from the narrative conventions of Western civilisation, springing almost unchanged from the pages of travel literature of the history of Western expansion on planet Earth. Alien presence is basic in another sense. It is the brooding menace of another kind of Gothic horror story. Alien creatures serve the purpose of ghosts, ghouls and things that go bump in the night – they are the dark antithesis that illuminates the patches of light within the structure of stories, throwing into relief what it is to be human. Aliens demonstrate what is not human the better to exemplify that which is human. Difference and otherness are the essence of aliens, for only then can they stiffen the sense of self and self-defence that completes the chain of science fiction as normative genre. Coming full circle, aliens are often devils incarnate, ready and willing to offer the Faustian bargain. Across space and time science fiction materialises the constellations of ideas and narrative tradition that personify and are distinctive of Western civilisation. Without aliens space and time, that is outer and future, would indeed be novel, unlike anything that had gone before. The possibilities of ethical questioning and morality plays would be limited, lacking the dynamics in which such questions present and have presented themselves within the history and experience of Western civilisation.

To understand the mechanics of how science fiction employs aliens one must not travel forwards but backwards in time. The very first alien encounter, H G Wells' *The War of the Worlds*, returns to the very beginning of Western storytelling. It is the story of the onslaught on planet Earth by an incomprehensible scourge bent on destruction. The aliens are unknowable, fanatic, equipped with superior technology, bloodthirsty, merciless and cruel. The sophistication that is taken for the acme of human civilisation is imperilled, on the defensive with its back to the wall fighting for its very survival. This *War of the Worlds* may be an imagined future, but it directly connects with the most familiar trope of the Western past. It is the Battle of Tours (Poitiers) all over again. It is the armies of Charles Martel turning the tide, its is Charlemagne and his paladins at Roncesvalles mustering for the first time a common sense of European identity, gathering the armies of Western Christendom to confront the Muslim hordes. It is the very familiarity of the structure of the story that makes the space and time elements used by Wells work so well.

European literature grows out of Tours and Roncesvalles, it is founded on the elements and motifs derived from that experience.

As Edward Gibbon, author of the *Decline and Fall of the Roman Empire*, informed generations of readers: but for the Battle of Tours Oxford would have been a city of dreaming minarets rather than spires. The romances of Charlemagne, in particular *The Song of Roland* about the hero who fell at Roncesvalles – a proto Custer's Last Stand – became entwined with Arthurian themes and were deployed as the popular and courtly literature of the Crusades.[4] This narrative tradition provides the foundational literary forms in all European languages where epics and mythic traditions coalesce with contemporary experience, moral and metaphysical ideas to become the collective repository of storytelling. The presence of an enemy, an external force that is difference and otherness, whose implacable opposition both defines the self and threatens the existence of space and time as it is known, is the beginning of European literary consciousness and political and socio-cultural formation. This basic understanding of space and time bounded by the presence of a hostile alien threat provides the backdrop, the metaphoric and allegoric themes, and the dramatic form through which all stories become comprehensible. The line drawn at Tours is the first frontier. It is the line in the sand, the conceptual place where heroes are made. On this frontier heroes set off on their unending quest for self-fulfilment, defending all that is enduring and valuable and making the world safe for the last best hope of humankind as known and personified in European thought. This essential narrative has structured not only the conventions of European popular narrative but also thought and knowledge.

This war of the worlds began with the Battle of Tours in October AD 732 near Poitiers in western France. The Visigothic kingdom of Spain had already fallen to Muslim forces in AD 711. In the next generation incursions were made across the Pyrenees, culminating in the initially successful invasion led by the Spanish Umayyad Caliph, Ab-ur-Rahman I, that overran Aquitaine, at which point Charles, mayor of Austrasia, the leader of the Frankish lands of northern France, came to the aid of Aquitaine. He defeated the Muslim army with great slaughter, though his own forces suffered only small losses. As a result of his exploits Charles acquired the epithet Martel, the hammer. Charles Martel was the founder of the Carolingian dynasty; his son Pépin rolled back the last remnants of a Muslim presence in southern France. His grandson, Charlemagne, carried the battle against Muslim forces into Spain. The medieval Chronicle of Isidore of Beja specifically refers to the Charles Martel forces at the Battle of Tours as Europeans, a defining battle defines a people. The romances of Charlemagne were a major literary compendium and source book for the Middle Ages and incorporated and conflated Charles Martel with the exploits of his grandson. Around Charlemagne gathered an order of knights, the paladins, prototypes for the Arthurian knights. The most enduring of the romances of Charlemagne is *The Song of Roland* whose eponymous hero fell at the Battle of Roncesvalles in AD 778, set upon by Muslim forces. *The Song of Roland* achieves literary form in the version by Chrétien de Troyes circa 1130, in the era of the Crusades. A contemporary conflict, the Crusades, that is pan-European and defines self-identity and the complete otherness of the foe is presented and anchored in an historical context. *The Song of Roland* draws on and elaborates the orientalist tradition founded by John of Damascus (d.748) of representing Islam as a pagan cult, dissembling the reality of the Other as something it could not possibly be. In this literary trope the Muslims are aliens, ideologically, metaphysically other than their Christian adversaries. As adversaries these Muslim aliens are fanatic, devoted to false consciousness, treacherous, untrustworthy, brutal and cruel.[5]

The crusading theme is another basic ingredient of the Western narrative tradition. It is the quest for secular fulfilment of metaphysical identity through territorial domination. The Crusaders seek to possess territory they have never occupied or owned on the basis of their superior claim and legitimating right, the just warrant of their Christian heritage. The animus of war and dominance is an epistemological and metaphysical demarcation of us and them, normality and otherness. In such works as *The Book of Wonders* and the immensely popular *Travels of Sir John Mandeville* the land sought by the Crusaders is intimately familiar to the basic understanding of Western Christendom and the quintessential land of miracles, wonders and marvels, a veritable outer space.[6] Intimately familiar because it is the land described in, and on which took place the events of the foundational text of all Western knowledge and understanding, the Bible. The land of miracles because here occurred all the evidences of the existence of a higher power the ultimate cause of all the suspension, interruption and rearranging of natural order that are miraculous. Questing, crusading and pilgrimage to these sought after lands includes the familiar Other, the Muslim peoples, and leads to encounters with all the other tropes of alien beings possible – the monstrous races who are none other than the extraordinary beings that decorate the sets of *Star Wars*. The imaginative aliens of 'a galaxy far, far away' have their inception in the anthropophagi, troglodytes, the dog-headed people and the beings with no feet but appendages so profuse they can function as sunshades when they lie on their backs.

The monstrous peoples are recurring themes acquired from the literature of classical Greece and Roman and endlessly recycled through medieval European letters. The monstrous races define the outer limits of the known, existing beyond the territory of the Other on the borders of the Western homeland, the Muslim adversaries. The crusading motif makes the sense of superiority and legitimating right innate to Western self-description. It is an impulse for exploration, seeking out, knowing and describing. It is a precursor of the scientific spirit. It is a warrant to lay claim to outer space, to colonise, re-inscribe and re-formulate this outer space. The paladins of Charlemagne, such as Roland, and the knights of King Arthur are in their own way the crew of the *Enterprise* or *Voyager*. Where the crew of *Star Trek* go they take the Federation with them and wield science as their warrant to colonise and control.

The medieval narrative tradition incorporated knowledge about the known world. It was constantly updated with newly acquired information as well as retaining and recycling the traditions of Greek and Roman knowledge, tales both fabulous and prosaic about far-flung peoples and places. So strong were these medieval conventions that they were used to inscribe, overwrite and provide a language to describe peoples and places newly encountered as Europeans travelled beyond the bounds of the homelands in what is called the age of discovery. Columbus and all who travelled in his wake, whether west or east, and especially all the stay-at-home writers who recycled the information made available by travellers drew more from the established conventions of European narrative tradition and its conventional knowledge than the reality of the other places or peoples encountered. As Percy Adams[7] has noted travel liars continued to be believed and preferred in both literary and 'scientific' literature long after what we would like to call actual fact became knowable and known. New Worlds were alien worlds, New Worlds were a conquest of space that immediately recalled and were described according to the essential drama of Tours and Roncesvalles. The expansion of Europe to become a global presence provided new detail to decorate the constantly recycled structure of narrative. The conquest of outer space as an imaginative form has re-inscribed this narrative tradition and all its conventions on a galactic scale. Aliens are always with us. Without aliens the conception of 'us' would lose meaning. The existence of aliens defines a boundary that is conceptual, epistemological and innate. The Crusades define a boundary line that has become constantly relocated, ever changing always the same, 'the final frontier'.

Early cinema serials, the comic books of the silver screen popularised two frontiers that were in effect exactly the same. Both built on and gave new expression to the embedded narrative tradition of Western civilisation. The Western frontier was matched by the frontier of outer space. The Wild West recalled the historic first frontier pitting the struggles of settlers as the forces of civilisation against the Red Indian menace. The space frontier had *Flash Gordon* struggling to save Earth and all space from the implacable forces of the Great Ming. It can hardly be lost on anyone that the Ming was none other than the yellow peril portrayed in exactly the same details, character notes and characteristics as were contained in the first of the Jesuit chronicles to come out of China. The reports of an early Portuguese voyage to China that resulted in the arrest and harrowing imprisonment of Galeote Pereira were circulated by the Jesuits, translated and rapidly spread across Europe. Pereira's tale focused on systematic routine cruelty, centralised tyranny, the unwavering obedience of a servile population. Marco Polo's Kublai Khan gave way before the enduring attractions of the images from which the Great Ming was fashioned. Earth and outer space, the past and the future were a continuous expanse over which the recycling of narrative tradition and its essential morality plays, storylines and dramatic structure provided weekly cliffhangers that kept the public coming back for more.

REWORKING THE OTHER

The alien presence in science fiction has undergone many transformations. It is such a basic metaphor, so primal an allegory that it can be reworked to serve in many ways. *Invasion of the Body Snatchers* has often been interpreted as science fiction prefiguring an entirely earthly and contemporary metaphor, giving a twist to Cold War neurosis. The idea of a society being taken over from the inside by an alien force and thus being made part of a hostile evil collective works precisely because the Cold War itself reawakened the most primal ideas of Western narrative tradition. What is the evil empire of totalitarianism but another incarnation of the original war of the world at Tours, or 'the present terror of the world' as Francis Bacon described the Ottoman scourge that beset Europe for centuries, or incorrigible empires encountered and marked for destruction like those of Aztecs, Incas and China? Civilisation, the civilisation of the West, is always on the frontier.

Like the virtuous homesteads in all those western films, the ones made iconic in *Shane*, they are constantly under threat, in danger of being overrun. The homesteaders define the ethic and innate superiority of the ideals of Western civilisation that have to be rescued from the ideological, alien threat that would undermine their rightful existence. Shane is the outsider, the lone questing knight re-embodied from all adventures of his Arthurian precursors, who uses his violent skills to defend the weak before leaving the land safe for civilisation. In science fiction, Shane becomes the lone scientist who battles to defend civilisation as we know it. And it all leads to the culmination of *Independence Day*: as Jan Mair shows, the storyline and ethic of *Independence Day* is a compound of all the alien inheritances that have fed the growth of the science fiction genre, right from the science fiction movies of the 1950s such as *Invasion of the Body Snatchers*, *War of the Worlds* and *Invaders from Mars*. Its message, however, is quantum-led beyond the old angst about communism, totalitarian regimes, and nuclear war. In *Independence Day*, 'aliens underline the total supremacy of America, their onslaught demonstrates the impregnability of American supremacy and its rightful leadership of the globe' – in one swift move, American ideology becomes the last bastion of universal independence.

The contending tradition in Western storytelling has been to use the Other to show up the failings, internal corruption and fall from grace of Western civilisation. The noble savage has always been a serviceable character. An entire genre of European letters developed around the idea of seeing European society through the eyes of a fictional alien. This style, originated by Sir Thomas More in *Utopia*, was also used by Voltaire, Montesquieu, Goldsmith, to name but a few. The alien reporter is, of course, irrelevant to the purpose of the satire or earnest morality tale. The prime focus of attention in using this device is Western civilisation itself. In the antithesis to *Invasion of the Body Snatchers*, *The Day the Earth Stood Still* uses the arrival of an alien spacecraft and its wise and benign occupant to offer a pacifist, internationalist moral. In the first flush of enthusiasm for the United Nations, in the aftermath of the Second World War, an old trope with a futuristically refurbished set of characters demonstrates how much science fiction is beholden to history. The alien traveller lands on Earth to caution its peoples of the dangers human violence poses to the proper uses of science. The alien holds up a mirror to humanity. The West has possession of immensely powerful new weaponry, the atomic bomb, the potential to destroy itself and planet Earth and invoke the animosity of aliens across the length and breadth of outer space. In light of these present dangers the way forward is adhering not to alien ethics, but the reputable and entirely earthly alternative ideas of the pacific traditions of Western Christendom.

It is important to note that the alien in *The Day the Earth Stood Still* could be interpreted as a biblical prophet, returned to rekindled the ethic internal to the West and thus save it from itself with its own ideas. This idea is a near relative of the various incarnations of idea of human origins being found in the stars, or the Erich von Daniken motif of the 'gods are aliens' down to the most recent *X Files* confabulations. Where once this trope made the Holy Land the patrimony of the West so by extension these recycled derivative tropes make outer space the real home of Western epistemology and metaphysics. But the alien of *The Day the Earth Stood Still* does not triumph. He is destroyed and chased off by human fear. What he leaves is a message that was already present within Western tradition that must be fought for and triumph by the effort of Western civilisation. A message that is now recycled in certain French science fiction films. As Sean Cubitt shows, the films of Luc Besson (*Subway*, *The Last Battle*) and Jeunet and Caro (*Delicatessen*) represent nature as the ultimate source of 'the good'. 'The theme of home and nature lost under the burden of transnational capital', notes Cubitt, becomes 'a sort of allegory of the struggles for land, now reinvented as nature'. Just as More used the New World as a mirror for the Europe of his time, the spectacle of reinvented nature is supposed to reflect the West's shortcomings to itself. This act of representing not only others nature but 'reinforces the ideological faith in a truly natural nature which exists as the object of scientific or artistic contemplation'. Nature is only good as long it is perceived as an alien Other – both in other societies as well as in 'the wild'!

The presence of aliens familiarises outer space and future time, orders these dimensions and makes them meaningful not only according to the history and experience of the West but according to the characteristic disciplines of knowledge developed by the West. Outer space, future time and aliens then operate in the conventions of science fiction to demonstrate the dominance of Western knowledge. Or to put it another way, outer space and future time become another reserved laboratory for anthropology. The diversity of lifeways and behaviours studied by anthropology is the repository of ideas from which science fiction writers fashion alien life forms and imagine alien societies and their cultural forms. Anthropology is the discipline that turned into a science the worldview of European expansion and its experience of other peoples. As a science, classical anthropology provides a holistic framework for explaining the dominance of Western knowledge as the product of a progress through evolution, stages and forms of savagery, barbarism and civilisation. The anthropological handbook employed by science fiction not only makes social evolution a pan-galactic phenomenon, it enables all evolutionary ideas to be cross-fertilised.

Mr Spock in *Star Trek* demonstrates this tendency. The rational Vulcans are a society dedicated to logic, it is the dynamic that structures their history, experience and social forms. But, in their mating rituals Vulcans as a people are driven by pure instinct. They are salmon, who once every seven years must return to the native hearth to breed or die in the effort. This is just one example of the way in which the original television *Star Trek* often played like an introductory anthropology course. It made not just the classification of planetary types but social forms a pan-galactic reality. M class planets are, in *Star Trek*, Earth-like planets. Societies were ranked, classified and described exactly according to the ideas of nineteenth-century anthropology. *Star Trek* storylines referred incessantly to the idea of parallel evolution so total that it enabled the crew to encounter Roman Empires, Chicago gangsters, Nazi societies and Greek gods in far-flung corners of outer space at future times. The point of perspective that orders these stories is the basic outlook, history and experience of Western civilisation, now reduced to the American Way.

The future worlds discovered on the final frontiers are nothing if not hierarchical. The top of the evolutionary ladder is occupied by none other than the all-American hero exemplified in television series like *Andromeda* where hope is still alive for the survival of civilisation as we know it. Patriarchal values remain intact, as Nickianne Moody demonstrates in her deconstruction of the television series *Space: Above and Beyond*. In *Space: Above and Beyond* an 'inverted millenarianism' is used to construct a near future where women work and fight alongside men as well as command men. But it is still 'Old Men' who direct the war, blatant discrimination is directed towards

InVitros and a noble humanity is pitted against an alien other. 'The price of gender integration into the military appears to be becoming an honorary male', notes Moody. But the hierarchy is not just biological but also conceptual, a point amply demonstrated by *Star Trek: Voyager*, whose Captain Janeway is clearly an honorary male.

In *Voyager* individualism as a value is placed at the apex of human achievement and notions of community are located diametrically opposite at the nadir. The extreme form of collective thinking is personified by the Borg, an evil fusion of organics, technology and the collective will of 'The Hive'. The Borg are the antithesis of what it is to be human. But what exactly makes a human human in a world of robots, cyborgs, and all sorts of aliens? The human itself, argues Christine Wertheim in her analysis of *Star Trek: First Contact*, is essentially artificial: it is 'always involved in a series of contingent technical "natures", its modes of artificiality are never fixed, but always in a process of becoming'. What then of the Borg? The Borg cease to be fantastic, category-breaking Other. Instead, they become 'a reflection of our own hybrid, freakish "nature"', 'their hybridity is our hybridity, their polymorphous heterogeneous becoming our polymorphous heterogeneous becoming'. Wertheim wants to go beyond Western possessive individualism to appreciate that the product of the synthesis between human and technical is not purely human, but transhuman, and includes the contribution of the technology itself. From this perspective, 'the Borg are indeed "other", but they represent the *otherness in ourselves*, that radical otherness which lies at the heart of our own artificially becoming, technical and multiplicitous "nature-s"'.

Elsewhere, I have noted that the Borg are the distillation, in its purest form, of all the orientalist stereotypes of Japan – they are the American fear of Japan writ large.[8] The represent a new form of techno-orientalism. In his exploration of 'Japanimation: Techno-Orientalism, Media Tribes and Rave Culture', Toshiya Ueno suggests that a techno Orient has been specifically constructed to 'define the images and models of information capitalism and the information society'. This new 'Orient' seems to be have become a standard backdrop to science fiction. From the classic *Blade Runner* to *The Fifth Element* to the television series of *Total Recall* – the swarming figures lurking in the background as well as the landscape are distinctively 'Oriental'. The presence of techno-orientalism both in Japanese animations as well as in certain Hong Kong films is particularly problematic. Ueno argues that it delivers a double whammy: by equating

'Japanimation' with Japanese culture, by insisting that traditional or ancient mythology is very significant in *anime*, techno-orientalism connects cultural identity in Japan with representations that are already orientalised. The layer upon layer of reinvented and re-invigorated orientalism shrouds everything but the Western prejudices about the Japanese other. So what is left of Japan as Japan actually sees itself? When transposed to Hong Kong, techno-orientalism reveals some surprising side effects. As Gregory Lee and Sunny Lam observe in the their analysis of *The Wicked City*, cyberpunks' celebration of multiple identities serves both as 'windows and mirror through which the ambiguities of our metropolises and the survival of marginalities are represented'. For culture where multiple identities are taken for granted, and where mainstream Hollywood products and their trumpeting of triumphant capitalism hold no real meaning, cyberpunk has its own unique value.

If cyberspace provides us an opportunity to explore real and imaginary identities, to become others, and if even the Borg are nothing more than others within us, what then is the difference between 'us' and 'them', West and the non-West, the poor and the rich, the privileged and the marginalised? Nothing. The 'Kiplingesque world of fixed meanings on East and West, on the self and the other', argue Kirk Junker and Robert Duffy, has now been replaced by a postmodern one where to quote Oscar Wilde, 'Most people are other people.' In the television series *Star Trek: Deep Space Nine*, Junker and Duffy see a world of otherness created through a dialectal naming of 'mine' and 'yours'. 'Since we may all be others what was "yours" could now be called "mine", and what was "mine" might now be called "yours".' This lack of distinction between 'yours' and 'mine', they suggest, 'can scramble a hierarchy of even Federation proportions'. Perhaps.[9] But this 'postmodern twist' would certainly make the appropriation of the cultural traditions and heritage of others a rather simple task – a point amply demonstrated by Peter Feng in his 'allegorical readings' of *The Matrix*, one of the most important science fiction films of recent times. *The Matrix* not only absorbs patented Asian cinematic technique of wire-fighting, it actually assimilates the very essence of Hong Kong: it is not just that inside the matrix everyone knows kung fu and race functions as narrative shorthand, but the fact that the matrix itself is Hong Kong personified. In the theological text that is *The Matrix*, we find transnational capital emerging as the new (yet very old) theory of salvation.

Wherever we look, the colonising, imperial mission of science fiction is hard to miss. Space, the final frontier, is the recurrent frontier on which Western thought has been constructed and operated throughout history, or time. Western thought not only constructed aliens to define itself better, it made constructed aliens essential to fulfilling its own moral purpose. As Dimitris Eleftheriotis observes in his contribution to this volume, the repressed historical and cultural identity of the Western civilisation resurfaces again and again in the science fiction visions of the future. In Wim Wenders' *Until the End of the World*, Eleftheriotis discovers all those elements that make Hollywood science fiction such a Eurocentric enterprise: individualism championed as a sacred absolute, humanism straight out of the Romantic tradition of modernity, Western experience projected as the universal and eternal, and the world reduced to little more than an exotic location for the consumption of the West. At the end of the world, we return to the beginning of Europe's colonial adventure. The white man's burden, so inherent in Western self-understanding, is ever present in the narratives and morals of science fiction cinema: it reiterates the dominance of the West as the source of the only stories worth telling; it operates as the driving force of mass popular culture and its merchandising, from *Star Wars* to *Independence Day*; it captures the mind and the markets of the Other for inclusion in the global economy; and it informs the ideas of all others about themselves. Without aliens, terrestrials and extra-terrestrials, civilisation as we know it just would not exist.

NOTES

1. See, for example, Joseph Needham, *Science and Civilisation in China*, Cambridge University Press, 1956 (six volumes); Roshdi Rashed (editor), *Encyclopaedia of the History of Arabic Science*, London, Routledge, 1996 (three volumes); and D M Bose *et al.* (editors), *A Concise History of Science in India*, New Delhi, National Commission for the Compilation of History of Sciences in India, 1971.
2. See Ziauddin Sardar, *Explorations in Islamic Science*, London, Mansell, 1989; Ziauddin Sardar, 'Above, Beyond and at the Centre of Science Wars: A Postcolonial Reading' in Keith Ashman and Philip Baringer (editors), *After the Science War*, London, Routledge, 2001; Susantha Goonatilake, 'The Voyages of Discovery and the Loss and Re-discovery on "Others" Knowledge', *Impact of Science on Society*, 1992, no. 167, pp. 241–64; and Susantha Goonatilake, *Towards A Global Science: Mining Civilizational Knowledge*, Bloomington, Indiana University Press, 1998.

3. There are odd exceptions to this general rule. There is one Indian science fiction film and a notable Thai one. For an analysis of the latter, see Amdan Knee, 'Close encounters of the generic kind: a case study of Thai sci-fi', *Screening the past 2000*, http://screeningthepast.media.latrobe.edu.au/archives/

4. See R W Southern, *Western Views of Islam in the Middle Ages*, Cambridge, Massachusetts, Harvard University Press, 1962.

5. See Ziauddin Sardar, *Orientalism*, Buckingham, Open University Press, 1999.

6. See M B Campbell, *The Witness and the Other: Exotic European Travel Writing 400–1600*, Ithaca, New York, Cornell University Press, 1988; and Sir John Mandeville, *Travels of Sir John Mandeville*, London, Penguin, 1983.

7. Percy Adams, *Travellers and Travel Liars, 1660–1800*, Berkeley, University of California Press, 1962.

8. Ziauddin Sardar, 'Science friction', *New Statesman*, 31 May 1999, pp. 35–7.

9. For a detailed discussion of the alternative view, see Ziauddin Sardar, *Postmodernism and the Other*, London, Pluto Press, 1998.

1 *Delicatessen*: Eco-Apocalypse in the New French Science Fiction Cinema

Sean Cubitt

There are Irish, Scottish and Welsh nationalists, Basque nationalists, Breton and Corsican nationalists – and French, German and British Greens. The old European imperial powers, or at least their liberal populations, are chary of nationalism after a century in which patriotism has been synonymous with racism, genocide and horror. Yet the love of the land, the geographical claim of identity, the faith in a natural source of the sense of self, still appeal deeply as political and ethical grounds of action. It is on this basis that at least a certain mode of conservation allies itself with a certain wing of conservatism, producing those unusual alliances between mud-caked New Age travellers and Labrador-walking bourgeois that have accompanied protests against the expansion of motorways and airports across Northern Europe. In some European science fiction, and especially in French SF films, the theme of home and nature lost under the burden of transnational capital has become a sort of allegory of the struggles for land, now reinvented as nature, as source of identity.

The best of these films, those signed by Jeunet and Caro and by Luc Besson, imagine futures of appalling anonymity, post-global cities plummeting into decay. While Jeunet and Caro are relentless in their pursuit of the logic of a decaying ecosphere, Besson has reached into another tradition to evoke the possibility of salvation for both humanity and the environment. That tradition, while it promises to reach back and return to new generations an ancient legacy, is in fact a modern invention with roots in Blavatsky's theosophy and Steiner's anthroposophy at the beginning of the twentieth century. It is best known to us today as the philosophy of the New Age. For the most part, those who do not share the neo-mysticism of New Age beliefs look down on it as gently quaint and morally neutral eccentricity. But, as even the entertainment industry in the shape of Spielberg's *Indiana Jones and the Last Crusade* reminds us, such mysticism has a darker history among the European powers. Wulfram Sievers, the

high-ranking Nazi officer whose task was to explore the bogus archaeology of the Aryans, was sent by the ideological arm of the SS to seek
out the ancient roots of the Teutonic culture in the Holy Grail and the
lost island of Atlantis. Part of a more than usually pseudo-science of
archaeology and anthropology, the Nazi quest for a race-historical
construction of the past still quivers in the undergrowth of European
New Age mysticism. Simon Schama's essays on the ideology of the
forest in Poland, Germany and England[1] likewise recall the pseudo-
histories which have allowed us to construct the wilderness as the
image of a folk soul. The heritage claimed by conservationists, by
national parks, by Green parties, by advertisers positioning
wholemeal and organic produce, even by the wave of caring
management consultants that arrived in the late 1980s[2] is all too
frequently based on a whitening of history. Proximity to the land
and racial purity are all too common bedfellows. The production of
national identity depends on a refusal to accept that nature is indeed
a social construct, not a historical given. The myth of a feudal
peasantry living in some idyllic communion with their environments, upheld in national legends from Robin Hood to the Serbian
oral epic tradition, produces the requisite authenticity, homogeneity
and natural status on which the ideology of nationalism can operate
without recourse to imperial histories. This is why it is so insidious,
not just at flashpoints like the Balkans but in the urban civilisations
of the great metropolitan powers.

The truism powering *Delicatessen* is, despite appearances, the same
neo-mystical thesis underlying Besson's *Fifth Element*, *Subway* and
The Last Battle: that the environment is the mirror of the soul.
Whether the corrupted environment of the city destroys the natural
health of the body, or moral corruption breeds the degradations of
the urban decay, the theme governing Jeunet and Caro's and
Besson's films is that which structures Eliot's *The Waste Land* of 1922,
a structure he derives from the earlier comparative religious studies
of J G Frazer and Jesse Weston,[3] and centrally the myth of the Fisher
King. In its basic form, the Grail knight comes upon a land laid
waste, whose king is wounded and in some variants castrated. The
healing of the land and of its ruler are the same quest, resolved in a
single act of courage, purity and moral probity. The difference is,
however, that while Besson's film shares the mystical belief in the
healing power of virtue (in *The Fifth Element* addressed as Love and
emblematised as sex), Jeunet and Caro's does not. Their corruption,
plainly allegorical of a general state of social ill-health in the present,

is fantasmatically projected on to an anonymous future but left there as a further stage on a downward spiral already begun in the late twentieth century. The ideological unity of moral purity and hearty land is then an ancient and powerful European myth against which the scenarios of degradation and depravity, human and ecological, can be played out as fantastic narratives in these recent French films. Echoes of it still remain in the immigration policies of ex-imperial colonies, in the stigma attached to tuberculosis and other diseases associated with squalor. It powers, I contend, a certain aspect of European Green consciousness, and in particular the apocalyptic visions promoted in these films. While the approximation of a life lived in accord with 'nature' is promoted as a good in its own right, it is fairly innocuous. Where it empowers the righteous to resolve what action is to be taken as a totalitarian response to what is promoted as an emergency, it is a dangerous political myth. In *The Fifth Element*, for example, the monastic cult is empowered, with our active encouragement, to play with unknown forces of nature in order to restore planetary health. *Delicatessen* sets its protagonists the more modest goal of survival, but at the risk of a fatalistic quietism in the face of enormity. In what follows, I want to analyse the principles underlying the *mise-en-scène* of the film's diegetic world (the fictional landscape it invents), the narrative response of the protagonists to its perils, and the role of the film's stylistics in proposing a more complex relation between human and natural worlds than either the diegesis or the narrative suggest.

In the version of Lovelock's Gaia hypothesis[4] adopted by Jeunet and Caro, the alien is Man (the gendering is significant, as we will see below), who has exiled himself from the Edenic innocence of a life attuned to nature. Innocently, nature will attack the denatured and vacuous culture of humanity, as an immune system would attack a viral culture. This cleansing work is the task of *natura naturans*, in the Kantian dialect, of nature going about its own work unobserved by science and unbound by the laws which science reads into it. But where Kant saw *natura naturans* opposed by *natura naturata* – nature turned into an object of knowledge and named in order to distinguish it from the human – this variant on the Gaia hypothesis reads the opponent as *natura denaturata*, the denatured humanity which, by seizing on technology for its salvation, has abandoned its link with nature and assaulted her into the bargain. Not only is this understanding of humanity as Man opposed to Mother Nature as woman an important gendering action that will structure the film's narrative resolution; it is a central theme of the loss of childhood and motherhood in the films of Jeunet and Caro. The lost ability to dream, the disembodied brain, the gormless unfathered clones of *The City of Lost Children* are all aspects of technology as denaturing. If nature is to be recovered it will be through the restoration of paternity, traced in that film in one's relation to the little girl, his protégée. In *Delicatessen*, a similarly important role is played out in the relation between the clown Louison and the two young boys whose antics enliven the film's action and add depth to its conclusion.

In the best known sequence in *Delicatessen*, the unexpected harmony of music, sex and work in the different rooms of the lodging house become a unified whole. But its claim to a utopian humanity against the backdrop of the inhumanity of the human, its alienation under conditions of eco-collapse, curtail it as an isolated instant. Indeed, technology, and capitalist war of each against all, envisioned as the dependent and determined upshot of over-technologisation, are portrayed as the spiritual as well as environmental pollutants that exacerbate the cannibalistic antagonism of contemporary society. The naïveté of our hero is comic and touching because he alone fails to fathom the depths of the depravity that surrounds him. In this way capital-technology appears as a false nature, an anti-nature usurping both ecological and human nature as they should exist – un-alienated. That innocence is what makes the construction of humanity as alien so distinctive a quality of *Delicatessen*. The satire of *Delicatessen* depends on an intuition of what a whole nature would be like. This ideological presumption of a shared intuition of wholeness, essential for the film to work as narrative and for it to meet its audience, is itself a construct and a dangerous one.

The danger is, in a curious way, particular to representational media when, as in Jeunet and Caro's film, they address us in the double mode of depiction and spectacle. Traditionally, cinema has been held to enthral us through its transparency – the effect based in photography that suggests to us that it does not illustrate the world but takes an impression, a mould, an objective likeness of the world as it is present to the lens. All the manipulations of the pro-filmic – the scene before the camera: light, performances, props and sets – are prior to the act of filming, and the film itself is merely a recordist of that (manipulated or otherwise) reality. That at least is the thesis of naïve realism underlying the naïve faith in film's native ability to depict unwaveringly. But at the historical conjuncture of film technology in which the presentation of the world can be further manipulated *after* the recording of the image, and especially in an era of digital treatment of the recorded image, then the medium begins to intrude into the act of depiction, not as Brechtian estrangement but as the spectacle of the medium itself.

This spectacularisation of the act of mediation itself – the gee whiz effect – is integral to the marketing, the attraction and the stylistics of the contemporary effects film. We go to certain films, rent certain videos or turn on specific TV programmes in order not to see the world transformed into its own image, but to see the power of the medium itself: to see Gotham City, Federation Starships or the seven plagues of Egypt rendered in such a way that the effect is not one of simple credulousness, but the double effect of enjoying both the fiction and the powers of the medium. This double effect produces a curious dialectic. On the one hand, we delight in the capabilities of the cinematic apparatus; on the other, we try to peer through it towards the pleasures of an impossibly pure depiction of an utterly unmanipulated reality, forgetting what we have always known about the factitious nature of the *mise-en-scène*, the preparation of the world for the camera. At a more ontological level, our knowing alertness to the post-production manipulations of compositing and computer-generated imaging promotes a willing mis-take of the world-for-itself, *natura naturans*, for the world as it presents itself to the camera. Because we feel we can distinguish between the spectacular cinema of effects and the documentary realism of the older cinematography, we have a greater faith in unmediated recording than before the advent of photo-realistic illusion. Perversely then, the more our films call to us with their displays of post-cinematic technique – in the sense both of film after photo-mechanical recording and of film subjected to post-production effects added after the moment of performance to camera – the more we hanker for an unmediated relation to the world. That yearning for the unmediated becomes the narrative goal of this eco-apocalyptic cinema.

A recent series of North American films suggests that the theme is not unique to Europe, though the directors of two of the key titles, *Dark City* and *The Thirteenth Floor*, are Greek and German respectively. Both films draw their dark, cramped visual design from the acid rain drenched cityscapes of *Blade Runner* and the neo-noir tradition. What they share, apart from a narrative premise based on dread of virtuality, is a presentation of a quasi-familiar if anonymous urban landscape as if it were entirely illusory: the theme is repeated in the best known of the cycle, the Wachowski brothers' *The Matrix*. In fact, the real for which the protagonists of the first two films hanker is that icon of ecological harmony, the seashore, where land and water, finite and infinite, meet as equals on a shifting border, and where the idyll of a re-naturalised humanity can be lived out, washed by the purifying waters of Ocean. At that dreamed of shoreline, the terminal beach, the human confronts the limitless forgiving of nature. But it also meets, far more importantly, its own forgiveness of its own past crimes. The idealised *experience* of nature is embodied in this unmediated meeting of the man and the waves. The curiosity arises from the fact that it is our most highly mediated narratives that most commonly and most frequently resolve themselves in the idealisation of the unmediated. Even if unmediated perception was a possibility, yet this construction of it would be deeply flawed, firstly because we meet it not as actuality but as depicted scene.

In the fantasy of a healed and reunified human nature, for whom the natural environment is posited as an absolute good and enjoyment of it as a moral right as well as an ethical obligation, what relation is being constructed between human and nature? The figure of the littoral man, the image of the man at the beach, is specifically a narrative image, and even more specifically a concluding image. As such it is not a resolution but the image of a resolution. There is something of a truism in film studies that the final scene defines the meaning of a film: we might call it the Rosebud thesis. But just as the rather ham ambiguity of the McGuffin in *Citizen Kane* tells us a great deal less about the film than almost any preceding scene, so the littoral man at the terminal beach tells us little about the pleasures and the conflicts which the preceding 90 minutes have offered and enacted. The meaning of a film very rarely resides in its conclusion. Dr Johnson observed of Shakespeare that he tends to huddle his endings – much the same is true of the commercial cinema. What makes moving pictures move, as both affective and narrative devices, is conflict. Resolution of conflict may be commercially necessary, ideologically desirable and rhetorically acceptable as a way of stopping that movement, but it is rarely the privileged moment that reveals the film's motivations. In our case, the felt antagonism between culture and nature, the built and natural environments, the biological and technological processes, is not 'resolved' in the figure of a man standing on a pier. Such images, deprived of their narrative rationalisation, would strike us as sentimental.

I take the nineteenth-century novelist George Meredith's definition of the term: the sentimentalist is he who would enjoy without incurring responsibility for the thing enjoyed. It is a definition which embraces our culture's constant recourse to images of starving children whom we have no intention of ever meeting, and the obligatory closing voice-over commentary on any wildlife programme pausing to deliver lamentations over the fragility of environments we have no intention of protecting. The terminal beach and the littoral man are sentimental because they invite us to enjoy their unmediated harmony *as spectacle*. Their spectacular harmony is the overdetermined resolution of a dialectic that we are nonetheless aware is far from resolved, and which is indeed dialecticised once more in the spectacular mediation of immediacy.

To their credit, Jeunet and Caro avoid that sentimentalism in both their French feature films. And yet, as Fredric Jameson argues of the transition from modern parody to postmodern pastiche, the parodic relies upon a shared system of values which, under conditions of postmodernity, can no longer be assumed. In the culture of the late twentieth century, one of the few values that the film industry can appeal to is the equation of nature with the good. The rise of green politics, indeed, disproves Lyotard's thesis that our epoch is characterised by the demise of master narratives: the Gaia hypothesis and similar apocalyptic ecological scenarios have become the most widespread basis for political action since the self-destruction of communism in 1956. The equation of the natural with the good strikes us, children of Darwin, Freud and Keynes, as self-evident. Nor is it adequate to argue that in some fashion the movie business misrepresents the truth of eco-politics. There are no truthful representations, in the sense that any definition is at once inadequate to the real it seeks to depict, and in the sense that every representation is external to the 'truth' it represents and is therefore unable to share the quality of truth which might otherwise be held to inhere in the world depicted.

My thesis here is that theories of representation are themselves doomed to spiral into the defeatist pessimism of simulation theory as long as they are determined by the belief that the purpose of communication is not to communicate but to depict the world. To be depicted, the world must be other than both the medium in which it is depicted and the agent – human or technological – that does the depicting. This is the burden of Kant's distinction: *natura naturans*, nature doing its own thing in and of itself is not the same as *natura naturata*, nature considered as an object and thus as the content of regimes of knowledge, of morality and of use. It does not matter if we take responsibility by making nature do what we wish it to, or refuse the responsibility and look at nature for its approximation to human aesthetic (picturesque) or ethical values. What counts is that nature is othered in that single action of representing. Jeunet and Caro pursue a fascinating course in showing us denatured nature, but since the film functions primarily as spectacle, that denaturing serves only to reinforce the ideological faith in a truly natural nature which exists as the object of scientific or artistic contemplation. Nature is only good so long as it is other. Its moral status depends upon its difference from the contemplating lens or eye. The very act of taking responsibility for nature, in the terms demanded by those wildlife documentaries, turns nature into an object over against the human subject.

The truth of good nature as it is depicted in cinema, mediated as spectacle, is as truthful, only and precisely, as the montage of wilderness views accorded to the dying Edward G Robinson at the close of *Soylent Green*: a painted paradise, an illusion within an illusion. On our behalf, Edward G witnesses a crucial turn of the dialectic: that nature has become spectacular for us. We stand, as humans, by definition outside and against nature, which exists for us, today, only as object. The spectacle is itself an effect of the commodity form in consumer capitalism,[5] so all-embracing that we have become accustomed to the policy statements implying that the purpose of factories is not to manufacture goods but to produce jobs – jobs having themselves become empty signifiers rather than productive engagements in the world. That nature against which our species fought so hard for so long is now so profoundly conquered that we permit ourselves the tourist pleasure of visiting our vanquished enemy in her chains, as we set off to ex-colonial possessions in search of an impossible authenticity. If, as green political thought has it, nature became object in the industrial revolution, in the consumer revolution it has become spectacle. It is my contention that the belief in an unalienated nature is an aspect of that spectacularisation of nature, and that faith in an unmediated perception of it is nostalgia for a state of affairs that never existed. In the end that nostalgic tone is what deprives *Delicatessen* of a politics, even as it provides it with an ethics.

Derived via the systems theory of Niklas Luhman from the environmental theory of information as poesis propounded by Maturana and Varela, the theory of communicative rationality proposed by Jürgen Habermas, arguable in many respects, provides us with a starting point for considering the process by which nature becomes spectacular: 'the self-relation arises out of an *interactive* context'.[6] The relation to nature as spectacle arises not as a quality of the world but initially as a problematic relation to the self. By posing the world as (spectacular) object, the self posits itself as subject of this spectacle. Specifically, in replacing the interactive relation with others by the relation with the world as object, subjectivity becomes, in that mirror, this troubled image of the entirely void and the entirely self-sufficient which are the conflicted characteristics of the spectacle. This relation to the self is an unhappy and unstable one. Unhappy because it is deprived of any relation but that of difference by means of its self-sufficiency, while by reason of its emptiness even that difference is rendered indifferent and so meaningless.

This unhappy consciousness is apparent most of all in Julie, the cello-playing daughter of the butcher, whose very existence depends upon the central operator of the cannibalistic system, whom she despises, refuses to forgive, attempts to kill, and yet whose gifts have allowed her to survive thus far, at the cost of a lack of self-esteem and, in her near-blindness, a cinematic mode of self-ignorance (a Lacanian might see her attempts to go without her spectacles as a failure of the mirror phase, and thus a lack of self-image by which to distinguish herself from her father or her environment, a different take on her clumsiness). The spectacular understanding of the self is unstable both because of internal contradiction between plenum and void, integrity and vacuity, and because the relation of objectivity which it depends upon and which produces the dialectic of absolute difference and complete indifference implies in turn at once dependence upon the other and the dependence of the other on the self, an irreconcilable opposition of freedom and necessity which cannot be resolved dialectically since the self must cling to the total premise of its own freedom at the expense of the world. That tragic failure of development is enacted in the film in the character of Aurore, who believes her suicide is dictated by internal voices, and though her admirer's brother confesses to being their actual source, she clings to her delusion and to her suicidal destiny rather than believe in the power of an external other over her internal freedom, however auto-destructive.

What Habermas' axiom offers is a way of making strange this now normative yet unhappy and unstable relation of self to self and self to world. The centre of this thesis, as we must rewrite it in order to avoid the temptation to eco-fascism, is interactivity. Where Habermas restricts interactivity to human agents engaged in rational discourse, we must extend it towards an understanding of communication that cannot be restricted to rationality because it embraces communication with the non-human and specifically with the natural environment. The sentimental relation with the environment merely regrets its degradation. The task to which we are invited by neo-liberal statements of ecological policy is to take responsibility for that degradation and its containment. But rather than assume imperialistic responsibility for the care of nature, the principle of interactivity, once extended to include an interactive relation with the natural world as an agent in dialogue, proposes that this responsibility is neither personal not exclusively human, but instead belongs to a polity that includes the environment itself as protagonist and citizen. In this sense, we can read the intertwining of community and environment in *Delicatessen* less as sympathetic magic and more as a dialogue between environment and inhabitants. The principle is then far closer to the old slogan that 'you are what you eat', given the fallen nature of the standard diet in the apartment block.

As we will see, *Delicatessen* has great difficulty in realising this dialogic conception of the ecological relation. But it does introduce us powerfully to a third partner, alongside nature and human society, that engages in the constitutive dialogue of ecological subjectivity: technology. The kind of humanism that excludes machines from dialogue with humans and environment is in hock to nostalgia for immediacy. Only a recognition of the technological mediation of that dialogue – from architecture to cinema, food to speech, clothing to music – can permit at one and the same time the centrality of mediation to the relation between environment and consciousness and of technology to our perception of the world, as object or, eventually, as agent. Understood as an active partner in the dialogue, technology, as mediation, constitutes that difference between self and world that might allow us to see ourselves from the perspective of the world. This position relates dialectically to that of the film theorist André Bazin for whom cinema transforms reality into its own true self. This transformation is normally read – as indeed was probably Bazin's intention – as the mission of cinema to redeem habitual perception, but it carries, in its echo of Mallarmé's sonnet *Sur le tombeau d'Edgar Allen Poë*, the implication that the world itself is positively transformed in its technologically renewed relation to mediated perception. Clearly *Delicatessen* is anything but a realist film in Bazinian terms. Yet in certain ways, and especially in its confusing of *mise-en-scène* (the staging) and post-cinematic, post-production effects, the film foregrounds the mediating functions of cinema as technology. In certain respects, this praiseworthy concentration of attention on the technological substitutes for the dialogue with the environment and sets the stage for the film's eco-political failure while offering a model of what a successful eco-ethical film might look like.

Caught up in a Catholic phenomenological movement informed by Sartrean existentialism and coloured by the critical theory of technology developed by the great Jesuit philosopher Pierre Teilhard de Chardin, Bazin permitted himself a belief in the world as objectively an object since it was created and known by a God to whom, as its creator, it was already primordially other. Without the alibi of a divine gaze in which the truth of nature might be thought as separate from humanity, we today have to understand nature as alien to us, and us to it. This is no longer, however, a matter of divine ukase issued at the doors of Eden as they clanged shut. Rather it is a materially and historically specific condition subject to all the usual social laws. Moreover, as *Delicatessen* adumbrates, that evolution is itself mediated by technology, which can be understood in this instance as the material form of our relations with nature or, more generally, of the interactions between nature and culture. Technology as it exists in this film is no one-way relation in which human will is imposed on a passive and objectified environment. Rather it figures the reciprocal imposition of natural laws on the extension and complication of human faculties. The cinematic technologies that *Delicatessen* embraces can be understood then not as barriers placed in between (subjective) perception and (objective) world but as active participants in the mutual construction of both. By placing the technological relation between subject and object centre stage, the emphatically technological aesthetic of *Delicatessen* throws the relation into conflict again. Neither Eisensteinian humanism nor Bazinian realism had been able to get beyond the binary opposition of perceiving subject and perceived object: *Delicatessen* learns from both how to render that opposition dialectical again.

The film, however, faces its greatest crisis in its need for a harmonious resolution to the conflict. Films must have a certain duration, and commercial considerations in Europe place that duration at around two hours. But there is also a deeply ingrained historical aesthetic sense that guides filmmakers towards a satisfying ending. The feudal narrative's conclusion arrives as *sententia*; as we have already noted, Shakespeare huddled his endings; by the time of Jane Austen and even more so of the great nineteenth-century novelists and dramatists, the ending has become closure, the culminating gestalt in which not only are loose ends gathered up and *sententiae* enounced but all ideological conflicts are brought to resolution with the finality of a Brahms symphony. It is a gestalt in the sense that the ending urges us to reconsider everything we have seen before, to reconsider apparent motives, to understand hidden causes, to unravel overlooked clues and to rewrite the opinions voiced by characters. If there is a certain brutality to this totalitarian gearing of narration to its conclusion, it is nonetheless conducted in the awareness that conflicts exist, and that out of conflict something new can be born.

What makes the lack of conclusion in unending narratives like those of television soap operas so depressing is that it substitutes for the dialectic of conflict mere binary opposition: irreconcilable, mythic, eternal. It is the mirror of that turn in the conduct of warfare from the pursuit of victory to that of stabilisation. The contained conflicts of Palestine or of the six counties of the North of Ireland are exemplary of this turn: victory, even peace, is unthinkable. Armed ceasefire is their nearest asymptotic pass to closure, just as is the case with the enduring situation comedy or soap opera. All we can hope for is to put a stop to things – to celebrate a Last Episode. At its worst, this is maudlin: the deaths that terminate *MASH* or *One Foot in the Grave*. At its best, the termination makes a virtue of its senselessness, as in the final charge in *Blackadder Goes Forth*. But that ending is absurd in the philosophical sense: it achieves meaning through meaninglessness, through the denial of meaning. In this way it does not close or conclude the narrative, but merely points up the difficulty of finding a narrative conclusion under conditions of televisual spectacularisation of narrative.

Among alternative modes of closure, we should fear the role of predestination in a number of recent American films, especially fantasy films like *Phenomenon*, and *Good Will Hunting*, in which genetic inheritance is the motive for conflict (not recognising your identity), and accepting that identity is the predestined resolution of the narrative. Related kinds of predestination inhabit films as diverse as *Titanic* and *Raging Bull*. Elsewhere, as if by accident, we find among the cinema's classical endings some which close the narrative conflicts by reopening them on another plane, the most famous of them all in *Casablanca* ('This could be the beginning of a beautiful friendship') and *Some Like It Hot* ('Nobody's perfect'). Among more contemporary films, the metamorphosis of the limp in the closing scene of *The Usual Suspects* and the recapitulation of the plot in the form of clippings on the police station wall bring with them a subtle sense of doom and waste to an otherwise almost comically perfect wrap-up. This comedy derived from the intensely tidy use of every idiosyncrasy of the diegesis, the narrative device deployed so successfully in *Lock, Stock and Two Smoking Barrels*, comes very close to *Delicatessen*'s strategy for closure. The loose stair, for example, is one of several motifs placed in the diegesis or the narrative in order to furnish devices through which the conclusion can be achieved with the highest degree of formal closure, in this instance paid off more than once in the unfolding of the plot. The bizarre auditory properties of the plumbing have similar multiple functions leading to critical functions in the concluding perepeteia. Here the orchestration of the ending is so perfectly set up as a function of the film's logic as to place its formality inside inverted commas, encompassing it in irony, and so mocking both the enormity of the characters' situation and the audience's engagement with it. It is a strategy of impotence.

Delicatessen sets itself small goals. Amelioration of the immediate problem – will Louison escape anthropophagy? – and personal salvation are the lonely goals of the narrative conclusion to a film that gives away neither the causes nor the solutions for its *mise-en-scène* of ecological disaster. Its proposition is that happiness is only possible in small things and among small people. A certain humanism guides this ending, Julie's cello and Louison's singing saw harmonising on the roof where surrogate children play. Like the children of Jacques Tati's *Mon Oncle*, these relieve the adults of the necessity for sex, and the children themselves of the guilt of generation. Meanwhile, the earlier montage of work, love and music as a single harmony endows this concluding scene with the symbolic value of an ideally innocent family. This closing shot, with its appeal to the romantic trope of the rooftops of Paris, sums up and redirects the film's echoes of Popular Front films like Carné's

Le Jour se lève, Pagnol's *Marius* (evoked not least by the Provençal accent of one of the cast) and Renoir's *Le Crime de Monsieur Lange*, with their evocations of community built around the geography of the apartment building and the camaraderie of the courtyard. But where both those films had very explicit political programmes, Jeunet and Caro only derive from them the chiaroscuro stylistics and the nostalgic sense of predestination characteristic of 1930s French poetic realism.[7] These derivations sentimentalise community in the sense defined above. We cannot therefore look to the ending for a summation of the eco-politics of the film. Instead, the ending strips the scenario of both ecology and politics. And while we can surely enjoy being beguiled by the disillusionment with politics, the abandonment of the diegetic world in favour of the protagonists that inhabit it cannot resolve the initial conditions that the film sets up. In so far as the ending is classically modernist, even surrounded by postmodern irony it fails the film as a whole. Most of all it fails the honourable mockery of resistance as futile, slapstick muddling-through.

Like Mr Tuttle the heating engineer in Terry Gilliam's *Brazil*, the troglodyte underground of *Delicatessen* are ineffectual buffoons, the creatures of a world they know enough to hate but which they have no means to revolutionise. The motor of the narrative then is not contradiction but self-contradiction, and its conclusion is only the vindication of the self as a the site of a mitigated, circumscribed, temporary but finally invaluable happiness. What this analysis leaves aside, however, is that the narrative is not the central charm of the film. The story, cunningly plotted as it is, does not serve as the core attraction for audiences. Rather, as I tried to argue above, that central role is performed by the foregrounded mediations through which the world of *Delicatessen* is presented. What fascinates is less the plot than the diegesis, the fictional world of the film, and that in turn depends upon a self-conscious process of mediation and spectacularisation of the mundane. This is achieved through compositions emphasising mechanical vision – the camera situated where no human eye could fit – but also by strictly cinematic means, notably the use of graphical and sound matches in the editing. The estrangement of the present, one of science fiction's honoured goals, is here achieved through a double activity of situating the everyday under that aspect that links it to the recent past (the *quartier*, the apartment, the local shop) and projecting it into the near future, a tactic of set design also deployed in *Brazil* and

1984. Notable by their absence are the multinationals. The lack of corporate logos strikes us as symptomatic of the characters' abandonment by their world. In place of transnational capital, we are presented with a politics of bosses and workers, a local politics against which the humanist anarchism of the film's conclusion is a suitable if unconvincing raspberry. Not only sentimental in its narration, the film is nostalgic in its *mise-en-scène*.

And yet it strikes me again that the film charms us as a kind of futurological statement, not for the optimism of its resolution, nor for the fatalism of its diegesis, but because of its mischief. The two small boys with their home-brewed technologies for making mayhem and their capacity for amazement: are these the signatures of the film's two directors? The renewal of community, so common as a theme in the cinema of the French Popular Front during the 1930s, returns here in a new guise, one in which the mediating powers of technology are emphasised rather than their alienating effects as tools of an external, instrumental logic of capital. Revelling in the technological, the boys and the directors can revision community under the guise of retroengineered objects like the talismanic singing saw. Throughout the film, technologies, especially ad hoc technologies like the painting machine formed from braces, embody the emotional and social relations between characters, while the shopworn psychologism of an older Hollywood and a still contemporary art house cinema is shuffled to one side, a matter of tokens, like the sensuality of the butcher's mistress or the Poujadisme of the postman. In other words, and this, I believe, is the film's great achievement, we have a humanistic view of the world carried out in the form of relations thoroughly mediated by technologies, instead of a world premised on bourgeois individualism and the psychological nonsense of deeply rounded character motivation. The drama is then not one of conflicts within individuals, but of conflicts within a community, and especially conflicts enacted through such emblematic technologies as the butcher's knife, his mistress' bloomers and his daughter's eyeglasses. The drama arises from these thoroughly mediated interactions, not from the subjectivities of the protagonists, not, therefore, from the problematic of the self. In this sense, this is a profoundly ethical film.

Yet since that ethics does not embrace the natural environment, we are left in a quandary. If the clown Louison gives us a model antithesis to the butcher – a vegetarian whose deepest relationship has been with an animal, his chimpanzee partner Livingstone – yet his triumph is still retailed in his adjustment to heterosexual and, more specifically, human romance. And meanwhile, although the sky has been tinted a paler shade of orange (the promised Age of Virgo), the impossibility of anything ever growing back, first announced by the butcher in dialogue with the taxi driver, is never contradicted. Nature is externalised from the new community, and what hope there may be is only that based in the oldest of all pre-destinarian technologies, the zodiac. With that exclusion of nature from the mutuality of dialogue and its othering as destiny, *Delicatessen* loses its chance to be a great film, remaining instead merely an excellent one, in which the full range of cinematic technique is brought into the foreground of spectacle in order to underline and exemplify a vision of humanity in dialogue with its machines and with one another. Of course, there is a sense in which nature will always enter into the dialogue, in the form of decay and damage to audiovisual media, a fact all too familiar to archival researchers and even to those of us who use our own video collections as a resource. The ageing of media has already become, for some artists, an ally in the production of new works, and the first inklings of what the twenty-first century's creative use of artificial life and bioengineering might be have already begun to emerge. But in the meantime, if cinema is to escape the mythologisation of nature, and the political legitimation of eco-fascism, we need to find a more positive entrance for nature into the dialogues of culture than the gnawing criticism of the mice.

NOTES

1. Schama, Simon, *Landscape and Memory*, HarperCollins, London, 1995.
2. Ross, Andrew, *Strange Weather: Culture, Science and Technology in the Age of Limits*, London, Verso, 1991 (especially Chapter 1).
3. Frazer, Sir J G, *The Golden Bough: A Study in Magic and Religion*, London, Macmillan, 1911–1915. Weston, Jesse L, *From Ritual to Romance*, New York, Doubleday, 1920.
4 Lovelock, J E, *Gaia: A New Look at Life on Earth*, Oxford, Oxford University Press, 1979.
5. Debord, Guy, *The Society of the Spectacle*, revised translation, no translator credit, Detroit, Black & Red, 1977 (1967).
6. Habermas, Jürgen, *Postmetaphysical Thinking*, Cambridge, Polity Press, 1992.
7. Andrew, Dudley, *Mists of Regret: Culture and Sensibility in the Classic French Film*, Princeton, Princeton University Press, 1995.

2 Rewriting the 'American Dream': Postmodernism and Otherness in *Independence Day*

Jan Mair

When the White House exploded in spectacular pyrotechnic special effects, movie audiences across America cheered. It was a brilliant fireworks display, and quite properly it celebrated *Independence Day* – both the traditional occasion for fireworks in the US, and the title of the blockbuster movie containing this iconic scene. The cheers were an ironic comment. The movie opened in the midst of the Clinton impeachment debacle embroiling the real White House. Yet, as a movie, *Independence Day* was genuinely designed to give America something to cheer about. In the words of the title song, 'It's the end of the world as we know it and I feel fine', *Independence Day* explicitly delivers the apotheosis of the American Dream. In this movie all that is not America does not so much fade away, it gets totally eradicated courtesy of aliens. What results from this apocalyptic conflict is a new global Fourth of July that subsumes every terrestrial being in Pax Americana.

The thesis of *Independence Day* is a neat reworking of the tradition of alien movies. While the film pays homage to the alien incursion sci-fi movies of the 1950s such as *Invasion of the Body Snatchers, War of the Worlds* and *Invaders from Mars*, its message is a quantum leap beyond their angst. The central theme of these B movies was fear: fear of communism, fear of totalitarian regimes, and fear of nuclear war. These elements fed into American political culture finding a steady reflection in contemporary film production.[1] Such fears were represented through the cultural metaphor of 'aliens', an all too familiar vehicle through which 'difference' and 'otherness' are deployed. *Independence Day* is nothing but an alien movie, but it is an alien movie of a very different political culture, a different time. Here aliens underline the total supremacy of America, their onslaught demonstrates the impregnability of American supremacy and its rightful leadership of the globe. In *Independence Day* the alien menace authors the ultimate feel good factor.

In science fiction, the 'other' as 'alien' is deployed to concretise the deeply divisive dichotomies of race and gender embedded in the repressive structures and relations of dominance and subordination. Modernity remains intact, the moral guardian of the future, whilst the 'other' emerges demonised and thus can be justifiably annihilated. 'The centre,' as John Rutherford has argued, 'invests the "other" with its terrors. It is the threat of dissolution of self that ignites the irrational hatred and hostility as the centre struggles to assert its boundaries, that constructs self from not self.'[2] Of all the categories of cinema, 'alien invader' films are the most prolific and conservative for, as Susan Hayward notes, 'They point at otherness as threatening to life and/or social mores' and 'represent the most "worrying" category of all with their innate potential for misogyny, racism and nationalistic chauvinism'.[3]

This is an apt summary of *Independence Day*. The film unashamedly elevates American ideology as the last bastion of universal independence, so that in one swift move America becomes both 'globo cop' and 'interstellar guardian'. This reification of American hegemony as the 'end of history'[4] is arguably just about tolerable as a piece of Hollywood fiction but American foreign policy and her military presence in the Gulf is metaphorically and symbolically vindicated via the narrative of the film. Put another way *Independence Day* becomes a libratory tract emphasising the 'moral' right to obliterate 'difference' – to annihilate all that is not Western.

Hollywood films follow, as Douglas Kellner has noted, 'the trajectory of US foreign policy: films are highly capital intensive and the producers of the culture industries closely follow political and social trends'.[5] If *Top Gun* prepared us for 'Operation Desert Storm' with its high tech military hardware, then what kind of apocalyptic future does *Independence Day* warn us to expect? It sets out to be a consciously postmodern epic gleefully showing its postmodern wares: an eclectic mix of styles, the parodying of so many science fiction and 'action adventure' movies, multicultural characters, smart special effects and stylistic spectacle on a grand scale. But there is no attempt at irony or to conceal its political message and the championing of Western liberal democratic modernity, which it presents as the apex of American culture. To champion their causes, Hollywood films must have an enemy, an evil 'Foreign Other' in order to galvanise rampant jingoism. Although Satan comes disguised as an extraterrestrial it does not take any great leap of imagination to decode this metaphorical illusion. Satan is alive and well, preparing again to fight the 'mother of all battles', he does not muck about but attacks and kills mercilessly and strikes terror into the hearts of every God-fearing, upstanding American citizen. Look no further than Iraq, here the devil's hands are never idle!

IDEOLOGY AND THE CULTURAL PRODUCT

Independence Day opens with the credits exploding into space; JULY 2 lingers on the screen momentarily, followed by an establishing shot which scans the surface of the moon. The camera slowly pans around closing in on the 'Star Spangled Banner' and then lingers on a granite edifice, which appears to be an epitaph, with the following inscription:

Here Men From The Planet Earth
First Set Foot Upon The Moon
July 1969 AD
We Came In Peace For All Mankind

The camera pulls back, highlighting the detritus of American moon landing missions. Imperceptibly at first a dark shadow begins to fall over the surface of the moon and a large spacecraft comes into shot. Shortly afterwards the voice of Michael Stipe can be heard singing the lyrics 'It's the end of the world as we know it and I feel fine' followed by interference on all the airwaves back on planet Earth. We are given a poignant shot of the statue of the raising of the American flag on Iwo Jima, and later a shot of the Statue of Liberty. These are significant metonymic devices deployed to immediately identify the ideological instrumentalities inherent in American cultural production – liberation, freedom, democracy – the peak of human civilisation. As Ziauddin Sardar powerfully asserts, 'America is a consciously created artefact, as is its self-image. The manufacture of this self-image must be sustained through its cultural products to imprint itself on a heterogeneous population, to forge them into a coherent body by passing them through not just a social melting pot but an ideological forge.'[6] *Independence Day* presents this conscious construction of America using a bulldozer: right from its opening shots the Light of America, the peace loving nation, is placed against the Darkness of the aliens, the barbaric killers. But this black and white ideology does not remain on the screen – it walks off the screen, just as the characters in Woody Allen's *The Purple Rose of Cairo*, into the real world.

It is interesting to compare how the dark, uncompromisingly evil aliens of *Independence Day* are shadowed on Earth. There are numerous symbiotic and ideological parallels between *Independence Day* (fiction?) and Pax Americana (fact!). For the West to manufacture consent and thus legitimate its actions, cultural production, specifically media production, both fact and fiction, must mobilise a propaganda war that induces panic and fear in the civilian population. This is where the dark aliens come in. During the Middle Ages, Islam was the darker Other of Europe – the alien Saracen who knew no mercy and cast a dark, spaceship like shadow over Europe. During the Cold War, communism acquired the mantle of alien Other. The post-Cold War West returns to Islam. During the recent Gulf crisis, Saddam Hussein and Bill Clinton were painted in the classical black and white colours of otherness. Consider this description by Paul Johnson:

> The French are selfish and slippery, the Germans slow and unresponsive and Japan is constitutionally incapable of leadership ... Would that Saddam Hussein were nothing more than a pantomime villain ... The ugly fact is that Saddam is a dictator ... ruthless ... Bill Clinton sometimes exhibits the sleaziest side of American Politics. ['Fornigate' – presumably?] ... But he is also the President and chief magistrate of the world's most powerful nation, and our best and most reliable ally. He is Commander-in-Chief of its armed forces. With all his faults, he is quite capable of rising to his responsibilities when the world needs strong leadership ... Bill Clinton, with or without his trousers, is still the leader of the free world.[7]

Of course, no one is suggesting that Saddam is not a power hungry despot; he has used chemical warfare against his own people, executed former ministers and attempted the genocide of the Kurds. He rules by sheer force of terror. But was Clinton the light to his darkness? The leader of the 'free world'? He was in fact a manufactured construction – just like *Independence Day* itself. The West has been instrumental in the maintenance of Saddam's regime. The West fears popular revolution in Iraq more than it does the continued irritation of Saddam. Many geo-political commentators concede that popular uprising in Iraq would inevitably lead to a 'Balkanisation' of the region and clearly this would not be to the advantage of Western imperialism, which would certainly not be able to exercise the same control over the area. While the UN has been instrumental in destroying a large arsenal of weapons of mass destruction found in Iraq, the capacity to engineer such military capability has always been dependent on arms sales to Iraq from the West and Russia. We thus have an ironic postmodern twist to this whole saga in that the West supplies Saddam with the wherewithal to produce his armaments whilst at the same time demanding he destroys them. This duplicity is very good for business: commodities must have a finite life span in order that a new purchase becomes necessary and the wheels of consumption continue to turn. The creation of an alien demon is essential to this process. But all the terrors and fears that the West invests in Saddam are projected on to the Iraqi people in general. Stereotypes are so tenacious and work so well precisely because they tell partial truths that are passed off as the whole truth. Saddam becomes the cipher by which imperial representation views all Iraqi people. Once the public has bought the necessary illusions of a demon, he has to be taught 'a lesson'; and, as Paul Foot points out, 'If this lesson has to be learned in blood and starvation not by the dictator but by children and civilians who detest him anyway, who cares?'[8]

Thus over time the threat of communism, in light of the end of the Cold War, has been conveniently transferred to the fear of the Middle East (Arab/Islam). The discourse remains essentially unchanged in that 'every telling of any tale must incorporate the journey of the manifest destiny of Pax Americana to dominate the globe with all that that implies about vindicating the marginalisation of all Others'.[9] Our erstwhile neo-alien, the demonised 'Vicious Oriental'/Arab is mythologised into the concrete ontological entity that threatens the very future and existence of humankind, and so any measures taken to neutralise this threat are rationalised through claims to global independence and freedom, even if this means *in extremis* nuclear, biological and chemical warfare. Turning around the American economy did not carry enough kudos for Clinton; he wanted his place in history and was hellbent on seeking out his 'Bay of Pigs'!

The demonisation process then serves a dual purpose by not only vindicating the military actions of the West but also by serving the needs of so called liberal democracy by producing 'necessary illusions'.[10] 'The bewildered herd is a problem', notes Noam Chomsky. 'We've got to prevent their rage and trampling. We've got to distract them'; and this can only be done by keeping them 'pretty scared, because unless they're properly scared and frightened of all kinds of devils that are going to destroy them from outside or inside or somewhere, they may start to think, which is very dangerous'.[11]

Otherness is also at work in the way *Independence Day* constructs its leading protagonists. Despite what appears to be a politically correct representative multiracial mix of identities (evidence no less of the racial 'melting pot' that constitutes America), these characters are beyond even lazy stereotypes. They are caricatures, vaudevillian, depthless, mere ciphers steeped as they are in the ideology of the American dream. Under the guise of celebrating multiculturalism and political correctness, *Independence Day* rapaciously devours and consumes marginal identities. The postmodern promise of multiracial empowerment is thus revealed as a sham, an act of (Liberal Democratic) appeasement that leaves the concentration of power firmly in the centre where it has always been. It is somewhat ironic that in the film the aliens are described as 'rapacious locusts' travelling from planet to planet, leaving each one only after they have consumed all the natural resources. This sounds rather like an allegorical description of imperialist colonisation tethered to the relentless march of global capital in which America is the major stakeholder. A point perhaps not lost on all those non-Western Others who, on the orders of the American president, prepare to defend the Earth from the aliens – including what looks suspiciously like the Iraqis! This shameless consumption of 'others' reveals the transparency of so called 'human rights', 'equality of opportunity' and tolerance of 'difference' that American foreign policy so boosts. 'Difference' and 'otherness' are not confined to the practices of signification and representation. 'Otherness' is lived through and by the body and experienced under repressive structures of power that cannot be glossed over by the clever marketing strategies of 'politically correct' image-makers.

'Difference' has become merely an expression of exotic consumer desirability. It is the selling point of the search for meaning in a postmodern dislocated temporal plane. The surface interplay of plurality on display throughout *Independence Day* is little more than trickery, a magical illusion designed to foster the belief that we are all 'Others' now. Others who, in the 'land of the free, and the home of the brave!' – remember the opening establishers? – can aspire to full human emancipation and independence. Not only does such a position sanitise history of the contestation of hegemony by the silent majority, it clearly points to the notion that the American

dream and 'Mom's apple pie' is a universal desire. Pass the Coca-Cola
– it's the real thing!

In terms of film criticism there are a number of ways in which
cultural instrumentalities can be identified and thus analysed
through reference to science fiction celluloid fantasy. These are not
necessarily discrete methodologies; indeed the analytical tools
overlap and coalesce. Nevertheless, it is possible to indicate loosely
alternative classifications of cultural instrumentalities. In the first
instance we can refer to the concept of 'reflections'. This approach
suggests that the overt contents of science fiction contemporan-
eously mirror the social trends and attitudes of the time. Thus such
films can almost be taken as sociological evidence, albeit metaphorically, as reflections of the preoccupations of particular cultures. The
second approach is the notion that science fiction films are ideological in that they are cinematic mediations of the concurrent social
order. Such films 'speak, enact, even produce certain ideologies,
which cannot always be read directly off films' surface contents'.[12]
The third approach is concerned with the role of the unconscious,
in particular the 'primal scene', 'repression' and 'Otherness'. The
fourth position addresses the 'spectator' and the role of pleasure and
fantasies that science fiction activates. Finally, there is the view that
science fiction films are 'actively involved in a whole network of
"intertexts" of cultural meanings and social discourses'.[13] *Independence Day* does little to obfuscate either social reflections or
ideologies. What is less obvious is 'repression' and 'Otherness'. The
impact of Ridley Scott's *Alien* is seminal here. Science fiction is
considered by many critics to be a sub-genre of horror, and by others
a sub-genre of fantasy. Such demarcations point to the difficulty of
categorising genres in general but science fiction in particular. *Alien*
is something of a synthesis of all the above and it marks a significant turning point, being at the vanguard of a renaissance of interest
in science fiction.

The original designs for the monster of *Alien* were conceived by
the Swiss artist H R Giger who drew on his work *Necronom iv*: 'a
malignant nightmare vision – part insect, part human, part
serpent'.[14] Giger explains:

In the beginning we had no idea what the alien should look like.
In most horror movies, the monster looks very unbelievable and
sometimes ridiculous – and once you see it the film is over because

it looks just like a man dressed in a suit ... we wanted a very unusual monster – a believable one ...[15]

The metamorphic changeling which constitutes the three different stages of the monsters form in *Alien* draws heavily upon nauseous primal fears of things that creep and crawl, the slimy miscegenation of insect, crustacean and snake succeeds utterly in inducing a response of stifling revulsion.[16]

Giger specialises in turning technology into erotica. So an added twist is that the alien emerges as the 'monstrous feminine'[17] – a complex, multi-laden representation of the maternal figure as conceived within a patriarchal ideology:

She is there in the text's scenarios of the primal scene of birth and death; she is there in the many guises as the treacherous mother, the oral sadistic mother, the mother as the primordial abyss; and she is there in the film's images of blood, of the all-devouring vagina, the toothed vagina; the vagina as Pandora's box; and finally she is there in the chameleon figure of the alien, the monster as fetish object of and for the mother.[18]

The monster's head as 'vagina dentata' ignites everyone's darkest sexual fears, our repressed desires are awakened and we are taken beyond the fear of death. The all-consuming vagina conjures up the horrifying spectacle of the 'archaic mother' phallic woman and castrated body. The spectator is confronted with the terror of the hell within and the hell without. Indeed the history of civilisation could be charted through our changing visions of hell and what it takes to survive. *Independence Day* posits a doomsday scenario of Armageddon, hell on Earth, but lucky for us all, a few plucky Americans are always there to save the world.

Since its release in 1979, Giger's alien has become culturally codified and conventionalised. In most science fiction (and horror) this way of representing alien life forms has become standard fare and thus the repressed unconscious of the spectator is automatically activated via internal reference to *Alien*. *Independence Day* borrows heavily from Giger's conceptual work. The primal fears of the spectator are heavily aroused during the alien autopsy scene in motivating sadomasochistic fantasies of mutilation and torture. The moral paralysis of postmodern times gives perverse attention to images of evil and suffering not to remind us of our humanity but to fuel deep seated fantasies of our inhumanity – taboo as an adjunct to moral behaviour has been jettisoned in favour of the pursuit of hedonistic abandon were nothing is sacred any more. The pornography of spectacle reigns supreme, and we are all voyeurs now desperately seeking out images of the unthinkable and unspeakable. Thus *Independence Day* adds yet more versions of 'Othering' to its glossary of the exploited. An examination of its characters reveals the extent to which stereotypical representations act as ciphers of power relations. Indeed it is the very detailed signifiers of each characterisation that demonstrate the exoticisation of 'difference', there to be plundered and commodified for the sake of polished entertainment and the profits of multimedia conglomerates. The film is both sexist and racist but it does not stop there!

CHARACTERS, CONSUMPTION AND CONSUMING DIFFERENCES

Independence Day has two leading characters: David Levinson (Jeff Goldblum) and Captain Steven Hiller (Will Smith). Levinson is our sensitive 'new' man evidenced by the casual dress and his sensitivity to his father; he is also a cyber genius and he wears the tortoiseshell spectacle frames to underline his intellectual and moral integrity. His laconic ambivalence and dry humour add colour to the portrait of a thoroughly decent politically correct 1990s man. So far so good except that as the narrative unfolds we learn that our new man has been abandoned by his one true love, Connie, so that she could pursue her career goals. Constance Spano (Margaret Colin) is a power-suited post-feminist who callously jilts her husband in favour of being the President's right-hand 'man'. In other words, our right-on good guy turns out to be an allegory for the backlash against feminism. Our Renaissance man has abided by the entire feminist parlance and, my God, we know he's in touch with his feminine side, doesn't he kiss his father? But, poor love, he still didn't get his girl! That is not until he has transformed himself into the knight in shining armour who slays the dragon and wins back the love of his woman. In effect he is nothing more than a male heterosexual fantasy disguised as the feminist ideal type. All that we women need is to be put firmly back in our place with the help of a good dose of machismo!

Captain Hiller is an ace fighter pilot and a one hundred per cent cool dude! Even down to his Calvin Klein shorts invitingly revealed over the waistband of his pants, his burnished and taut torso is charged with homoerotic frisson, displayed as it is in all its animal magnetism. And herein is the crux! His semi-nude body becomes sexualised and objectified, and we are transported back in time to images of the 'noble savage' – a creature of rare beauty just waiting to be tamed and civilised by modern (white) man. Notice how the white guys never get their 'kits off'! Who wants to look at pale flaccid flesh when we can gaze upon the exotica of black skin! Race and sex now firmly overlap discourses in the West. In the cinema, the sexualised imagery of the black male is constantly exploited, by both white and blacks. The 'Black Stud' is a recurrent feature in Hollywood films, from the 'blaxploitation' films of the 1970s to *Miami Vice* and the films of Eddie Murphy and Spike Lee.[19] To which we can now add the films of Will Smith.

So Captain Hiller turns out to be another token. He might well fly the craft that saves the planet but this in itself is what is so problematic. If someone has to die for the clarion call of 'Uncle Sam' it is much better for it to be the expendable body of a black; after all, modernity itself has been built on the bodies of the 'blacks'. All the stereotypes of race are stitched together in this one character – funky, rhythmic, athletic, graceful and sexually charged. In the cultural politics of postmodernism, capitalism must deliver the goods, and black bodies, especially black male bodies, have obtained a kind of mythical status – they stand as a primitive sign of wildness.[20] The commodification of difference appeals so much because it offers an alternative 'lifestyle' to white people who are in the throes of a crisis of identity under postmodern conditions. But under the guise of plurality and diversity this fascination and respect of 'Otherness' and 'difference' is just a crude marketing myth. In reality an obsession with different and 'primitive' Others has a long established history in the West, most often with negative undertones, which leads inexorably to a consideration of Jasmin Dubrow (Vivica A Fox).

Jasmin is the fiancée of our black hero, Captain Hiller. She has a young son from a former liaison and in order to support herself and her son she works as an 'exotic' dancer. Of course we all know that 'exotic' dancing is merely a euphemism for sex work. For feminists, both in the current wave of the feminist movement, beginning in the 1960s, and in the earlier wave which began in the 1860s, sex work has been a difficult issue. Feminists abhor the exploitation of women's sexuality by profiteers and some feel instinctively that sex work supports the objectification of women's sexuality and is somehow related to the pervasive violence against women.

However, there is a growing voice among many feminists that the stigma imposed on sex work keeps all women from determining their own sexuality.

But *Independence Day* revels both in its patriarchal ideology as well as its positioning of the 'male gaze'. The scene of Jasmin stripping is just plain gratuitous, there only to titillate the male spectator and remind the female audience of their objectified status. But probably more telling is the scene were Jasmin's fiancé, Captain Hiller, receives notification that despite his excellent credentials he has been turned down by NASA for space flight. Being an astronaut is Captain Hiller's dream ambition but as his colleague pointedly reminds him, 'Man, you're never gonna get to fly a space shuttle if you marry a stripper.' Thus the double standard of morality between male sexual behaviour and female sexual behaviour lives on. Jasmin is in fact the 'fallen woman', the 'whore' whose binary opposite is crystallised in the 'Madonna' symbolisation of the First Lady, a point I will return to shortly. But just to pile on the stereotypical weight, Jasmin is not only black – the exoticisation of black female sexuality is an invidious marker of 'Primitive Otherness' from the 'Hottentot Venus' through to Josephine Baker to Tina Turner *et al.* – but she is also a single parent threatening the very wholesomeness of American family values! Her only path to redemption from her 'sinful' ways is through being upgraded to a respectable/honourable married woman. Congratulations, Mrs Steven Hiller, and welcome to the double shift!

Marty Gilbert (Harvey Fierstein) the token 'gay' man in the film is similarly two-dimensional – decidedly camp and ludicrous. His ineffectuality means he can be easily dismissed. This begins to expose the limits of the film's pretence at representing different identities. Marty paints a thin veneer which barely glosses over the rampant heterosexism of the film; and when he utters the line 'I'd better call my mother' we are back to the hackneyed myth that homosexuality is the result of an over-domineering mother (monstrous feminine!). At the same time this phrase capitalises on all those familiar stereotypes of American Jews – WASP values permeate!

In contrast to Jasmin, First Lady Patricia Whitmore (Mae Whitman) embodies the 'virtuous feminine' patriarchal ideal, the vanilla accompaniment to the masculine WASP. Her role is to remind the audience of God's (men's) natural intended 'rightful' role for woman – *Kinder, Kirche, Küche!* There is no need here to rehash the crudity of biological determinism but suffice it to say that the myth lingers on. Her appearance in the film is minimal and even then for the most part she is prone and helpless, the defenceless woman who suffers with dignity and in silence. But that is the whole point. Her fatal injury inflicted by the aliens serves to galvanise our WASP President into acting not just as a political decision-maker but to participate fully in military combat. For in yet another ironic twist we discover that the President is in fact a Gulf veteran but his 'wishy-washy' liberalism has received mounting criticism.

In an early sequence in the movie, we are witness to a studio debate broadcast from the presidential suite in the White House. Two political commentators exchange the following comments:

Leadership as a pilot in the Gulf War is completely different from leadership in politics ...

That's the problem: they elected a warrior and they got a wimp ...

Thus the battle against the alien invaders becomes for the President a highly personalised quest not only for political vindication but also to avenge the death of his wife. Saddam Hussein accused Bill Clinton of deflecting criticism from his domestic affairs (particularly the many sexual scandals that have dogged Clinton's presidency) by single-handedly exacerbating tensions in the Gulf. No marks here for identifying the parallels between fact and fiction. A war of any kind has always been the answer to a domestic crisis in Western democracy as well as fulfilling the primary aim of imperialism. In *Independence Day*, President Whitmore is elevated to the apex of universal power, just as during the Gulf crisis President Clinton behaved like the 'Global Emperor' that he aspired to be. The speech made by our fictional President prior to the battle to save the world could just as easily have been made by Clinton if war had broken out with Iraq:

Good morning.
Good morning.
In less than an hour aircraft from here will join others from around the world and you will be launching the largest aerial battle in the history of mankind.
Mankind – that word should have new meaning for all of us today. We can't be consumed by our petty differences any more. We will be united in our common interest. Perhaps it is fate that today is

the Fourth of July and you will once again be fighting for our freedom.

Not from tyranny, oppression or persecution but from annihilation.

We're fighting for our right to live and to exist and should we win the day, the Fourth of July will no longer be known as an American holiday, but as the day the world declared in one voice:

> We will not go quietly into that night
> We will not vanish without a fight
> We're going to live on
> We're going to survive
> Today we celebrate Independence Day!

Notice not just the Dylan Thomas rip-off ('Do Not Go Gentle Into That Good Night') but also how the speech is reminiscent of George Bush's address prior to 'Operation Desert Storm' in which he referred to

> an historic moment. We have in this past year made great progress in ending the long era of conflict and Cold War. We have before us the opportunity to forge for ourselves and for future generations a new world order, a world where the rule of law, not the law of the jungle, governs the conduct of nations ... I am convinced not only that we will prevail, but that out of the horror of combat will come the recognition that no nation can stand against a world united ...[21]

In essence the only objective behind American foreign policy is maintaining the status quo; and the question of who will contain America in her role of globo cop is unequivocally oxymoronic.

X FILES, UFOS AND MILLENNIUM MUSINGS

Cultural production is not a neutral sphere, just innocent entertainment. Moreover, the artefacts of cultural production are thoroughly ideological, bound up with political discourse, struggles, agendas and policies.[22] I have been concerned largely with deconstructing the ideological underpinnings of an alien invader movie. Such 'readings' of Hollywood cinema are now more or less taken for granted, yet it is striking how alien invader narratives have over time been so thoroughly bastardised since the seminal prototype of H G

Wells' *The War of the Worlds* was first published in 1898. Wells' novel was actually written as a critique of Western imperialism, so moved was Wells by the plight of indigenous Tasmanians who were virtually wiped out by Western colonisation. Wells wanted to demonstrate to the West how it might feel to be invaded by a strength far superior to their own whilst at the same time suggesting that earthlings should not feel too harshly towards the Martian invaders as they are themselves guilty of insinuating the same colonial forces on others. *Independence Day* makes a frail attempt to recover this all but lost concern of science fiction; but it overindulges our fear of invasion to the neglect of examining the inherent power that underpins relations of 'Othering'. What it does do, however, is to tap readily into the cultural psyche of a de-divinised West whose quest for meaning in an age of meaninglessness once more turns its collective gaze towards the heavens. But now the search is not for the Omnipresent being but for something quite different. The collective postmodern hallucination is saturated with narratives of UFOs, alien visitors and alien abductees. 'The truth is out there' but it is not a truth that anyone but the Americans would recognise.

Independence Day is a direct outcome of the phenomenal success of the television series the *X Files*. During the 1990s, the culture of the *X Files* had a tremendous hold on the Western psyche. A central theme of the show is alien invasion, alongside its ever-present twin, alien abduction. Indeed, as we learn in the first series of the *X Files*, the sister of our hero, FBI agent Fox Mulder, was herself abducted by aliens. This, however, is not just a product of cinematic imagination: an estimated 23 per cent of Americans believe in aliens and 10 per cent actually claim to have been abducted. The *X Files* is a product of an industry relentlessly pushed by certain sections of the American media that has recognised and fed the public's fascination with the subject. The prime source of much of this material is the now famous, or if you like infamous, alleged incident at Roswell:

According to enthusiasts, a UFO crashed in Roswell, New Mexico, in 1947 and believers claim the investigation into the crash has been deliberately kept from the public ever since. They also insist that US government agencies have conducted experiments on both the craft and the dead aliens found in the wreckage at a top secret location called Area 51 in Nevada Desert and that information leaked from there substantiates their claims.[23]

Independence Day succeeds so well in suspending disbelief by cap-
italising on the Roswell/Area 51 conspiracy theories. In a crucial plot
twist we are taken into the deep bunker where a crashed alien
spaceship has been secreted for study purposes. It is possession of
this spacecraft that permits the final victory over the alien threat.
Here the entire project of Western knowledge, knowing about the
Other the better to subsume, subjugate and suppress them, finds its
cinematic endorsement and vindication. It is knowledge equals
power in comic strip guise. We also have the character of Russell
Casse (Randy Quaid), a 'white trash', single parent, Vietnam veteran.
He is hopelessly alcoholic on account of being abducted by aliens
and no one believes his story. Woven together, these two themes
connect with a form of mass hysteria that almost become an
everyday occurrence in postmodern USA.

By elevating the death of certainty in all areas of cultural, philosophical and scientific paradigms, postmodernism, with its dedicated
reliance on relativity, has amputated all meaning from human
existence. Lost and bewildered, the unanchored masses thus seek out
new ways in which to invest meaning into the purpose of life.
Having abandoned God, science and enlightenment, we now look
beyond the stars for truth. As each new generation comes of age there
is, and perhaps always will be, a resurgence of interest in the
paranormal, of which alien narratives offer the most irresistible hook.
But at the present time there is much more than intergenerational
angst at play. The millennium provided a focus for the alternatives
to the triumph of the individual over society, the main characteristic of modernity. The lure of Armageddon and Judgement Day is the
credence it gives to the visions of mystics, religious philosophies and
all forms of certainty. The millennium is the moment to contemplate that humanity might have taken a wrong turning, thus
ushering in its own destruction. Or, humanity might have allowed
its righteous defences to fall into decay, making it an easy target for
the lurching menace of unreconstructed evil. *Independence Day*
exploits these fears; it then provides an unequivocal answer.

The end of the millennium has not only brought us paranormal
madness. It has also returned us to the beginning, to the days before
feminism, before the recovery of the non-Western history, identity
and futures began, before the Western representations of the Other
and notion of Otherness were deconstructed and shown to be imperialist in nature – to the days when men were mostly white and
did what had to be done. The past becomes the only future and its

moral is: 'It's the end of the world as we know it and I feel fine.' Out of Armageddon comes certainty, a very particular form of triumph. The purpose of the Other is to define the self. What the alien invasion defines in this movie is the dominant self, destined to reign in the new millennium, ending all doubt, eradicating all complications such as wishy-washy dabbling with empowerment of Others. The feel good factor could not be clearer: I have looked into the future and it's American; no thought, amendment, reassessment or change necessary. As it was in the beginning, so shall it be, world without end, for ever and ever. The future is the old Western frontier: all that does not submit will be destroyed. When the Other is eradicated insularity becomes total. America talks to itself, of itself as the only global reality. In which case, *Independence Day* is a backward step for us all!

NOTES

1. Hayward, S, *Key Concepts in Cinema Studies*, London, Routledge, 1996, p. 303.
2. Rutherford, Jonathon, 'A Place Called Home: Identity and the Cultural Politics of Difference', in Rutherford (ed.) *Identity: Community, Culture, Difference*, London, Lawrence and Wishart, 1990, p. 11.
3. Hayward, *Key Concepts in Cinema Studies*, p. 305.
4. For a wider exposition see Francis Fukuyama, *The End of History and the Last Man*, London, Hamish Hamilton, 1992.
5. Kellner, Douglas, *Media Culture: Cultural Studies, Identity and Politics Between the Modern and the Postmodern*, London, Routledge, 1995, p. 83.
6. Sardar, Ziauddin, *Postmodernism and the Other*, London, Pluto Press, 1998, p. 108.
7. Johnson, Paul, 'Should Blair Back Clinton Over Saddam – Even If It Means A War?' *Daily Mail*, 4 February 1998, London, p. 8.
8. Foot, Paul, 'Bombs away, let's kill a few children', *Guardian*, 9 February 1998.
9. Sardar, *Postmodernism*, p. 113.
10. Chomsky, Noam, *Media Control: The Spectacular Achievements of Propaganda*, New Jersey, Open Media, 1991, p. 4.
11. Ibid., p. 7.
12. Kuhn, Annette, 'Cultural Theory and Science Fiction Cinema' in Kuhn (ed.) *Alien Zone: Cultural Theory and Contemporary Science Fiction Cinema*, London, Verso, 1990, p. 10.
13. Ibid.
14. Shay, Don and Norton, Bill, *Alien: The Special Effects*, London, Titan Books, 1997, p. 9.
15. Ibid., p. 12.
16. Ibid., p. 27.
17. Creed, Barbara, 'Alien and the Monstrous Feminine', in Kuhn, *Alien Zone*, p. 128.

18. Ibid.
19. Jordan, Glenn and Weedon, Chris, *Cultural Politics: Class, Gender, Race and the Postmodern World*, London, Blackwell, 1995, p. 267.
20. Ibid., p. 313.
21. Breidlid, Anders *et al.* (eds) *American Culture: An Anthology of Civilisation Texts*, London, Routledge, 1996, p. 353.
22. Ibid., p. 93.
23. White, Michael, *The Science of the X-Files*, London, Legend Books, 1996, pp. 1–2.

3   Displacements of Gender and Race in *Space: Above and Beyond*

Nickianne Moody

During the 1990s exploring the place of women and war through the detective/thriller genre became more popular. Here the deceased woman officer such as the medevac pilot in *Courage Under Fire* (1996) or the victim in *The General's Daughter* (1999) can be debased and then exonerated or excused against a background of political and military deceit or intrigue. Even when living, the characters played by Demi Moore (*A Few Good Men*, 1992, and *GI Jane*, 1997) bear the full weight of traditional military hierarchy and political alliances that prevent them from doing their job and proceeding from auxiliary to combatant. The films are grounded in the realities of military protocol, the Gulf War and twentieth-century gender politics.

On the other hand science fiction has always provided a narrative space that allows the reader to consider alternative ways of living, typically through the creative representation of the future. Although it is commonly understood as a masculine genre because of its pre-occupation with technology and warfare, science fiction has become increasingly popular with women readers. This is particularly the case with televisual forms. Both male and female writers have used the fiction to explore the possibility of women's experience removed from patriarchal mores and oppression. This discussion considers the extrapolation of women's involvement in a gender-integrated military during a fictive time of total war. *Space: Above and Beyond* provides the diegetic space to consider the relationship between women and war, but the series uncomfortably elides the gender issues that it raises. Instead it follows its other agenda which accepts gender equality as a given and denies the exploration of struggle and contention through which this new social organisation and cultural experience has been achieved. As science fiction negotiates the present through its representation of the future then *Space: Above and Beyond* (*S:AAB*) is rooted in the same cultural anxieties as the military thrillers as well as the prospect of social change manifest in our own time. Therefore, although the military thrillers engage awkwardly with the weight of traditional patriarchy, tacking on text epilogues (*The General's Daughter*, 1999) to valorise female military personnel, *S:AAB* is actually more interesting for what it chooses not to say about women, work and war. This absence is just as significant to understand how the popular imagination considers either the inevitability of gender equality or patriarchal order.

The extent of its failure as a science fiction series makes *S:AAB* a curious object of study. This discussion, however, is not going to dwell upon the political or practical reasons that led Twentieth Century Fox to make the decision not to commission a second series for the 1996–97 season. Instead it will concentrate on the unsettling future diegesis that contributed to the show's demise but will probably ensure that it lives on in re-runs. As it does so it will record a continued uneasiness in the last decade of the twentieth century with both an integrated workforce that results in the presence of women in armed conflict and the suitability of young men in the same role.

It is not unusual for science fiction series to be threatened by cancellation. They are exceedingly vulnerable as an unpredictable genre that requires an enormous initial investment and has an imponderable audience. This is particularly the case now when special effects demand exceptionally high budgets and the services of additional specialists. Moreover, science fiction series are difficult to market and very often, as in the case of the seminal series *Star Trek*, take a long time to recoup their production costs through syndication and the licensing of merchandise. Advertisers and programmers are often uncertain whether science fiction is for adults or children, whether its content is pulp or intellectual fare and thus are unable to gain a clear sense of a homogeneous audience. *S:AAB* does have a committed fan following on the Net, but even their discussion, analysis and interaction register an uncomfortable uncertainty with the series in marked contrast to fans of *Babylon 5* or the very confident and impious episode dissection of contemporary *Star Trek* fans. Discussion is predominantly focused on technology and training, especially the spacecraft and special effects. Secondary discussion is directed towards the enigmas present in all narrative episodes and then speculation on the potential romantic involvement of characters and the general attractiveness of cast members.

Part of the reason for the series' awkward reception comes from the fact that it belongs to a new narrative mode in televisual fantasy and science fiction, one that does not meet with the needs of television schedules or the pattern of heterogeneous consumption that ensures the popularity of programmes such as *Star Trek*, that is, conclusive single episodes which draw on a wide variety of generic and formulaic narrative. *S:AAB* is part of a characteristic group of programmes which expresses great anxiety in the lived cultural experience of the contemporary period and explores this in fiction through drawn-out serial narrative. The narrative drive of each episode in the series is predicated on the development of doubt rather than on resolving a dilemma through narrative certainty. These series produce demanding single episodes which rely heavily on the audience's knowledge of prior narrative accounts for their maximum emotional and intellectual impact.

To create this effect and achieve such audience responsibility or interaction the series has to be developed cumulatively and not as separate episodes but as a distinct entity and consistently developing narrative. This reaches its apogee in *Babylon 5*, which relies not just on sequences of episodes forming narrative clusters within a season but attempts to produce a five-season storyline. In *Babylon 5*'s case this was thwarted by interference from the production company, the contractual obligations of actors and the instability of finance in producing television narrative. Straczynski, the creator of *Babylon 5*, has criticised other science fiction series as relying on a 'backwards continuity, so that when you refer to something that happened in a prior episode it makes sense rather than actually foreshadowing and the development of actual serial narrative'.[1] Technically, *S:AAB* fails to strike a balance between the exposition needed to develop characters which interest the writers and the clichéd dialogue and action-adventure one suspects appealed to the backers. The first episodes of *Babylon 5* very carefully lay down a science fiction *mise-en-scène* and relatively standard science fiction dilemmas and conventions in free-standing episodes as the story gradually opens up. *S:AAB*'s overall pace is too slow and its introduction to the emotional dilemmas which characterise the main protagonists leans towards the melodramatic. *Babylon 5*'s initial episodes stand alone as recognisable science fiction conundrums gradually leading the series into a battle narrative. *S:AAB* opens with the advent of war which becomes the permanent dramatic situation.

Cult television very often manifests itself by requiring the audience to fully engage in the narrative construction, for example, *The Prisoner* (1967–68), *Twin Peaks* (1990–91) in particular and the development of programmes such as *The X Files* (1993–) and *Millennium* (1996–). The initial publicity for *S:AAB* and its first episodes attempted to target a young audience with the prospect of interstellar dog fights. However the storylines and pace of narrative development actually require great sophistication and dedication on the part of the viewer. Along with the series previously mentioned programmes yield more in second viewing and in discussion with other viewers. Therefore, cult narratives foster popular appeal because they have to be read rather than consumed and they are open to many different readings. They are heterogeneous and able to appeal to different audiences across class, race, age and gender. Glen Morgan and James Wong, the creators of *S:AAB*, were previously co-producers and writers for *The X Files*, and for the *S:AAB* pilot they collaborated with the director David Nutter. It is clear that the high production values, densely constructed plots and interest in character studies from their previous work is a priority for the space series. However, obvious space-faring science fiction is difficult to market in comparison with *Star Trek* and *Babylon 5* or without using the cult television press, which was exceedingly critical of the series and did not really consider it after the first five episodes.

S:AAB shares many of the traits and preoccupations of these programmes, but it failed to attract a big enough audience to justify the costs of its CGI budget and thus secure a second series commission. Reviewers attempted to acknowledge the quality of the special effects and production standards of the programme, but seemed to be either confused or unimpressed by the writers' preoccupation with the fallible rather than heroic qualities of its characters. Pre-publicity stressed that *S:AAB* was a series following the exploits of three heroes, but the two male heroes lack the dignity, reliability and commitment implied by this title, leaving Shane Vansen, the career soldier and the more worthy candidate. Vansen does live up to this role but her competence even when she is hysterical in the third episode, 'The Dark of the Sun', exists in comparison with the lack of maturity evident in her male peers and makes remarkable, even unprecedented viewing.

The premise governing the series is relatively straightforward: as the Earth starts a space colonisation programme, it comes into conflict with alien life which escalates into a bitter and long-running war. The series follows the missions assigned to the very young 58th Marine Squadron. These are inexperienced pilots, two of whom are defined as having very non-patriotic motivations for working in both space and the military. In its initial publicity, *S:AAB* promises computer-generated star battles, but its warfare was not a shiny special effects extravaganza and was billed as a 'futuristic Vietnam' with an 'action-packed cyberpunky feel'.[2] In an interview given by the writer/producers prior to the launch of the series, a great effort was made to establish that emphasis had been placed on the characters and that the producers intended to make creative use of the evolving *S:AAB* diegesis:

> 'I think our tone is more intense action adventure,' says Wong. 'It's a character study of people under pressure, and it's an action-adventure show set in the future, so you have dog-fights in space, aliens and other weird stuff. The backbone is "We're at War" more than anything else.'[3]

Although the references that hold the developing narrative together come directly from the history of warfare, especially replaying military dilemmas of the Second World War, *S:AAB* is set in a future which imagines a different set of cultural tensions. In concluding their pre-production interview, Wong and Morgan intimate that they wanted the viewers to discover more than just another glossy science fiction series. The 'more' referred to here was an apprecia-tion of sophisticated character development and the consideration of faith as a motivating issue:

> Not necessarily religious faith, although that's fine, but nowadays officials get elected and whether you're on the left or the right you say 'that's the guys for me', and then, in what seems like a matter of weeks, they've let you down. That's why we went back to the World War Two films, where there was that mood of 'I'm willing to die for a cause' that's the element that we want to explore.[4]

To do so the producers extrapolate a military service in which both sexes serve without apparent segregation, sexism (or racism) and through which the writers can pursue developing fraternal rather than romantic or sexual relations. The series focuses on a group of very young recruits in a situation of total war. The first episodes therefore are exacting as their fan criticism and commercial reviewers suggest. They are grim and humourless, striking a very discordant note in contemporary science fiction. Nevertheless, the pilot and its subsequent episodes are criticised for being derivative, as there is a desperate need to link this 'science fiction' to other programmes. However, the real focus of criticism was its use of 'dysfunctional personalities', and after the first month of screening in Britain it became the concerted critical opinion that it was too much effort to watch the programme in the hope that these characters would develop.[5] The hope, it seems, is that the teenage angst reviewers perceived in the realisation of the young marine corps would resolve itself through romantic entanglement, hence their disappointment when this did not become a narrative direction.

These reviews compare *S:AAB* so readily with *Top Gun* and *Full Metal Jacket* because it is composed of an all-encompassing patriarchal environment. The pilot's director, David Nutter refers to the space carrier Saratoga where the bulk of the action is set as '*Das Boot* in outer space'.[6] This is a future which is very claustrophobic with only fleeting reference to the Earth society for which they are fighting. It also has the uneasy tension of a western, which recognises that its hero is a killer outside of a civilisation to which they can never return. There is a fluctuating moral alignment between East and West or in this case old and new, space and Earth. Space is full of deadly terror and the prospect of taming it or colonising it is lost at the same point that Earth is revealed as a home for political corruption in the aftermath of a sterility plague.

Nutter also saw the series outlining something other than an 'SF-Future', that is, one where 'people dressed in tight polyester suits and no shadows, darkness or grime'.[7] The genres that have been drawn upon to correct this vision of the future are not necessarily narrative spaces that offer especially pliant roles for women. Yet the mission leader of the squadron is female and she undergoes complex character development and career advancement, which contrasts significantly with the treatment of female characters in other science fiction programmes.[8]

To achieve the intensity required for this exploration of long-term and bitter warfare, the writers have to establish the Earth for which each character is fighting. The back story views the Earth in a dystopian manner using three current science fiction conventions to map out its future history. The Earth has been depopulated by a fertility plague in the early twenty-first century (2004). In response to this the remaining humans created artificially intelligent androids known as 'Silicates' in order to rebuild after the global economy has collapsed and world leaders have opted for the unification of the Earth. As well as the Silicates, Earth science attempted to build up the workforce through the production of genetically designed, artificially gestated humans known as 'InVitros' (2027). Both of these groups are used in indentured service. Although this scenario is very familiar in science fiction narrative, it is explicitly not the case that the resulting culture responds to the crisis of sterility by enforcing gendered divisions of labour. Usually such a threat to the human population results in the removal of women from work in the public sphere to ensure their focus on reproduction, for example, Margaret Atwood's *The Handmaid's Tale* (1987). In the *S:AAB* diegesis the lack of a 'human' workforce makes women more acceptable in the workplace. The identification of a new underclass enables women to be ascribed as human rather than 'Other' but of course this is implicit within the series rather than the subject of discussion.

The next stage in this future history is another virus known as the 'Take a Chance' virus which infects the Silicates and allows them to act independently. They decide to rebel and the AI wars commence in 2047. The InVitros are conscripted but unwilling to fight as they have developed outside a social or familial situation that might engender patriotism or a desire to protect family and/or community. So although women are in the armed forces following a debate and social action which we do not witness, family values continue to be upheld as virtues and necessary for social cohesion. The war ends when the Silicates flee the Earth. The androids were originally designed to prepare for outward human colonisation, taking advantage of space flight theory and technology developed in 2014. After stealing spacecraft, they leave the Earth in 2057. The humans return to their plan for colonisation, which has an overtone of pacifism, but the first colony unwittingly invades planets owned by aliens from the Reticulus sector (2063). The aliens' experience of Earth life is the extremely unpredictable, volatile and amoral Silicates with whom they seem to have joined forces. Their judgement of humans by the actions of their creations leads the aliens to commit themselves to total war.[9]

The three central characters that are presented to us as potential heroes in this war have motivational outlines connected to each of these three Earth life forms. There is a human colonist (Nathan West) who has lost his place on the mission to an affirmative action programme for InVitro (IV) participants. There is also an InVitro (Cooper Hawkes) who has been conscripted and needs to learn social skills in order to function as part of a marine squadron. The third character, Shane Vansen, has an exaggerated fear and hatred of

Silicates. She witnessed her parents' murder by Silicates during the AI wars and joined the military in a complicated gesture towards retribution. All three join a recognisably patriarchal military service, but sexism is not its defining characteristic. Instead the military is far more preoccupied by simulacra of racism inherent in the InVitro storyline. The InVitros, identifiable by the gestation navel on the back of their necks, are considered as second-class citizens, discriminated against and subject to violence. Their treatment and the emotional register and language used during these scenes follows conventions established by various media for articulating abusive racial antagonism. However, it lacks a historical perspective for this experience, presenting the violence and exchanges as arbitrary responses.[10] The visual difference which marks the Other is absent rather than disrupted even though Hawkes' immature behaviour and lack of loyalty is no different from West's. Attitudes to race become conflated with class as the narrative logic distinguishes between the two men because of their social place and status within a future world which is moving into a further phase of colonisation. Instead of unity the war which the Earth fights apparently for its very survival divides evolved humanity on a piecemeal basis but integrates women and blacks unquestionably into the army.

Thus the presence of women within the military is not an issue for the series and how this acceptance has been achieved in just over fifty years of future history is never accounted for by the diegetic narrative. The emotional tenor and graphic injustice, abuse and violence of the military thriller is directed at the IV characters and increasingly the alien enemy. Shane Vansen is established by the first two episodes as a natural leader for the 58th Marine Squadron. She is both the choice of the group members themselves and its InVitro commander. Vansen is presented as an exceptional soldier and is promoted at the conclusion of the first and final series. Her gender is neither a source of strength nor weakness. Moreover, she is the member of the squadron who is the least likely to question the patriarchal hierarchy governing the military at war. Unlike other representations of women within the military her commitment is unchallenged by questions of gender politics. Her belief in the system and its ideals allow her to manipulate the conditions under which her group is fighting. This is significant because it presents Vansen as succeeding by accepting the patriarchal and traditional values of the military. She is not hampered in the execution of her duties by civilian or feminist politics, which present themselves to others.

Vansen's presence and activity in this science fiction series is therefore unlike most other SF representations of women. Programmes such as *Stargate SG-1* (1997) are quite typical; they are able to use diegetic conventions to create situations where gender inequality can be narratively resolved in either an alien, historical or virtual environment. In 'Emancipation', the third episode of the first season of *Stargate SG-1*, for example, the programme chooses to establish the credentials of the female member of the exploration team. The group travels through the stargate to a planet where it encounters a tribe very akin to the Mongols. In a male-dominated society, the female team member (who is both a soldier and a scientist) is required to dress in female attire. She is later sold as a concubine and has to resolve the narrative dilemma through hand-to-hand combat with a larger and stronger male opponent.[11] *Star Trek: Voyager*, on the other hand, establishes female leadership as resting significantly on age and experience as well as education and training. *S:AAB* has neither of these strategies to draw upon; Vansen is an inexperienced recruit working with an untested team who cannot rely on historical precedent or alternative realities to explore her position as woman and soldier. Therefore the dramatic proof that her gender does not preclude her from active military service simply is not an issue.

OPERATIONAL EFFECTIVENESS

In the early twenty first century, the extent to which women serve in the armed forces is still determined by considerations of operational effectiveness.[12] Generally, although women can be armed and are given weapons training for the purpose of self-defence, they are not permitted to engage and kill the enemy in an offensive role. The principles of operational effectiveness are built upon rationales of the rights of decency and privacy as well as concerns regarding women's lack of physical strength and the aggressive instincts required for combat. The implications here are that being a woman requires access to sanitary and personal living conditions which are different to those that can be tolerated by men. These considerations also stretch to a woman's reliability in terms of expected length of service and unwillingness to contravene cultural assumptions about women and war.[13]

It is women's mental and physical operational effectiveness which is being explored and assessed in the military thrillers. These films impact and mediate the experience of actual military service because decisions concerning appropriate roles for women in the military are subject to vociferous public as well as media debate. Cogent beliefs held by religious and political groups also shape the policy decisions made within the service. Foremost of these is the firm impression that mixed gender teams in combat areas would undermine the unit and the bonding necessary for battlefield performance. None of these issues are addressed directly in *S:AAB*, but they do appear to make up the underlying considerations of the ponderous initial episodes. Shane Vansen has to be tested in the field and resolve her fears by assuming the role of a warrior mother. She proves her leadership capabilities by establishing the group as a family rather than setting up collegiate bonding. The squadron relies on teamwork but it is not necessarily acting as a team whereby each member is equal and performing a role (which may have a higher or lower status) that must be undertaken for the group to succeed. The 58th Squadron identifies itself as family and thus binds different interests to a common cause. Moreover, a family is understood as a network which can accommodate learning from experience and which acknowledges that each individual has strengths and weakness and that these may change as they develop and grow. It is Vansen who becomes the focus for this style of management which is seen in contrast to other squadrons. Often the 58th lacks a sense of professional deployment, preferring an amateur approach that allows it to deal with the emotional and technical crises of unprecedented events the way one must do within a growing family.

Despite her role of 'mother' Vansen is generally desexualised although one woman reviewer criticises the programme for the regularity with which the actress in this role takes 'pointless strolls around the ship wearing nothing but Ripley-style undies and a sheen of designer sweat'; gender performance in this series is curiously neutered and Vansen is particularly asexual.[14] The books aimed for adolescent reading which accompany the series make much of Hawkes' attraction to Vansen and her ability to defend herself physically from his tentative sexual advances.[15] Her role as mother and then as colleague within the military context begins to construct her as a taboo object or suggest that she is autonomous. Combat narratives in fiction generally have a specific relationship to the symbolic process of being a man.[16] Therefore discourses of combat should differentiate men from women. It does not in *S:AAB*, and Vansen does not become more of a 'woman' through her combat experience although she clearly becomes a better marine. The narrative does not attempt to probe the ideological constructions of masculinity and femininity as complementary but distinct spheres of experience. Instead it sets up hierarchies of age and a dichotomy between human and alien.

Through their youth and inexperience, all of the members of the 58th pass through trials instigated by a military hierarchy that is itself struggling to come to terms with the ideological impact of this future war. *S:AAB* chooses most strikingly not to act out the life giver/life taker dichotomy of the mythology surrounding women and war. This distinction is made plain by contemporary military discourse in the words of General Robert Barrow,

> ... combat is finding ... closing with ... and killing or capturing the enemy. It's killing. And it's done in an environment that is often as difficult as you can possibly imagine. Extremes of climate. Brutality. Death. Dying. It's ... uncivilized! And women can't do it! Nor should they even be thought of as doing it. The requirements for strength and endurance render them unable to do it. And I may be old-fashioned, but I think the very nature of women disqualifies them from doing it. Women give life. Sustain life. Nurture life. They don't take it.[17]

Although it is this exact scenario of combat experience, requiring a grim rather than glorious heroism which the programme diegesis attempts to realise, the latter part of Barrow's assertions here are completely effaced. The women in *S:AAB* are presented as committed both to the army and the squadron while their male peers have to learn through socialisation and realignment of allegiance how to function as part of that team. Hawkes attempts to live up to the example set by an 'older brother' and make sense of his death by conforming to military hierarchy and learning what it has to teach him. West abandons his quixotic quest to find his fiancée and can thus give his full attention to the missions assigned to the squadron. Both therefore become reliable and responsible members of the squadron rather than liabilities. Gender in this fictional world is not an issue as each character is seeking maturity through combat experience. The situations in which the female characters find themselves prompt them to question their humanity and not their femininity. *S:AAB*'s assessment of war as dehumanising uses fiction to explore the experience rather than obscuring it through straightforward heroic narrative. The programme confirms war as a brutal, traumatic and alienating experience with only fleeting moments of heroic valour to give a semblance of control and purpose. Despite the CGI spectacle present in each episode, the programme does not deliver the cultural or formulaic expectation of combat narratives. The series framework also precludes a shift into another genre in order to relieve the tension of a scenario of total war. It is unremitting and there is no space afforded to consider alternative lives for female (or male) characters. The 58th gains success and status from very shaky foundations, and as the squadron negotiates military politics and combat situations effectively and without interpersonal strife, the debate regarding women and the military does not develop.

This situation arises from the way that the war which is being fought is fully narrativised by twentieth-century allusion. The fundamental question regarding women and the military relates to the nature of future war. In the early twenty-first century, gender integration into the armed forces is taking place through the need for suitable labour and equal opportunity policies but more significantly through the increasing adoption of technology. Beyond science fiction the imagining of future war is very limited, especially the effect that it will have on personnel. In the late 1970s Major Michael Andrews specifically outlined how changes in the nature of combat will make the exclusion of women from the services an increasingly illogical proposition:

> The future battlefield will require unprecedented technical expertise. Manoeuvrable craft, hovering command modules, 'smart bombs', laser guns, spaceships, missiles, neutron bombs, satellites, 'brain waves' and biocybernetics will be involved. Civilian population centers will be targets.[18]

Therefore, debates relating to such gendered categories as 'upper body strength' become irrelevant. Andrews identifies through a quote from Margaret Mead that undisclosed concern about the military and not necessarily women underpins the gender politics regarding combat.

> It is possible that the historic refusal to give women weapons may be due not to a rejection of putting the power of death into the hands of those who give life, but rather because women who kill … are more implacable and less subject to chivalrous rules with which men seek to mute the savagery of warfare. It may be that women would kill too thoroughly and endanger the negotiations

and posturing of armies, through treaties and prisoner taking, with which nations at war eventually manage uneasy breathing spaces between wars.[19]

Separate spheres and the ideology of motherhood support unequal power relations, which have been institutionalised in the sexual division of labour. The logic of private and public spheres is ultimately played out in the continuing exclusion of women from military service. However, the desirability of eradicating discrimination which would place women in combat situations has split feminist opposition to blatant policies and practices of inequality in the military. Theorists such as Jean Bethke Elshtain have proposed a particular mode of feminist consciousness, which is referred to as 'maternal thinking'.[20] The position is an outcome of the experience of mothering or being mothered. Elshtain describes it as 'a way of knowing' which links the individual with the social whole and thus prompts critical reflection. She argues that this perspective places contemporary feminists in a powerful theoretical position from which they can challenge the militarist stance and militaristic policies and thinking. In S:AAB the crisis engendered by infertility has rendered any objection to women in combat zones null and void. Moreover the Earth government is clearly represented as lacking choice in this engagement with war. Women are also seen as making new contributions to military practice. Both women in the 58th learn to depend on instinct or the development of psychic intuition to cope with and survive battlefield situations,[21] a situation encouraged by the unreliable nature of the equipment that has been issued to them and the men that serve with them. The significant aspect of the programme's representation of paranormal experience is that it is included without being denigrated as a female attribute. The military hierarchy is specifically interested in this ability and the male members of the squadron come to trust and depend upon it. There is no contradiction between 'female logic' and 'male rationality'. The military is faced by a new situation whereby it must adapt to the present circumstances rather than rely on traditional dichotomies. Of course this does not necessarily imply that this is the preferred reading made by the predominantly male audience of S:AAB.

MODES OF EXTRAPOLATION: S:AAB AND STARSHIP TROOPERS

In her analysis of science fiction film in the late 1970s and 1980s, Vivian Sobchack identifies a visual screen aesthetic which she terms 'inverted millenarianism'.[22] The term refers to a popular account of the future, which litters the diegetic world with the residue of a commodified culture. Sobchack accounts for a pleasure and a sense of realism found in the perception of a future which does not comprise bright colours, shiny technology and a successfully evolved human society, images which were predicated in science fiction series and films of the 1950s, 1960s and early 1970s and which have their origins in pulp fiction illustration in the pre-war era. The near future is given the grimy feel that Nutter was striving for because it is subject to decay and an incentive for repair and recycling. The lack of replicator technology or instantaneous transportation produces a deceptively low-tech combat situation which can emulate cinematic representations of the Second World War. Sobchack notes in a number of films, the epitome of which is *Blade Runner* (1982), 'the visual trashing' and yet operational functioning of what used to be shiny future technology that is part of the 'post-future' science fiction film's adoption of film noir conventions.[23] Progress is not a given in this articulation of the future. Gender equality was often seen as part of the imagined future that 'inverted millenarianism' contravenes. Such equality would occur naturally through the benevolent enlightenment demonstrated in the *SG-1* episode. 'Inverted millenarianism', therefore, posits a future of loss rather than libertarian gain. The significance of this pessimistic articulation of the future is its acknowledgement of popular anxieties about social trends. Part of this expectation of the future is women in combat and women as heroes. However, the dark future is also ambiguous about the political or moral meaning of this eventuality, especially its desirability.

Children's science fiction television has accepted active female protagonists and allows them to participate both in terms of intellect and physical prowess. There are moments when the pace of narrative imperative blurs gender distinctions, but this is not a tactic which is necessarily employed by *S:AAB*. In early reviews, *S:AAB* is persistently criticised for being dull. Even those supporting the series have to concede:

> It's often slow, grim and humorless, and strays into hokiness given the slightest opportunity. But it's also made with conviction, which its high production values, strong acting, superb effects and interesting characters pulling it through the less inspiringly written episodes. Meanwhile, the better scripts, which are

becoming more common, are providing densely constructed, intriguing, multi-layered plots for the cast and crew to really get their teeth into.[24]

S:AAB's style and mode of presentation are very important to the statements that it makes regarding gender. S:AAB lacks the postmodern irony which allows similar future war narratives such as Paul Verhoeven's *Starship Troopers* (1997) to achieve immense box-office popularity. S:AAB cannot avoid the implicit reference to gender politics which is embedded in its premise and resulting storylines. Verhoeven's account of the near future in films predating *Starship Troopers*, such as *Robocop* (1987), parody welfare capitalism and the relationship between business and government. This ironic sensibility counters 'inverted millenarianism' and allows the bright shiny future to be playfully re-inserted into the adventure narrative. S:AAB has a tendency to offer an inadvertently silent pastiche of older non-science fiction films which in effect fails to give the audience a strong enough indication of their role regarding the construction of serial plots. Moreover, it reveals that it is critically bankrupt regarding issues of gender because it will not acknowledge that it has instated female marines in a pastiche of a period in which they had no place.

A comparison between *Starship Troopers* and S:AAB demonstrates that, whereas both assume a gender-integrated military (which *Starship Troopers* visualises as an unselfconscious mixed shower scene), *Starship Troopers* is heavily reliant on a mythology of heterosexual romance to structure its storyline. S:AAB's use of the same trope (such as Nathan West's search for his lost fiancée) has to be abandoned before the series can fully develop its dramatic impact. Therefore we have to consider a number of variables in the presentation of sexist narratives concerning the representation of women and war. Both West in S:AAB and Rico in *Starship Troopers* join the military in the hope of sustaining a romantic relationship and both develop to maturity through the combat narrative. It is form rather than theme which allows a more detailed examination of gender issues or the acknowledgement of their absence. Televisual science fiction offers far more narrative space and potential than the shorter format of popular cinema. S:AAB has longer to explore characters; *Starship Troopers* of necessity is much more reductive, determining them by the dynamics of class and the vicissitudes of love.

Starship Troopers delivers the narrative that *S:AAB* is so anxious to avoid, that is the competition of different accounts of femininity for the clearly recognisable hero. This is the case because *S:AAB* has problems in the representation of masculinity in the same way that *Starship Troopers* raises anxieties about contemporary femininity. The two women in the love triangle with Rico in *Starship Troopers* do not develop skills, qualities or maturity of character. They remain exactly as they appeared to Rico in high school; the girl next door, Dizzy Flores, who follows him into the Mobile Infantry, and the unattainable object of his desire, Carmen Ibanez, whose near perfect maths score allows her to join the fleet and train as a pilot. The regular male members of the squadron West, Hawkes and Wang are presented as juvenile for most of the *S:AAB* narrative, whereas the female members, the engineer Damphousse and leader Vansen, demonstrate greater maturity in their negotiation of emotional and practical dilemmas. Although *S:AAB* is accused of melodrama and banal sentimentality the celebration of cliché is an accepted part of *Starship Troopers'* narrative style. The romantic narrative in this film perpetuates itself through scenes such as the way Ibanez watches her two suitors fight over her. A more significant example is the way that Ibanez's rival dies in Rico's arms declaring that her life was fulfilled because she 'got to have him'.

Ibanez then takes on the role of cinematic heroine/love interest. As her position in the military is characterised by structure, science and her attractiveness to the male officer who has trained her, her femininity has not been in doubt and she can easily take on the role of victim. In this film gendered relationships in the military are seen as uncomplicated because adolescent sexuality is not necessarily related to parenthood. Being in the military is explicitly a way for women to gain citizenship and thus a licence to have children in the future. One could assume that the sterility plague that forms the back story to *S:AAB* also changes the meaning of adolescence, sexuality and gender roles yet these issues are not explored. At the beginning of *Starship Troopers* Rico has a disagreement with his parents regarding his relationship with Ibanez. Although she is special to him the confrontation confirms her as ordinary and marks her as a potential wife and mother. She holds this meaning when she has to be rescued by Rico at the conclusion of the film. In accordance with a more traditional war narrative the hero has risen from the ranks, found his purpose and reached a level of maturity.

Both *Starship Troopers* and *S:AAB* look at women, work and romance in the context of the military. It is here that they make very different statements about the future. Ibanez chooses very early on to try for a career, she wants a command and piloting makes best use of her extraordinary mathematical abilities. She is enabled to participate in the military not through female solidarity or struggle but through benevolent patriarchy. The film constantly belittles her achievements rather than celebrating them. Early on Rico's mother describes her as 'some little girl who wants to look good in a uniform', and this comment is reiterated during the film. In contrast with Dizzy, she is humiliated by her squeamishness during a high school biology dissection. Her rise to the status of pilot is apparently effortless and guaranteed compared with Rico's (and Dizzy's) promotion in the field. Her insensitivity to the hero is explained by her characterisation as a career woman which codes her as naive and immature. In contrast to Dizzy in terms of class she is also coded as frigid. Dizzy is seen as an unexceptional girl who can satisfy the hero's needs and share the same cultural experience and background. Ibanez in comparison is able to achieve her professional goals by controlling her sexuality. Her contribution to combat is rarely heroic, and when Rico goes to rescue her it is a distraction to his battlefield responsibilities. Moreover, towards the film's conclusion, her superiority as a pilot is voided because class segregation has kept her away from the combat zones, from which Rico draws his more legitimate status. The two interventions that she does make into combat both reveal her to be remarkably passive. Piloting does not make her a leader and she does not train among men. She is gradually represented as a technician and therefore does not compete with Rico. Neither does Dizzy; although she is capable of action and decision-making she remains subordinate to him. Thus women have a specific place in warfare which is defined by contemporary imagery and discourse concerning their operational effectiveness. It is not seen as a problem in this future war scenario, which is still a narrative about men with women as extras.

The *S:AAB* diegesis and narrative declines to emulate this structure, hence its ratings failure. Its consideration of an integrated army sees the assimilation of women as existing without complication and with equal opportunities. 'Never No More' is an episode of *S:AAB* which provides narrative space to consider the biography of the female lieutenant and her choice not to marry, which has left her free to join the military and avenge her family. Crucially, unlike her male peers Hawkes and West, Vansen is seen as adult and not adolescent. She has had the responsibility of raising her sisters after the death of her parents. The retelling of her youthful decision is a revelation of character for the audience. By episode 15, the audience for *S:AAB* finds itself committed to each mission of the war without ellipses of time which speed up the contemporary science fiction adventure. *Starship Troopers* resolves a very similar total war scenario very quickly and with four main missions. 'Never No More' is a poignant interlude in the development of the war. The episode opens with the death of a female pilot and Vansen's confession that she has had a premonition. This episode details a turning point in the war, which is manifest in the discovery of the enemy's home planet. The appearance of an alien ace pilot is the main focus of the story; so although we follow a personal storyline it is integrated with the developing narrative about the course of the war. Vansen has a reunion with her high school sweetheart, Captain Oakes of the 38th Squadron, who is mourning his colleague and lover killed by the new alien fighter. Although she is unsure of her emotions, Vansen volunteers to replace the dead pilot on an important mission. She faces her feelings through a masculine gesture of solidarity.

At the briefing, Vansen falls into reverie and recalls the marriage proposal that Oakes made to her before the war. Romantically, he had played a Patsy Cline record, significant to him as it was playing when his father had proposed to his mother 95 years before. Vansen declines to become part of that tradition. She tells Oakes that she does not believe in forever, and we later learn that they drifted apart. As they reconcile after the mission he tells her that he himself has come to believe her words, but she replies that she regrets acting upon them. Her reasoning is extremely enigmatic; she says, 'When something seems inevitable the harder I fight it. Giving your life to someone doesn't mean dying; I wish I'd given you mine that night.' *Starship Troopers* uses romantic imagery to perpetuate the masculine hero as a survivor in a world where women have become contenders. The stratification of roles upheld by contemporary military service is predicated on the traditional notion that believes in the sanctity of unegalitarian gender roles and in a gendered morality. *S:AAB* generally replaces issues of gender with those of humanity in opposition to the alien other. However, in this episode it suggests that there are alternatives to the social organisation of formal heterosexual relationships which underpin these assumptions. To equate marriage with death is an extreme statement, to then reconsider its value and possibility of negotiating such a relationship is equally radical. *S:AAB* cannot articulate the political, social, personal and economic concerns resonant in this statement but it sees them as being of interest to its audience and their contemplation of the future. Despite asking the question *S:AAB* turns to traditional romantic narrative to avoid answering it. All the pilots on the Saratoga are called out to destroy the alien fighter and Oakes flies with the 58th. His fighter is disabled and as he crashes he knocks the alien craft out of combat. It had locked its sights on to Vansen's craft and his demise saves her life. The alien craft is not destroyed and Vansen's war must continue.

As the example has shown, *S:AAB* wants to explore the emotional aspects of total war at a very different pace to other science fiction series or visual products. Its depth is incommensurable with the combat narrative of *Starship Troopers*. Yet narrative potential is contained by the same discursive matrix. We do not see the relationship between women and war in any context other than the military or high level political intrigue. During wartime, discourses of femininity which deny women a place in the public sphere become problematic and reveal their inherent contradictions. Women must work outside the home and become part of a team replacing the men called away. Femininity, particularly during the Second World War, was a promise to women of normality and the brighter future of homemaking to come. Vansen is in effect re-fighting the Second World War but femininity or the return to femininity is not at issue in this fiction. The apparent unwillingness to confront these issues makes the programme even more unsettling with regard to gender issues. The presentation of the narrative in 'Never No More' emphasises Vansen's long hair and Oakes' height and size, but every time Vansen speaks it confuses the romantic imperative. Vansen is in love and Vansen is sexually attracted to Oakes, but she is still able to do her job. As women are increasingly portrayed as competent in the workspace, unreconstructed men are infantilised and shown to be unstable. Oakes is churlish and overacts to Vansen's assumption of command in the field. Hawkes and West can only watch Vansen as she goes about her mission. They are powerless to intervene in her emotional life as it lies outside the military discourse upon which they intersect. An impression which is accentuated by the way they are present as she leaves for the mission but can only sit behind a viewing screen, the contribution that they may make to such a serious situation is not even considered.

Furthermore, Vansen's maturity and agency confirm that gender roles have changed. On the mission, access to privileged information motivates her to take command from Oakes, which he greets initially with anger and then with recognition that her actions were valid. He is left holding on to a romantic ideal that is meaningless to Vansen. He does sacrifice his life for her but the crucial point here is that she is also in combat and not a victim waiting for rescue. Gender thus appears to be a less contentious issue than others raised by the diegetic future. 'Never No More', with its naming of the alien fighter 'Chiggy von Richthoffen', illustrates the way the series replays legends of the First and Second World Wars which were undertaken with a sustained ideology about a better future and the defence of ordinary lifestyles. The narrative takes place on the *Saratoga* which references both the turning point victory over the British in the American War of Independence (1777) and Theodore Roosevelt's speech on patriotism in July 1918: 'There can be no fifty-fifty Americans in this country, there is room here for only one hundred percent Americanism.' During the American War for Independence, Linda Grant de Pauw argues, tens of thousands of women were engaged in active combat.[25] Their service and those of women nursing in the First World War and flying in the Second have been effaced by the maintenance of discrimination at the end of the twentieth century. Although they may not have been equal in the chain of command those nursing on the battlefield were just as subject to the brutality and physical reality of war which was perniciously ignored by those advocating that women should not be involved in the combat zones during the Gulf War.[26] *S:AAB* has produced in effect a gender correct version of the Second World War in space without any consideration of its inherent contradictions.

During the Second World War, the call for unity was also directed at perceived divides between class and in terms of national identities. A sense of unity in Britain was built upon the promise of a better future. Gender equality was not part of that future and was heavily felt by women who turned to reading science fiction in the 1950s and 1960s. Talking to North American women in the late 1980s about how they started reading science fiction, many reported that they appreciated the opportunity offered to female characters in space.[27] Most pleasurable and reassuring was the respect given to women's use of scientific knowledge and initiative in the juvenile fiction written by Robert Heinlein, which would have included *Starship Troopers*. This is a significant function of science fiction. However in this fiction the gender roles open to women beyond adolescence are actually limited. What is remarkable is the respect for the roles that they hold and the acknowledgement of the contribution they make to colonial society. These narratives of colonisation and war do legitimate active females of all ages, but egalitarian notions of citizenship require them to conform to parental roles as required by an underpopulated society. Gender equality in *S:AAB* is achieved in a world dominated by war and through which hope for a better future is gradually eroded, since the potential for colonisation is lost.

S:AAB's use of 'inverted millenarianism' and construction of a near future where essential patriarchal values remain unchanged marks a sense of uneasiness about this visualisation of gender equality. Women are equal in the ranks and work alongside as well as in command of men. The squadron that we follow, 'The Wild Cards', is led by a 'Queen' with a 'King' clearly second in command.[28] They are not an unusual squadron, except for their success and survival. Military life is not a temporary expediency for these women. The military framework has been used particularly in comedy as an unnatural environment for women – for example, *Private Benjamin* (1980) – which effects a maturing process before the woman can leave it for other roles. The future scenario offered by *S:AAB* provides greater potential than the static, closed narratives of *GI Jane* (1996) and *Courage Under Fire* (1996), but the acceptance of women in the military belies the political nature of this far-reaching transition. Questions of whether the integration of men and women in the combat zone is a stable proposition are displaced by a generational opposition to the hierarchy of 'Old Men' who direct the war, a reconfiguration of racial politics around the blatant discrimination directed towards InVitros and the ultimate but unstable definition of noble humanity against an alien Other. The price of gender integration into the military appears to be becoming an honorary male, an inevitability that Vansen does not seem to want to fight and indeed the series did not have the chance to explore. The full potential of women in the future is an issue which has been addressed over and over again in feminist science fiction writing since the 1970s. Visual renditions of these narratives are few and far between. However, their consideration of responses to future war that include pacifism, separatism and conflict would make an interesting contribution not only to how we consider warfare but also as a basis from which to speculate on a non-fragmentary egalitarian future.

NOTES

1. Straczynski, J M, 'The Profession of Science Fiction 48: Approaching Babylon', *Foundation: The Review of Science Fiction*, no. 64, summer 1997.
2. Nazarro, Joe, 'Entering a Futuristic Vietnam with Space Wars', *SFX*, no. 5, October 1995, pp. 34–6. The introductory description of the series is '*Top Gun* meets *Full Metal Jacket* in space ....' Another account in the same magazine saw it as '*Star Wars* crossed with *Top Gun* plus a dash of *Melrose Place*', p. 26.
3. Nazarro, 'Entering a Futuristic Vietnam', p. 35. The writing production team comprise Glen Morgan and James Wong who established their reputation as co-producers and writers for *The X Files*.
4. Ibid.
5. Levell, Karen, 'Beyond burn after the first month's decidedly dull episodes', *SFX*, no. 23, 1997, p. 81.
6. Nazarro, 'Entering a Futuristic Vietnam', p. 35.
7. Ibid.
8. For a further discussion, see Moody and Schofield, 'Reconsidering Gender and Heroism' in James, E and Mendlesohn, F, *The Parliament of Dreams: Conferring on Babylon 5*, University of Reading, 1998. Vansen's role is defined by her work and she has no other status or life path. Other female protagonists, such as Delenn in *Babylon 5*, are conferred power through class, hierarchical status or indeed psychic ability.
9. This outline uses data compiled by Stoneburner, C *et al.* 'Space: History and Timeline' from the *Space: Above and Beyond Mission Status* site http://www/.planetx.com/space:aab/encyclopedia
10. See Jan Nederveen Pieterse, *White on Black: Images of Africa and Blacks in Western Popular Culture*, London, Yale University Press, 1992.
11. The female character's responses to her situation are treated as quasi-comic. However, the back story to the episode is even more interesting. The narrative insists upon the initial tribe that the group meet as being in process of repealing mores/laws which restrict the activity of women in the public sphere. This radical change is prompted by the tribal leader's realisation that he had married for love and that this made him a strong ruler. It is the reasoning of men rather than political activity of women which motivates this bid for social change. Moreover, the gendered roles and status as well as cultural practice are justified anthropologically as a tradition that protects women from capture by aliens using the stargate. As the team leaves, the sense is that the tribe will now conform to fairer gender relations as the product of progress.
12. For example, women in the US Army are subject to Direct Combat Probability Coding: 'Women will be assigned in all skills and positions except those which, by doctrine, mission, duties of the job, or battlefield locations involve the highest probability of direct combat with enemy forces.' For a further discussion, see Hooker, Richard D, 'Affirmative Action and Combat Exclusion: Gender Roles in the US Army', in Duke, Lois Lovelace (ed.) *Women in Politics: Outsiders or Insiders*, New Jersey, Prentice Hall, 1993. In Italy national legislation prohibits gender discrimination; however, it does not apply to the armed forces. Women are

currently excluded from the military. See Stanley, Sandra Carsen and Segal, Mady Wechsler, 'Military Women in NATO: An Update', *Armed Forces and Society*, vol. 14, no. 4, summer 1988, pp. 589–95. In Israel once a crisis situation has been defined the Israeli Defence Force is exempt from law and women are not permitted in combat zones for the express concern that they will distract their male counterparts.

13. See Dandeker, Christopher and Segal, Mady Wechsler, 'Gender Integration in Armed Forces: Recent Policy Developments in the United Kingdom', *Armed Forces and Society*, Fall 1996.

14. Levell, 'Beyond burn after the first month's decidedly dull episodes'.

15. The novelisation of the pilot episode *The Aliens Approach* (HarperTrophy, 1996) is published by the children's book division and is written by Easton Royce which is stated to be the pseudonym for a well-known children's book writer. Later books in the series are written by established children's writers who use female pseudonyms.

16. See a further discussion of this in the final chapter, 'Recognizing the Gendered Warrior', of Merryman, Molly, *Clipped Wings: The Rise and Fall of the Women Airforce Service Pilots (WASPS) of World War II*, New York, New York University Press, 1998.

17. Barrow, General Robert, *New York Times*, 21 July 1991.

18. Andrews, Michael, 'Women and Combat', *Military Review*, 1979.

19. Mead, Margaret, 'Women in National Service', *Teacher College Record*, 21 August 1972, p. 51.

20. See 'On Beautiful Souls, Just Warriors and Feminist Consciousness', *Women's Studies International Forum*, vol. 5, no. 3/4, 1982, pp. 341–8.

21. The 58th Squadron has another permanent female member, Vanessa Damphousse. She is a highly trained engineer, but the narrative suggests that she has clairvoyant precognition. The 58th has other female (and male) pilots assigned to it, but its personnel has a high turnover through combat casualties.

22. Sobchack, Vivian, *Screening Space: The American Science Fiction Film*, New York, Ungar, 1987, p. 246.

23. Ibid.

24. Golder, Dave, 'Space: Above and Beyond', *SFX*, no. 12, May 1996.

25. See 'Women in Combat: The Revolutionary War Experience', *Armed Forces and Society*, vol. 7, no. 2, winter 1981, pp. 209–26.

26. A good example of this was Field Marshall Sir Nigel Bagnall's 'A Call to Arms in the Battle of the Sexes', *Independent*, 28 August 1990, who opened an impassioned plea for women's inherent pacifism and our (sic) duty to protect them from the harrowing scenes of war in this fashion; 'Stomachs will still be ripped open and the non-supported entrails exposed ... .' His statement belies women's involvement in medical intervention on the battlefield and their work with aid agencies in times of crisis engendered by war or natural disaster.

27. These interviews were carried out as part of the author's postgraduate work researching empirical method in the sociology of literature.

28. Each member of the 58th Squadron has a call sign: Damphousse is Ace of Hearts, Wang is Joker, Hawkes is Jack of Spades, West is King of Hearts and Vansen is Queen of Diamonds.

4 *Star Trek: First Contact*: The Hybrid, the Whore and the Machine

Christine Wertheim

Picard, captain of the *Enterprise*, lies dreaming: embedded in a gigantic matrix that weds flesh and technology in a radical synthesis known as The Borg. It is 'definitely not Swedish'.

'Six years ago they assimilated me. They had their cybernetic devices implanted throughout my body. I was linked to the hive mind. Every trace of my individuality eradicated. I was one of them ... I can hear them.'

Flash of alien face: skin glistening wet. A transparent membrane of indescribable delicacy. Veins throb blue under alabaster whiteness. Glossy lips purr sensuously red. 'How could you forget me so quickly?' The whisper slides over him like liquid silk. 'We were so close you and I.'

But I get ahead of myself.

Back in the present, Earth looms into view on the screen of the *Enterprise*. 'Atmosphere: methane, carbon monoxide, fluorine. Population approximately 9 billion. All of them Borg.' Determined to assimilate all species to their collective, the Borg have created a temporal vortex and travelled back in time to absorb humanity before it develops warp drive. The task for the *Enterprise* is to prevent this disaster by following the Borg back to the past.

The main plotline of *First Contact*, the 1997 *Star Trek: The Next Generation* movie, is neither interesting nor original. Humanity must develop faster than light flight because only this is significant enough to attract the attention of aliens and encourage them to make First Contact, paving the way for our entry into the Space Federation. The crucial date is 5 April 2063, when one Zephram Cochrane makes the first such flight. It is he and his ship which must be protected in a story that is half *Terminator*, half *The Right Stuff*, for Cochrane is modelled on Chuck Yaeger, not spam in a can, but a 'real' man who flies a real ship, all thrusting phallus with rock 'n' roll blaring over the intercom. There is a lovely scene where the first officer Reiker, played by Jonathan Frakes, also director of this epic, and Jordie, the engineer with cybernetic eyes, are cooing over this artefact, touching it in awe like two little boys wanking a giant collective member. The counsellor, Deana Troy, walks in on them and excuses herself with the question, 'Would you three like to be alone?' This theme of the 'real' man is a constant refrain in a movie that, at least in its main storyline, is utterly predictable. The Borg die. The *Enterprise* wins. History reasserts itself. Flyboy takes his spaceship up. The aliens recognise that we are no longer so uninterestingly 'primitive'. They descend to Earth. They wear druidic costumes. They have pointy ears. They make First Contact. And a new era of peace, love and Space Federation dawns, as all humanity is suddenly united in the realisation that 'they are not alone in the universe'. If the history of humanity is anything to go by, it is more likely we'd unite round our common sense of difference from the aliens and treat them as invading others, not friendly brothers. But this is *Star Trek*, not George Orwell. However, if the basic plot of this saga is as dull as dishwater, two things make it thoroughly satisfying, the Borg enemy, and the subsidiary storyline in which they/it capture Data, the android equivalent of Spock in the *Next Generation*. I shall discuss the Borg first, before examining their/its interest in the android.

THE BORG: THE OTHER AS (THE) UNCATEGORISABLE

The Borg, 'man's deadliest enemy' and the best *Star Trek* bad guys ever, as entertaining as Q and infinitely more deadly, are a synthesis of every cliché about the Other: a complex (con)fusion of insect-virus-commie-machine, with a hive mentality in which each will is absorbed into the collective drive to 'assimilate' the universe. The most frightening aspect of the Borg is that they do not so much kill their enemies as absorb them. 'If you see a crew member who's been assimilated,' asserts Picard at one stage, 'do not hesitate to fire. Believe me, you'll be doing them a favour.' Better dead than red. The means by which the Borg effect this miraculous assimilation is not brainwashing, but implants. Once they've got a body they proceed to invade it, inserting their cybernetic devices into every orifice, possessing it from within. This invasion of the body, this penetration of self by other is what makes the Borg, to a Western mind raised on the credos of individualism and an absolute distinction between self and other(s) so suspect, so alien, so Other.

Are they/it one or many? Singular or collective? They/it blur the boundaries between every category of being, singular/plural, animate/inanimate, insect/animal, disease/host, human/machine. For they/it constitute a heterogeneous dis-unity in which the main characteristics are a radical fluidity and an absolute lack of discretion between identities because, instead of a separation between discrete selves and categories there is what de Sade called 'a universal prostitution of all beings'.[1] Indeed, in many ways the Borg are the inheritor/s of de Sade's transgressive fantasies whose philosophical point is to urge a 'transgression of the limits separating self from other, man from woman, human from animal, organic from inorganic'.[2] What could be more transgressive of the limits separating self from other than the Borg, when their whole *modus operandi* is to absorb their enemies, not so they may cease to be, but so their uniqueness can be added to the gradually evolving totality that is the Borg?

It is this fear of absorption into another, rather than possession by it, that makes the Borg so frightening, for at least in possession, though one is turned into an object, one still has a sense of discreteness, of a self that is separable from others. In the case of absorption one loses even this, as one is incorporated into, and becomes a part of a greater whole. To a creature like 7 of 9, the Borg drone captured and forcibly disconnected from the hive in the *Voyager* series, this is a noble position as one takes part in something greater than oneself. But she wouldn't know any better because she was assimilated as a child. To fully grown adult minds (from a modern Western culture), this proposition is utterly abhorrent in its implication that one is *merely* a part, not (a) whole in oneself, as if being a part of something greater than oneself reduced one's (self-) importance as an individual. But this is the problem for the 'Western' mind, which may now be found in many non-Western geographical locations,[3] because in Western-style societies the 'social contract' has been reduced to a competition in which whoever doesn't definitively come out on top must be seen as having 'lost', there being no principle of co-operation by which the whole collective could be seen as gaining simultaneously.

In this sense the Borg represent the opposite of the Thatcher principle. Where the prime minister thought there was no society, only individuals, to our eyes the Borg appear to have only society and no individuals. They/it are the embodiment of the Western fantasy of communism/socialism, as well as virtually all Asian cultures, especially Muslims in their current incarnation. This fantasy is both a misrepresentation and absurd, for it opposes 'individual' to 'society' as if it were a simple matter of the one or the other. Indeed, one could argue that this fantasy of exclusive disjunction in which there is an absolute choice between individuality and sociality, with no possibility of having both simultaneously, is the ultimate ideological weapon of capitalism, triumphant over democracy as much as it is over socialism.

In reality, in all cultures the individual subject comes into being through a complex set of social relations which ontologically and epistemologically precede it, and the shifts in the constitution of that totality known as society are always at least partially effected by the personal intentions of its subjects. The problem for people raised in a Western-style society, wherever this be located, is that we cannot accept any parameters whereby the relations between individual and society are negotiated in ways other than our own. When we encounter such differences we automatically assume that these others have no concept of the individual at all. As this is our most valorised idea, notwithstanding the fact that only some individuals are really valued in our social structure, not all, our projected perception of their 'lack of individuality' scares us to death. Of course there is to the Western mind a 'real' physiological foundation to this view that the Borg/Asian/communist other has no regard for, or even concept of, the individual. They all look the same, whereas 'we' are each clearly different.

But the Borg offer another take on this matter, for even leaving aside the possibility that all Caucasians look alike to the people of other races, or that, as Andy Warhol famously said, people in capitalist societies often look more alike than their socialist counterparts,[4] there is the question of what it *means* to look alike, or even to be alike. What is interesting about the Borg in this context, and another point they have in common with de Sade, is that the assimilation of different beings to the collective does not produce a dull homogeneity in which all become the same. It produces a radical heterogeneity in which every being gets to share in the real differences of all the others. From this perspective, the reason 'individuals', in our sense, cannot be identified in the Borg collective is not that they have all been reduced to an order of the same, but that the collective as a whole has absorbed so many different aspects from so many different species that it has become too complex to categorise, and so too complex to be partitioned in the ways we are used to.

In this sense the Borg are like the great hybrid figures of Bosch's *Garden of Earthly Delights,* figures that are such a complex fusion of building, insect, instrument, animal, plant, human, machine and costume, it is as impossible to say what each is or is not, as it is to say where one starts and another begins. And yet, the whole world composed of these strange hybrids is infinitely more diverse, complex and fascinating than the easily categorised and individuated world of our everyday lives. To de Sade, this state of radically shared heterogeneity, of perpetual metamorphosis in which there are no fixed identities only a constant translation of one form or body into another, substitutes for God. It is the primordial reality to which he would love to return, for in his materialist atheism all social order, ethics, morality and institutionalised activity are seen as 'unnatural' constructs imposed upon a natural *disorder*.[5] From a Freudian perspective, the attraction of this state is that it recapitulates the original polymorphous sexuality we all experienced prior to the limitations imposed by our entry into the social order. It is a state in which the veil of repression is lifted to reveal the original fluidity we lost in being subjected to 'castration', that process which constitutes us as individuated 'subjects' positioned in a social order precisely by separating and distinguishing us from our 'objects'. For de Sade, though neither the 'I' nor any distinguishable 'object' can be said to 'exist' in this state, it is this, not social order, which constitutes true reality.[6] Nearly 200 years later, the French writer Georges Bataille came to the same conclusion in his concepts of 'base materialism', the *informe* and 'heterology'.[7]

It is because they/it evoke this desire to return to a more primordial, un-self-conscious state that makes the Borg so thoroughly fascinating to us the viewers. But it is what makes them repellent to minds like those of the *Enterprise* who come from a culture so perfectly conformist, so thoroughly repressed, it makes every one of them, in their prissy self-righteous individualism, absolutely the same. Just as in Bosch's work we love the hybrids from hell more than the well-categorised creatures of Eden, cute as these are, so in *Star Trek* we love the complex Borg more than the simplistic individuals who make up the *Enterprise* crew. It is an interesting fact of many fantastic artworks that the 'bad' guys are the ones universally loved, while the good guys are loathed, for these, like the *Enterprise* crew, are just too conformist, when the whole purpose of fantasy is to break down or transgress the cultural frameworks by which we habitually make sense of the world. As Rosemary Jackson says in her excellent introduction to the topic *Fantasy: The Literature of Subversion*, '[p]resenting that which cannot be, but *is*, fantasy exposes a culture's definitions of that which can be: it traces the limits of its epistemological and ontological frame'.[8] This is precisely the de Sade–Bataille project, to expose the limits of our social ordering systems by transgressing them, not so much to bring order down, as to open it out to critique. From this perspective the Borg offer viewers an opportunity for the sort of genuinely critical self-reflection that is prohibited by the repressed and narcissistic conformism of the *Enterprise* and the Space Federation. This is the value of all 'Others', that through their very *difference* they enable us to see ourselves more clearly, because in *not* reflecting us they enable us to see ourselves from the outside.

But, if the Borg as a totality are fascinating, their Queen is even more so, for She is *The* Borg. It is also her capture and seduction of Data that constitutes the subsidiary, and by far the more interesting storyline of this saga.

THE OTHER STORY: THE MAKING OF A 'REAL' MAN

'Are you ready?' a silky voice purrs through the ether.

Data lies prone on a table, head encircled by a halo of green light. He has been captured by the Borg, and their Queen is taking an interest in him. I would too if I were Her, he is by far the most interesting member of the *Enterprise*. 'Who are you?' he asks, both curious and polite.

'I am The Borg.'

A beautiful torso floats into view at the top of the screen, face perfectly chiselled, forehead high, skin radiant white, lips ruby red, shoulders bare. It is held by a network of thin tubes that guide it across the space in a gently arcing curve. From its underside a gleaming red tail flexes. Half-spine. Half-phallus. All bio-techno-logical.

'That is a contradiction', Data counters. 'The Borg have a collective consciousness. There are no individuals.'

'I am the beginning, the end, the one who is many', she replies calmly.

The torso is lowered into its casing, a gunmetal grey skin covering a body that is half well-cut muscle, half electronic implants. The head shifts into place, and She utters a sigh of pleasure as the bionic 'buttons' round her décolletage lock top and bottom together in a chain of bio-technology that looks like an elaborate piece of costume jewellery. In fact, the overall effect is of a high-tech Elizabeth I, for with Her dazzlingly white skin, high forehead and off the shoulder costume The Borg is every inch a Queen. (Somehow only capitals will do for this magnificent creature.)

So begins the other storyline of the film, where, instead of a typical bang-'em-up-and-shoot-'em saga, we are given a complex story of interpersonal relations in which the question of what it is to be human is deftly interwoven with an exploration of sexuality and gender. Indeed, what is most impressive is the way this plotline shows how these two issues are inseparable; that to be a human subject is to be a sexed subject. The specific 'subject' around which these questions turn is Data, the man(made)-info-machine, whose problem is that he's never sure if he is 'really' experiencing anything or just processing inputs that can be categorised in a certain way. It is through his capture by the Borg Queen that Data finally experiences the real sensations he has so long craved. And, in representing this encounter, the film raises many questions concerning Data's position as a 'subject', or lack thereof, and what it is to be an Other, both the other of humanity, and the other in a sexual relationship. For, whatever the relation between Data and the Queen, it is definitively sexual. The ultimate irony of this film is that the sexiest encounter the *Star Trek* saga has known comes between an android and a ... well, what exactly is the Borg Queen? But we shall deal with Her shortly. For now, let us examine how their relationship evolves.

The encounter begins well. The Queen is courteous and magisterial, if enigmatic. Data is his usual polite, perky self. (Being an android, Data doesn't have to go into that boring how-dare-you-degrade-my-dignity routine that Picard feels compelled to perform every time he is tied up by a woman.) They banter a while, politely, Data trying to figure out the contradiction represented by this unique Borg Queen, She trying to convince him of the virtues of the Borg way of life, for She wants Data to add his uniqueness to the collective's heterogeneity. Unable to imagine the pleasures such a state could potentially bring, Data resists. However the Queen is wise and has powers beyond his wildest dreams. So instead of trying to reason with him She unclasps the cuff pinning his arm to reveal a few square inches of skin suspended above a bionic net of wires and blinking lights.

'Do you know what this is, Data?' She purrs.

'It appears as if you are trying to graft organic skin on to my endoskeletal structure', he answers correctly.

'What a cold description for such a beautiful gift', She replies. Then, adopting Her most beatific smile yet, She bends Her beautiful head and, pursing Her lips, blows lightly on t/his skin. It is a haunting image, this combination of shivering skin and bionic circuitry turned on by the touch of a woman's lips. For whatever else The Borg may be, She is all woman, right down to Her treacherous desire which does not balk at preying on men's needs in order to satisfy Her own demands.

'Was that good for you?' She whispers, as Data splutters, smiling, confused, delighted, embarrassed. Never has he felt so human, either to us, or to himself.

On returning to this scene some time later we find Data still prisoner, as a Borg drone carefully sews the new organic skin in place and locks his arm back up. He is chattering away, in his best nonchalant, rationalistic, I'm-not-emotionally-affected manner, quizzing the Borg about what they are doing to him, reverting to the certainties of science in a desperate attempt to stave off another encounter with the 'real', even though that is his most cherished desire. This completely exasperates The Borg and She finally loses her royal cool. They argue about perfection, She, Nietzschean to the core, trying to convince him that the synthetic mixture of biological organism and technological invention is superior to the merely human, or, for that matter, the purely machinic, as he is. Data refuses to be swayed, despite the fact that his whole aim is to become more human, more organic. Given the pleasure he so clearly derived from the previous scene, we can only assume that his program to protect the *Enterprise* overrides his more personal desire for real physical sensation. But The Borg knows that actions are more convincing than words. So instead of arguing, She unlocks the clasp on his arm, again offering him sensation, bodily sensation, human sensation, not the shallow electronic simulations of sense he has had to make do with until now. However, Data has had time to prepare for this encounter and springs into action before Her 'stimulations' can subvert his programmed goals. Consequently, instead of pleasure he receives pain, as a defending drone slashes through his newly grown skin. This brings him to a halt, his personal feelings and sensations at last overriding his programs, as he clutches his arm in pain and confusion.

An interesting philosophical point is made here: that the essence of being human is not certainty, but confusion, for it is only when Data is forced into a state of confusion, when the certainties of his programs are overridden, that he at last experiences something 'real', something human. And precisely because She knows this, it is just here, when Data is at his weakest and most vulnerable, that The Borg steps in for the kill. Drawing closer, eyebrows arched, She asks him, nonchalantly, almost innocently, 'Are you familiar with the ... physical forms of pleasure?'

Data backs away, breath coming quickly. 'If you are referring to sexuality, I am fully functional, programmed in multiple techniques.' (The mind boggles.)

'How long is it since you used them?' She purrs.

'Eight years, seven months, sixteen days, four minutes, twenty-two ...'

'Far too long!' She reaches forward and kisses him, then draws back slightly. This time Her stimulations completely override his software, and he pounces, instantly drawing Her to him in a tight embrace as the camera dissolves to another scene. We can only hope that future generations of *Star Trek* producers will not be so shy, and that the question of Data's multiple sexual techniques will be more fully explored in later episodes.

Much could be made of this little scene from a psychoanalytic perspective, specifically that it is a classic, even literal, example of the psychoanalytic thesis that femininity and masculinity are isomorphic with hysteria and obsessionality, the two principal forms of neurosis. For where the hysteric is overly alive and needs calming down, the obsessional is mortified and needs enlivening. What could be more mortified than an android, or more alive than this beautiful Borg? As we shall see, this theme of mortification is not unconnected with the notion of Otherness. But before we discuss that, we must first examine the final scene in this storyline, for Data is not the only (obsessional) man to be seduced by our Queen.

Flash to Picard. The battle is over. The Borg have fled. The *Enterprise* recaptured. Flyboy's erupting into the sky in his phallic-shaped rocket, rock 'n' roll blaring. But Data is still in the grip of the Queen, and Picard 'can hear them'.

'I must save my friend', he tells his companion, the black female engineer who built the first faster-than-light craft, even if she didn't design it. She is a sort of all-purpose PC Other, a black female technician who nevertheless remains permanently a sidekick, supporter to the two white male heroes, Picard and Flyboy. We must wait for the later *Deep Space Nine* series to get a black man as hero and star, and for the *Voyager* series before we have a woman as the central character.

Picard enters the zone the Borg have assimilated on the *Enterprise,* all murky atmosphere, suffused with 'alien' green light and hollow electronic growlings. The walls look like a combination of the inside of a stomach and a Visigoth tavern decked out in gunmetal grey, the current fashion of the future in sci-fi movies. (Do all aliens really hire the same interior designers?) For those not in the know, Picard was once assimilated into the Borg collective, and he has harboured a personal hatred for them/Her ever since. Spying Data standing quietly in a Borg niche, face now half covered in 'real' organic skin, he shouts at the Queen

'Let him go. He's not the one you want!' Says who? Why do men always think they know what a woman wants, even a Borg woman?

'Are you offering yourself to us?' She is quizzical, bemused.

'Offering myself? ... That's it!' The bubble has burst. The light switched on. 'I remember now', he continues in a self-righteous rage. 'It wasn't enough that you assimilated me. I had to give myself freely to The Borg. To you.'

'You can't imagine the life you denied yourself', She counters sarcastically.

A fight ensues and, inevitably, predictably, disappointingly, The Borg is killed, Picard gloatingly breaking Her neck/spine/phallus/ source-of-power, which is now exposed as pure machine, its organic component having been burned off by poisonous fumes. All the drones are instantly deactivated, and the *Enterprise* is restored to its normal state of peace and order. We can only hope the producers of the film were thinking 'three dimensionally' and that The Borg will return in all Her glory in future episodes. But what has all this got to do with Otherness? Indeed, what kind of Otherness are we talking about here, for we have already examined the uncategorisable Otherness of the Borg as a collective? There are two issues at stake, the Other as feminine, and the Other as machine. Both revolve around the issue of sexuality. Both involve the Borg Queen. The latter also involves Data. I shall deal with the former first.

THE BORG: THE OTHER AS WOMAN AS WHORE

As one of the collective The Borg Queen is other because She is part of the confusion of insect-virus-commie-machine that constitutes the collective. But as *The* One of the collective, She is, as Data says, an outright contradiction, and a wholly different kind of other. She is the collective that is also an individual, the one who is many, the 'I' which is the All of the-m-others. But if an 'I' is of the-m-others, then it is of an order other than the 'I' that we normally associate with individual subjectivity. It is an 'other-I' which is multiplicitous and relational, whereas, since the Enlightenment, the 'normal' subject has been seen as definitively singular, autonomous and self-contained. It is here that sexuality becomes an issue, and the issue of sexuality becomes entangled with the notion of Otherness, for this 'other' subject is clearly the feminine one. The problem is that femininity is definitively excluded from the notion of subjectivity if it is equated with the relationality of the-m-other's function. In this case, we need another way of defining femininity. But even if we dissociate it from child-bearing, the main characteristics of the feminine mode of being still seem to be relationality, equivocality, splitting and a porousness of boundaries (precisely the qualities of The Borg), all of which go against the entrenched definitions of subjectivity as founded on a fixity of meaning, a unity of identity, and an absolute separation of self from (the-m-)others.

The problem of the feminine subject is even further complicated by the fact that she is constantly confused with that other quite different entity called 'The Woman'. According to the French psychoanalyst Jacques Lacan, 'The Woman doesn't exist'. Lacan did not mean by this that anatomically female bodies don't exist, or even that there are no feminine subjects. He meant that the concept of 'The Woman' is a fantasy existing exclusively in people's minds, a fantasy that both men and women think feminine subjects should conform to. In the psychic structure of the masculine mind 'The Woman' is the fantasy that occupies the position of (his) object, the cause of his desire, and that around which his psycho-sexual life revolves. In the psychic structure of the feminine mind there is a problem, for she cannot take herself as object. Or can she? And if she did, what would it mean? In other words, if the masculine subject revolves around 'The Woman' as object, at least his subjectivity is clearly separable from that object. But in what sense can we talk about the feminine subject being separable from 'The Woman' as object? This is one reason why subjectivity is seen, in patriarchal society, as masculine *by definition,* for the patriarchal subject is defined in relation to an object named 'Woman'. This is also why 'The Woman' is other. She is the other-of-the-subject.[9]

But what about the feminine subject? Clearly she is a problem only if we do not have another definition of subjectivity. But this is the problem of patriarchy, that it does not provide the conceptual apparatus for defining subjectivity in other terms. Indeed, one could define patriarchy as the social state in which a 'feminine subject is excluded because subjectivity *per se* is defined in relation to an object conceptualised through the trope of "The Woman"'. The challenge for both feminism and psychoanalysis is to develop a more complex view of subjectivity which, through reconceptualising the relations between the subject's I and its object(ive) Other, is able to embrace other forms including the feminine.

However, we do not live in the future. We live here and now, and in the future-now of *Star Trek*, a woman, even a Queen, cannot take a man as her object, for a man is, by definition, not an object, but a subject. This is what makes Picard so angry in relation to The Borg: that She treated him as an object, demanding that he 'give' himself to Her. (And he can't imagine the pleasure he denied himself.) The problem here is not so much that The Borg is/are collective, and that in giving himself he will lose his individuality, for as he himself says, in his (unique) case, She did not want just another 'drone'. She wanted a human being with a mind of his own, 'a counterpart'. The problem is that She takes for herself the active part and puts *him* in the position of passive object, the position of non-subjective Otherness. The name for women who do this is 'Whore'.

A whore is a woman who has her own desire and pursues it. She is a woman who does not wait for men to come and proposition her, but actively goes out seeking them, stalking them, pursuing them. And when she finds them she seduces them, insinuating herself into their affections, their minds, wearing them down. In short, a whore is a real other, a woman who upsets the 'natural' order by turning herself into a subject and putting men in the position of objects. This is why all whores must die, including The Borg, for they are unnatural and excessive in the assertion of their own desires, which should naturally be subordinated to the desires of men. This 'unnaturalness' is symbolically marked in a most acute manner in our first view of The Borg. Remember Her torso sailing majestically overhead, spinal cord dangling below. This member is not so much unnatural because it is clearly half machine as because it looks like a phallus. The woman, whether in fantasy or fact, does not have a phallus. Indeed, in psychoanalytic theory, if 'The Woman' is merely a fantasy object, at least she is a 'natural' fantasy, for 'The Woman' is precisely the one who is in want of the phallus. But the woman who believes she actually has a phallus is not fantastical, she is an object of derision, for she is the most deluded of all creatures. As Data says in his argument with the Queen, 'Believing yourself to be perfect is often the sign of a delusional mind.' In being the ultimate in perfection, the fantasy of a woman with a phallus is also the ultimate delusion. This is why The Borg must be crushed, because She behaves as if She really has a phallus. It is the man who has the phallus, not the woman. And it is (the bearer of) the phallus which desires. The other is (merely) the cause of (t)his desire, its object but never its subject. As the subject's other, its object, the woman's 'natural' desire is simply to arouse the man's, not to have any ideas of her own. This is the reason a woman's desire should be subordinated to a man's. So at last we come to the desire of a man, the only proper subject for an enquiry into Otherness.

DATA: THE OTHER AS MACHINE

The problem is that the 'man' in question is Data, not a flesh-and-blood, born-of-woman man, but a man(made)-info-machine and, it has to be said, he handles his relations with The Borg infinitely more graciously than Picard. But this is probably because Data's problem is not so much with women, as is Picard's, but with humans. As a man(made)-info-machine it is almost irrelevant that Data is designed to look, and programmed to behave, like a male, complete, apparently, with multiple sexual techniques although, it has to be said, we are not told which role/s he is programmed to play in these.[10] But if Data's problem is not women, neither is it the problem of a subject in relation to an object. Data does not want to possess a human; he wants to become one. His problem is thus not whether he is or is not a subject, or is properly recognised as one by a woman-object-other. His problem is simply that, whatever he is, his sensations are limited in relation to humans. Where they are clearly aroused in all sorts of pleasant and unpleasant manners, all he experiences are inputs he can categorise as pleasure or pain. What he never actually does is *feel* pleasure or pain, that is, until The Borg gives him the gift of humanity, by properly stimulating him. But it is not Her stimulations, Her actions, that are the gift here; it is the sensory apparatus to respond to them.

This is what makes the relation between Data and The Borg so much more interesting than that between Her and Picard. Where Picard turns everything into the typical, 'I-must-be-on-top, I-subject,

You-object' struggle, Data is quite happy to play the object-role, for in this position he gets what he has always wanted, to feel like a 'real' man. Which just goes to show that these two positions are not mutually exclusive, as Picard so desperately insists on asserting. In this sense, there is something genuinely radical in the relation between Data and The Borg, for in his acceptance of this role reversal play in which he becomes the passive object and She the active subject, he engages in a kind of sexual experimentation that, for Hollywood, is really quite subversive. Perhaps he really has been programmed with multiple techniques.

But if Data can liberate himself from the constricting sexual codes of his culture it is because he understands that there is something much more precious than the assertion of one's subjective position, something other men take for granted, namely, *life* itself. For it is clear that Data treasures his flesh, all few square inches of it, as much as his life, because this is the only thing he has ever known as *real* life, not just a simulation of it. Thus, not only does one feel very sad in the final scene where he and Picard are fighting and killing The Borg, one also does not quite believe it. In fact, one feels betrayed, in the same way we were betrayed in *Fatal Attraction* when, in a desperate attempt to relieve us of the sympathy we felt for the Glenn Close character, the makers of the film had her boil the family bunny. In other words, this is one of those cases where the movie makers illegitimately manipulate the plot by having a character act in an unbelievable manner. (Cynics would say the whole thing beggars belief, but I mean believable on its own terms, not those of 'objective' reality.)

What is not credible here is that Data would willingly give up his precious life-giving skin, for at the end of this scene he is shown with circuitry exposed on his face and arm where he has ripped off the organic skin grafted by The Borg. We are not shown the act itself, precisely because it is not believable. We are only shown its effects. As Picard helps him to his feet, Data says in the hushed tone of true appreciation, 'She was unique. She brought me closer to humanity than I've ever been. And for a time I was tempted by her offer.'

'How long a time?' Picard demands, callously sizing up Data's loyalty rather than showing the slightest concern for his loss, a loss Picard cannot even imagine, though clearly The Borg did.

'0.68 seconds,' Data replies efficiently, before adding quietly, 'and for an android that is nearly an eternity.'

The question is: why did he do it?

The answer, according to the logic of the plot, can only be that having real-life sensations would make him value himself above the others he is designed to protect, those human subjects to whom all his own desires must be constantly subordinated. There is a very telling scene in this respect early on in the movie when, along with others, Data and Picard are heading towards their first encounter with the Borg. Data opens the conversation with a delightfully childish outburst of enthusiasm over some newfound feelings.

'I believe I am feeling anxiety. It's a fascinating sensation', he burbles.

Picard is annoyed at this and responds tetchily, 'I'm sure it's a fascinating experience. But perhaps you should deactivate your emotion chip.'

Ever obliging, Data complies, only to have Picard mutter gratuitously, 'Data, there are times I envy you.'

What is there to envy? Every one of his own pleasures must be nipped in the bud, virtually before they've begun, if they even vaguely look like interfering with the demand that he place others' needs before his own.

So we come to the real problem with Data: why is he the true Other in this piece? Data is not a subject, not a 'person' at all, either masculine or feminine. He is a slave, reduced to the condition of a living death, because he has to give up his feelings, his sensations, his *life*, in direct opposition to his own personal desires. And this is not because his loyalty or sense of duty, which after all are pleasures, override his other desires, but because he is *programmed* to. Inside his being Data has the equivalent of the device implanted in Alex from *A Clockwork Orange*, a device that makes him physically sick if he even so much as thinks about sex. Data isn't made sick by his programming, it just asserts itself over his desires, overriding them so that he has no opportunity to pursue his own goals. In this case Data is as one possessed, for he has no control over his own actions. He cannot make choices of his own free will, for good or bad, but is completely enslaved to the will of others, to the point of not even being able to have feelings and sensations of his own. It may be argued that this is what the Borg do to those they/it conquer. But while each new recruit has their will absorbed into the collective, there is no suggestion that they stop feeling, stop having sensations. Data by, contrast, is the walking dead, and after his brush with life, courtesy of The Borg, he must know this in an even more painfully acute manner than ever before.

What is most horrific about this state is that, as one possessed, he still has his own consciousness intact. He is not in control, but he is conscious of himself as a discrete individual. The point is that although the state of Borgdom may appear frightening to those on the outside looking in, to the ones actually experiencing it it would not be nearly as horrific as the kind of possession Data has to endure. Though as a Borg one may lose the sense of separateness as one becomes mingled with the All of the-m-others, being a part of that vast collective consciousness is potentially, as the Queen asserts, an unimaginably great experience. On the other hand, though it may appear less unappealing to (Western-minded, and masculine) outsiders, to those undergoing it, as so many women and colonised 'subjects' have attested, absolute possession by an other is living hell, for it places one in the position of being an absolute object, the complete opposite of a subject. The paradox here is that those placed in this position are precisely *not* pure objects. If they were they would have no desires of their own and hence no objections. It is only because those put in this position, whether women, androids or 'primitives', are *in themselves* subjects that they can feel their objec-tification-in-relation-to-others as a confinement.

The problem with Data, or with his position in the symbolic order of *Star Trek: The Next Generation*, is that the producers of this saga want to maintain the same duplicitous fantasy that haunts psycho-analysis, namely that someone can be a fully (self-)conscious 'subject' in-relation to itself, and yet completely objectified in relation to other, more 'real' subjects. In the case of women the objectification occurs in relation to men. In Data's case it is played out in relation to humans. In this sense, Data represents the other side of the Sadean contradiction, for though de Sade's libertines get to experience the pleasures of a life dissolved and dispersed into other beings, the heterogeneous mixing together of all things, including subjects and objects, in order to achieve this experience they must first turn these others into pure objects by robbing them of their own subjectivity. Remember all those children captured and held in chains to do the libertines' bidding?

If there is a liberatory way of viewing this fantasy, there is also a paradoxical price to be paid for it. It's all very well for those who want it, those who are its subjects, however much they might be trying to become Other. But what about those who don't, those who are *forced,* precisely because they don't want it, to conform to these desires? It is this negative side of the Sadean fantasy that so troubles us in the Borg, even if, like Sade, we love the fantasy at one level. On the one hand we want to see them, like 7 of 9, as proud and happy in their extraordinarily heterogeneous collective consciousness. On the other, at the level at which we continue to view them as individuals, we can't help feeling they are being held against their wills. One could argue that this is a flaw in the design concept, for if we take the logic of the Borg literally then, like Bosch's hybrids we should not be able to delineate them into discrete individuals at all. In the case of the Borg then the contradiction is only an effect of the lack of imagination on the part of the show's designers and writers, not of their actual being. But in the case of Data, as with women and those forcibly colonised, the paradox is real, and as such, like men and colonialists, the makers of the series must make up their minds. Either he is a real subject, in which case he must be allowed to develop his emotions and sensations as *he* wishes, not having to switch them off whenever others require it, or he is not, in which case it should be honestly admitted that he is in a state of possessed servitude, the slave to others' wills, however conscious and intelligent he may be. If the latter is the case, it will be a miracle if he doesn't end up like Marvin the paranoid android from *The Hitchhiker's Guide to the Galaxy*. As Marge Piercy shows in her novel *He, She, It*, if we ever do develop robots that are fully *self*-conscious, we do not have the right to put them in this position, especially not one so charming, so playful, so multi-techniqued as Data.

CONCLUSION: THE TRANS-HUMAN

There is, of course, another reason why Data must give up his cherished flesh. If he did not, there is nothing, in principle, to distinguish between him and The Borg. If he kept his skin, he would be the same hybrid fusion of organics and technology. And we couldn't have that, now could we? But, then again, Jordie has technological implants. So what does that make him?

This brings us to what I believe is the truly radical point of the movie, for there is perhaps a more complex reason why we are so fascinated by these hybrid creatures, one that bears on the very definition of what it is to be human. As Keith Ansell Pearson argues in *Viroid Life,* his marvellous defence of Nietzsche's theory of the trans-human, humans cannot, as Western philosophy has so long assumed, be defined as self-contained subjects using tools that may be conceived as objects external to their being.[11] Rather, following Nietzsche, we must recognise 'that from its "origins" the human has been constituted by technical evolution'.[12] Whether these techniques be sticks and bones, printing presses or the VCR, whether evolved in thatched huts on desert plains or in the high-rise towers of concrete jungles, as Pearson persuasively argues, the human is something absolutely distinct from the natural because it is essentially *artificial*, even if this artificiality plays itself out around and through a biological core. Furthermore, not only is the human always involved in a series of contingent technical 'natures', its modes of artificiallty are never fixed but always in a process of becoming. From this perspective, the fantastical, category-breaking Borg are not other at all. They are actually a reflection of our own hybrid, freakish 'nature', our *Doppelgänger*. Their hybridity is our hybridity, their polymorphous heterogeneous becoming our poly morphous heterogeneous becoming. As Pearson so succinctly sums us up, '[t]he human being is the greatest freak of nature and the only features we can be certain of are monstrous ones characterised by perpetual mutation and morphing'.

However, arguing that humanity is a monstrous technical becoming is not the same as opting for an uncritical acceptance of the technological commodification foisted on us by unbridled capitalism. Rather, it is to argue for a 'critical in-humanity' which goes beyond the ethics of possessive individualism by recognising that the thoughts and other creations generated at the interface between the human and the technological – beginning with the originary mnemotechnics constitutive of human thinking – are not purely human, but *trans*-human, for they include the contributions of the technics/techniques themselves, and the pluralities of becoming these bring into (our) being. Viewed from this perspective the Borg are indeed 'other', but they represent the *otherness in ourselves,* that radical otherness which lies at the heart of our own artificially becoming, technical and multiplicitous 'nature-s'. It is precisely because this instability, this plurality, this extended, non-body-bounded becoming threatens capitalism that it is defined as other, and repressed. For only through the repression of this relational and equivocal otherness can we be maintained as passive, discrete and possessive individuals; that is, as subjects of enlightened consumption. Fortunately, as Freud said, that which is repressed always returns in the real. With any luck the Borg might just turn up one day and assimilate us for real.[13]

In any case, as all the hybrids presented in this movie – Data, the Borg and The Borg – suggest it may never be possible to make an absolute distinction between subject and object, (hu)man and machine, the I of the self and the All of the-m-others. Perhaps the truth is that each and every one of us is penetrated by an Otherness from which it is impossible to properly distinguish ourselves, ever.

NOTES

1. De Sade, quoted in Rosemary Jackson, *Fantasy: The Literature of Subversion*, London and New York, Routledge, 1988, p. 73.
2. Ibid.
3. See Ziauddin Sardar, *Postmodernism and the Other: The New Imperialism of Western Culture*, London and Chicago, Pluto Press, 1998.
4. See 'What is Pop Art? Interviews with Eight Painters (Part 1)', *Art News*, New York, November 1963, and John Russell and Suzi Gablik (eds), *Pop Art Redefined*, London, 1969.
5. Jackson, *Fantasy*, p. 74.
6. However, if there is a positive, unrepressed side to this fantasy or even to its actual realisation, there is also a very negative side for, as de Sade himself shows, an absolute un-self-consciousness reigns here. The problem is that, though in fantasy this may be desirable, in actuality it would not only make society untenable, it would make survival itself impossible, for those in such a state would require others, who are themselves self-conscious subjects, to take care of them. An excellent account of such a state is given in *Watt*, Samuel Beckett's finest novel. The other aspect of this state only touched on here is the fact that, though to some people it appears as liberatory, to others it simply induces stark terror. For an excellent, if thoroughly nasty account of the terrible side of this fantasy, see *The Event Horizon* (1997, directed by Paul Anderson (III), Golar Production/Impact Pictures/Paramount Pictures, 95 minutes, USA).
7. See Georges Bataille, *Visions of Excess: Selected Writings, 1927–1939*, Minneapolis, University of Minnesota Press, 1985. See especially 'Base Materialism and Gnosticism', pp. 45–52.
8. Jackson, *Fantasy*, p. 23.
9. For an excellent account of this problematic, see Juliet Mitchell and Jacqueline Rose (eds), Jacqueline Rose (trans.) *Jacques Lacan and the Ecole Freudienne*, London, Macmillan, 1982.
10. There really are too many questions raised by this issue of Data's sexual programming for the producers of the saga not to enable us to explore it more fully in future episodes.
11. See Keith Ansell Pearson, *Viroid Life*, London, Routledge, 1997, p. 4.
12. Ibid., p. 5.

13. Either that, or we end up in some boring 'post-' not trans-human fantasy where the elite look like Ethan Hawke and Uma Thurman and everyone else is a troll. For an excellent critique of this possible future, see Marge Piercy's *Woman on the Edge of Time*, New York, Knopf, 1976. Piercy's point, along with Pearson and so many others, is that the media, medical and pharmaceutical industries notwithstanding, *we* make the future, not some impersonal evolutionary drive that will only realise itself in some 'post'-human purely machinic future. This myth of a post-human goal for evolution is merely a device employed by these industries to repress a far more radical and active engagement between humans and technology that might upset the passive consumerist logic of Late Capitalism.

5 Japanimation: Techno-Orientalism, Media Tribes and Rave Culture

Toshiya Ueno

I wish to examine Japanimation (Japanese animated cinema) from the perspective of two notions: techno-orientalism and media tribalism as depicted in rave culture (especially psychedelic trance techno). Just as the discourse of orientalism has functioned to build up the identity of the West, techno-orientalism is set up for the West to preserve its identity in its imagination of the future. It can be defined as the orientalism of cybersociety and the information age, aimed at maintaining stable identity in a technological environment.

Globalisation and tribalisation seem to be completely mutually dependent. Media tribalism can be defined conceptually as parallel process or a reverse side of globalisation. Once McLuhan predicted that the world would become a global village where people could live as members of a tribe despite geographical distance. But his prediction hit on only half of the reality. Certainly, globalisation brought about tribalisation, but there is no single, common tribe, but many tribes with all their potential conflicts. Globalisation includes, and is constituted by, a mosaic patchwork of different kinds of tribes. Generally, tribalism is depicted negatively, for example, with reference to the ethnic war in ex-Yugoslavia or the tribal war in Rwanda: tribalism is equated with Balkanisation or Lebanonisation. But these impressions are wrongly combined with a geopolitical imagination in an ideological projection of the cultural into the geographical sphere. This kind of projection should be deconstructed as soon as possible so that the significance of tribalisation can be analysed in a positive or tactical way. French sociologist Michel Maffesoli in his book *The Time of the Tribes* emphasises the factor of affect and emotions in subculture and the aesthetic articulation of sub-groups in contemporary society. Unlike other agencies like class, ethnicity, gender and race, the 'new tribes', according to Maffesoli, are very temporary, fragile, plastic and unstable. Some other sociologists, such as Zygmunt Baumann and

Kevin Hetherington, also employ the term 'tribes' in their analyses of postmodern, global, information society.[1]

URBAN AND MEDIA TRIBES

By urban tribes, I refer to the small social groups based on urban (youth) subculture. Urban tribes formalise the relationship between people out of styles, tastes and fashion choices within popular cultures or subcultures, as mediatory moment. Thus each subculture can have its own tribe: *Anime-otaku*, football hooligan, techno, house, reggae, punk, skinheads, neo-mods, and so on. Hence, to belong to a certain tribe is to invent rather than to follow a common interest. The experience of shared rituals in everyday life can create something new to be shared. But sometimes tension or conflict can arise between different styles and tribes. This sort of eventual antagonism is constituted in subcultures themselves. Each urban tribe has a sort of community of sense, but generally urban tribes violate so-called 'common sense' (parent culture or mainstream popular culture) because of their subcultural and counter-cultural origins. Besides this opposition to a mainstream culture, subcultures intrinsically maintain antagonistic relationships among themselves. For instance, the heuristic of the cultural struggle between Mods and Rockers in the 1960s was structured by oppositions between suits/leather jackets, The Who/the old rock 'n' roll, amphetamine/marijuana, Italian Vespa scooter/American motorbike. Each subculture invents its own tribes through their rituals (cultural customs and practices) in everyday life. But it should be noted that no single taste or style can have total hegemony in a scene: one tribe always presupposes the possible (co)existence of another. There are no privileged and transcendent tastes and styles. Instead, tribal segments are articulated in their various relationships. Despite the antagonism and oppositions between urban tribes (for instance, Punk vs. Skinhead, Trance Techno vs. House, Manchester United vs. Dynamo Zagreb) at least they do not try to deny their opponents totally. Instead, limited and overlapped zones act as a buffer or shock absorber, which is also one of the effects of tribal formation.

Nor can one imagine a subculture not relying on some kind of media. In other words, urban tribes are always already presented, articulated and constituted by and through various types of media, which, in contemporary cities, are based on the artificial tribal sense and affiliative solidarity constituted in the accumulation of commodities. For this reason I would like to call urban tribes 'media tribes' specifically. The age of globalisation, and of urban tribes, is the age of media tribalism and tribal media. Thus the notion of media tribes stands in a complementary or even equivalent relation, depending on context, with the concept of urban tribes (with the term 'media tribe' perhaps even broader and vaguer than the term 'urban tribe'). Moreover, it is easy to find frequent use of the terms 'tribe' or 'tribal' in subcultures themselves, especially in club culture and its flyers, regardless of musical genres, and its implications seem to be quite positive. The crucial points for tribes and tribalisation in subculture are, first, that urban and media tribes are always plural and multiple, and no one tribe can ever exist by itself alone. If there were only one tribe, there would be no articulations and no cultural differences, so that neither solidarity nor community distinct from others could appear (in principle, although any media culture could make its own tribes in contemporary cities and society, not all of them necessarily express 'tribal' solidarity because of the variety of tribal formation). And second, one can traverse subcultures and travel from one tribe to another: theoretically, one can be Rastafarian in the daytime and a Heavy Metal fan at night.

The Japanese novelist Shintaro Ishihara, who later entered national politics and became the president of Tokyo's metropolitan government, published a novel called *The Season of the Sun* in 1957. This novel featured the outsiders of the young generation of the 1950s and became a bestseller. The 'Sun Tribe' (*Taiyo-zoku*) came into being as a result of the sensation caused by the novel. From the late 1950s to the late 1960s, Japanese subculture produced a great number of films, some of which depended on Ishihara's novels and the image of the Sun Tribe. Ishihara's younger brother, Yujiro, appeared in such films as an actor and became a very popular film star. Interestingly, even after this sensation subsided, the term 'tribe' (*zoku*) has remained in discussions of Japanese subculture. When older people are confronted with a new phenomenon in subculture or youth culture, people try to label the young generation adopting strange behaviour, fashions and tastes as a tribe: Speed Tribe (*Boso-zoku*, biker gangs), Bamboo Tribe (*Takenoko-zoku*, street dancing groups in the 1980s), Crystal Tribe (*Crystal-zoku*, Japanese yuppies in the 1980s), Otaku Tribe (*Otaku-zoku*, info-mania tribe), and so forth.

Why are the Japanese so crazy about tribes? Japanese society, at least to the superficial glance, is quite homogeneous. It is difficult to set out visible markers for distinguishing and discriminating between others. On a superficial level, there are no physical differences of skin colour, hair, eyes; hence the use in Japanese animations of bizarre hair colour, hairstyles and strange forms of eyes in their graphic characters. Additionally, many Japanese think that there are no class or ethnic communities within 'Japan'. Of course, this is just disavowal rather than misrecognition. I suppose, then, that these media tribes are supplements or surrogates for class, ethnicity and other agencies. But mainly, urban tribes and media tribes seem to have been reduced to mere generation gap or co-opted into market segmentation by public relations corporations.[2]

Japanimation is a neologism referring to animation work made in Japan: the alternative term *anime* is already quite popular even in Europe and North American. However, I use this term to emphasise both geography and the particularity of its characteristic styles, for these are quite different from animations in the general sense. Now Japanimation can be seen through TV and video distribution around the world and many gadgets and toys derive from it. Enthusiasm for and interest in Japanimation has remained powerful even after the economic recession and crisis in Japan. Screened and broadcast in other Asian countries as well as in Europe and North America, even in Eastern Europe, its influence is visible in fanzines and electronic game cultures. In one way it is just one more result of the globalisation of capitalism, but at the same time it can afford an opportunity to analyse and interpret it critically.

If the Orient was constructed and invented by the West to build up its cultural identity, then the techno Orient has been invented to define the images and models of information capitalism and the information society. It is one of the bases of techno-orientalism as an unconscious ideology.[3] I have been investigating the reasons why Asian landscapes excite the cyberpunk imagination. Certainly it would be possible to answer the question by mentioning the influence of Asian languages, lifestyles and urban designs in the film *Blade Runner*.[4] But Japanimation itself marks the mutation of global capitalism by appropriating the illusion of Asia or Japan, just as the shift of capitalism from Fordism to post-Fordism is frequently presented as 'Fujitsuism', 'Sonyism' and 'Toyotaism', and so on. These corporations are famous for highly sophisticated divisions of productive labour in factory developments such as the *kanban* (small board) system for subcontracting at Toyota. The small factories for replicants (androids) in *Blade Runner* should be noted as fictional counterparts of the same mode of production. The coexistence of high technology with slums and ruins is never simple fiction, but rather addresses actually existing societies. For instance, East Palo Alto in Silicon Valley was seen as a very dangerous city with poor educational and residential conditions; and a large number of Asian regions are faced with the dilemma of simultaneous modernisation and de-industrialisation, which also causes the amalgam of high-tech city and 'quasi-ruined landscape'. Some Japanimation and Hollywood films caricature the reality of this world.

The post-Fordist economy is inextricably tied up with the labour forces of Asia. In this context, it should be noted that many Japanimations have been produced by animators in other Asian countries with relatively cheaper labour costs. Japanimation itself is a symbolic result of 'Japanisation' in capitalism or Japanese (sub)imperialism or (post)colonialism. During the 1980s, the 'Japanese way' of management was overestimated in Western societies and their corporations. But the success of Japanimation is linked not only to the Japanese way of management but also to the intrinsic nature of contemporary capitalism. New orders of information capitalism and colonialism achieve hegemony not only through military and diplomatic politics but also through economic and cultural politics. Indeed, rather than simply pursue cheaper labour, Japanese corporations move into Asia largely to avoid the risks of changing currency rates and constructing new networks of production, sales, distribution and R&D for more rapid access to world markets. Moreover, they need a model of information capitalism, and use images of Asia to point towards the new era. Other Asian areas become a resource for Japanese capital as images of the future as well as its economic base. In this sense, techno-orientalism in Japanimation can function as a cultural apparatus or unconscious ideology to cover and disavow the reality of global capitalism. In techno-orientalism, Japan is not only located geographically, but is also projected chronologically. Through the futuristic images of Asian cyber-landscapes in Japanimation, audiences can be mobilised and even overadapted for the information society and cyber-technology. The landscape and atmosphere of Japan, as typical model of over-adjusting to the high-tech built environment, are constantly referred to as signs of the near future. Thus Japanimation is defined by the stereotype of Japan as an image of cybersociety.

The West is seduced and attracted by this model, but at the same time Japan is looked down upon rather than envied by the West. Even in theoretical discourses, sometimes we can find examples of techno-orientalism. American sociologist Antonia Levi's *Samurai from Outer Space* is an example.[5] Her analysis implies that *anime* is more interesting for 'Western' people than for the Japanese because of its cultural specificity. The orientalism reappears when she insists that, in Japanese animation, traditional or ancient mythology is very significant, so that *anime* is assumed to be closely connected to cultural identity in Japan. The frequent deaths or sacrificial fatal attacks of heroes and heroines in *anime*, for Levi, drive from moral codes based on Shinto and the spirit of *hara-kiri* or *kamikaze*. Evidently, from the title of her book, she is still fascinated by an illusory image of Samurai which never existed but has been constructed as an interface for understanding the heterogeneous culture.[6] Similar examples are only too common Although in his article, 'Transformational Magic', Tom Gill analyses Japanese SF action heroes of special effects dramas, his argument is deeply caught in cultural essentialism and collapses into a silly putative theoretical prejudgement of the other culture. He also tries to combine Japanese *anime* and SF drama with an imaginary cultural background of Zen Buddhism, spiritual endurance (*gaman*) and group mind in Japanese society. Furthermore, although he explains the frequently used red–white colour combination in Japanimation and SF by tracing it back to Japanese tradition, I do not believe there is any such connection. Indeed, it is surprising that some non-Japanese scholars construct an imaginary Japanese culture.

PSYCHEDELIC TRANCE AND CULTURAL DIASPORA

In the 1970s, the German band Kraftwerk pioneered techno-pop using computers, rhythm machines and sequencers. In live gigs, they imitated robot-like gestures, pretending to be Japanese businessmen in Düsseldorf. In the 1980s, African-American musician Africa Bambaata launched his legendary Planet Rock by sampling Kraftwerk's Trans Europe Express. This exchange is one of the founding moments of hip-hop and also the basis of house music. In the mid-1980s the Japanese techno-pop band Yellow Magic Orchestra released several albums played and composed in techno-orientalist style. Their versions of Martin Denny or traditional Asian music styles in the form of techno pop were followed in the late 1980s by house and electronic sampling music genres. Around the late 1980s and early 1990s in Europe, rave culture, including trance techno started. German trance in Germany, the golden days of acid house and hardcore open air parties in the UK: these are now crucial chapters in the legend of techno. After the Criminal Justice Act was brought into law in the UK, it became more and more difficult to organise rave parties in British and other European cities, but the psychedelic trance scene was still powerful all around the world including Eastern Europe, Australia and Japan. Goa, on the west coast of India, already well known as a major hippie destination since the late 1960s, had hosted progressive rock and new wave gigs until, in the 1990s, people started to play techno and Euro-trance. So Goa became the home of Goa trance or psychedelic trance. Ironically, since Goa was first colonised by Europe in the late fifteenth century, it is necessary to analyse and interpret Goa trance techno through postcolonial discourse. One of the influential organisers and record labels in this scene, Matsuri, based in London and Tokyo, has become globally famous, and its video clip featuring Asian religious symbols and mythical icons seems to be also very techno-orientalist. Actually Goan techno-psychedelic trance has appropriated many musical elements from all over Asia, including ethnic melodies and tribal rhythms from India, Japan or Turkish-influenced Bosnian traditions. Moreover, this genre is based on electronic equipment – turntable, rhythm machine, bass synthesiser, mixer – which are mainly made in Japan such as the legendary Roland 303 and 808 machines.

The process of globalisation is based on the constant circulations and exchanges of materials, information, cultural elements and human resources in the form of the labour force. In other words, it has always required 'cultural travelling' and cultural diaspora. In using these terms, one should keep a critical distance from their use in globalisation theory more generally. Originally, diaspora has its background in movement and migration forced by economic, political, religious, ethnic or other factors. But in so far as cultural elements like dreadlocks, T-shirts and music move, one can apply the term 'cultural diaspora' to interpret their circulation.[7] Certainly diaspora presupposes a sort of cultural travelling and risks the problems of travelling theory, but it should not be confused with the effects of postmodern pastiche and mere eclecticism. On the other hand, it is now becoming difficult to maintain the rigid dichotomy between real refugees, illegal migrants, asylum seekers and others who have 'suffered' diaspora, and rave aficionados, hooligans, New Age travellers, indeed some tourists who undertake a 'cultural diaspora'. In some contexts, it is no exaggeration to say that it is now hard to distinguish precisely between forced settlement and voluntary migration, dwelling and travelling. There is a grey and blurred zone in the variety of ravers, hippies and New Age travellers, anarchists and squatters, some of whom maybe migrant workers or otherwise extra-legal.

Obviously, the positivistic, empirical and 'academic' view is insufficient to grasp such a complicated reality. Needless to say, the concept of diaspora is always circumscribed by histories of suffering and catastrophe. But even in our more or less stable everyday life in the 'First World', sometimes quite unmetaphorical suffering or catastrophe can be found. What is important for diaspora is maintaining and inventing memory networks of 'original' cultures beyond the formation of nation states and powers. In such networks, first and foremost, the power relations, economics, politics and ethics have come from the positions, decisions and wills of those who have suffered diaspora. In other words, the fact and actuality that one cannot help being in exile does not exclude the willing decisions of individual agency. What is crucial in thinking about diaspora is to avoid separating politics from lifestyle, and focusing rather on cultural politics and the empowered relations within it. Gestures and behaviours seemingly dependent on tastes and styles can lead us to political positionalities. While paying attention to the immense differences between the dangerous lives of migrant workers and journeys of willingly exiled intellectuals and mere tourists, one should also be aware of the transverse horizon they share. It is not romanticising drifters as diaspora to insist upon the transversality between 'wannabe' and 'forced to be' in diasporic situations.

Travelling cultures (or cultural travelling) of globalisation are fundamentally motivated by 'synthetic reason'. I do not wish to underestimate the dialectical reason elaborated by Hegel and Marx and its potential for critical and cultural theory, but, at the very least, dialectical reason can be said to be based on linear and hierarchical structures. Where dialectics, for example, resolves binary oppositions in a third 'synthetic' term which acts as a kind of goal for otherwise spontaneous social or cultural phenomena, 'synthetic reason' is based on non-linear dynamics and logic.[8] Needless to say, some aspects of dialectic reason can be truly 'synthetic' or even 'synergetic', but for now, in the interest of clarity, I will adopt as a hypothesis this dichotomy between dialectic and synthetic. In synthetic reason, emergent forms of stability within a given system can occur in terms of strange attractors, butterfly effects and chaotic processes in general. Of course, it should be noted that these terms have to be defined scientifically and rigorously distinguished from one another. One should not forget that the concepts drawn from natural science and adopted into the cultural field are sometimes only metaphors. But at the same time, it is also a truism that some theoreticians appropriate concepts from the natural sciences for cultural and social phenomena with proper logical and structural frameworks. In fact, some scholars in cultural studies use terms derived from synthetic reason to explain globalisation and its cultural effects. For instance, it is quite noteworthy that Paul Gilroy occasionally explains diasporan (sub)cultures by adopting the terms from chaos theory. Citing Du Bois, he writes:

> This change of perspective is aimed at transforming the more familiar unidirectional notion of diaspora as a form of dispersal which enjoys an identifiable and reversible originary moment, into a much more complex 'chaotic' model in which unstable 'strange attractors' are also visible.[9]

The contingent character of diasporan cultural propagation across dispersed locations is rendered understandable by concepts addressing unexpectable, unpredictable phenomena. Thus, the key notion in cultural diaspora is an emergent behaviour in which cultural elements can arise out of the organic interactions of heterogeneous cultures without appeal to any top-down effect. On the contrary, the aim of both cultural travelling and diaspora is to push forward towards a synthesis of cultural elements through bottom-up procedures. In this context, synthetic reason can be said to be synergetic.

It is easy to recognise the elements of techno-orientalism in psychedelic trance's party decorations, the design of flyers, clothing, CD sleeve designs, the names of bands and the titles of their songs. First of all, its music style itself commonly refers to 'Oriental' atmosphere by using some particular instrumentation, melody or rhythms. Of course, in this case, the 'Oriental' is purely conventional, addressing Asia, Africa, the Middle East or South-East Asia as imaginary objects. Tibetan religious objects, tepee tents of Native Americans, Balinese, Japanese or Siberian shamanistic implements, South or East Asian clothes are common in Goan trance raves. Flyers and installations of party events continuously cite cultural designs from totally different backgrounds. Taoist calendars, images of Buddha, Chinese ideograms from the I-Ching, feng shui schemas are used to build the atmosphere of tribal culture, even when they have nothing to do with the tribal. In one way, it is merely a Western dream of Asian and Oriental cultures, a longing for the Rest by the West, in which media tribalism coincides with the techno-orientalism of the information society.

But I have to say that the taste for the tribal never means a return to premodern society or archaic civilisations. Certainly, past, 'native' and 'primitive' societies exert a powerful attraction, in some ways like a revival of psychedelic movements of the late 1960s. But Goa or psychedelic trance tribes are pretty aware that all kinds of tribal moments in their culture are a sort of illusion, an idealised model whose purpose is criticism of their actual civilisation, since while adopting tribal (premodern) tools and styles, they are also expertly over-adapted for electronic and other high technologies.

Although so far in Japan, hugging one another has been rare until recently, and despite the lack of an ultimate model to imitate, I have been wondering why Goan trance's very specific style of dance has propagated all around the world. It is unlikely that the entire psychedelic trance tribe has been 'educated' by the travellers from Goa. It is more likely that particular steps and actions could circulate alongside the distribution of records and CDs and through organised parties. In this way, many ritual behaviours and customs specific to rave could have gained their everyday popularity. One can also suppose that the music itself encourages the 'transversal' distribution of both dance and rituals. Trance parties are full of practices of hospitality, kindness and giving (drink, dope, food, and so on). In other words, it is deeply based on the 'gift economy', which encourages the movement of style and ritual around the world. This is also enabled by some media, one of the most interesting in this scene being the magazine *PLUR* (the name means Peace, Love, Unity and Respect) published by active party organisers and DJs in Taipei. This bilingual quarterly magazine was also distributed in Europe, Japan and the USA. Containing articles on trance culture, the history of electronic equipment and critical reviews, it was the first magazine exclusively focusing on psychedelic or Goa trance. *PLUR* is rumoured to have disappeared as a result of police pressures, perhaps the counterpart of the Criminal Justice Act in Taipei. But before this disappearance, the members of *PLUR* invited Croatian unit Dogma to play live in Taipei where their club EDGE also hosted other famous groups like Astral Projection from Israel.

It is significant to appreciate this new type of inter-East connection. Trade in music software and technologies had already established some global links: is the sharing of acts, rituals and dance styles just a concrete result of globalisation? Certainly one needs to be careful in interpreting the detail of the current situation. Recently, psychedelic trance music is beginning to be remixed with other genres like breakbeat, drum 'n' bass, jungle, gabba and hardcore techno. In fact, in recent raves and parties in this scene, trance music seems to be arriving at new beginnings which are not yet named as one genre. Some participants are calling this new trend 'Tribal'. This may reflect the long-term effects of the Criminal Justice Act: a weakened rave culture divided between recuperation and co-option by big beer and tobacco corporations on the one hand, and less legal but less political dissident parties and events on the other.

JAPANIMATION AND RAVE CULTURE

Meanwhile in Japanese animations, works inspired or 'contaminated' by techno-orientalism are increasing. *Gasaraki*, for example, features near-future war and politics in Japan and globally. Robots in powered metal suits take a significant role in this political suspense science fiction. The battle in this piece is inspired by images from television news during the Gulf War and the story includes a debate on the participation of the Japanese army, constitutionally bound to self-defence. The strange mobile suits called *gasaraki* are very similar to samurai armour, and their power is summoned up and released by a trance dance resembling the dance of traditional Noh theatre. *Gasaraki*, constructed by unknown technology and handed down in one particular tribe through history, is at the centre of a narrative of conflicts among an international secret society, a right-wing philosopher and his sympathisers in the army of self-defence, the US army, illegal migrants and the special tribe controlling *gasaraki*. Conservativism and traditionalism in Japan also contribute to the world of this story, as does the amalgam of high technology and Oriental culture.

A second Japanimation called *Brain-Powered* features a war between cyborgs over the huge space colony Orphen. There are two kinds of cyborgs: 'Grantures' fighting for and 'Brain-Powereds' fighting against Orphen. These mechanical organisms are not mere robots even though they are driven and manipulated by humans: they have their own will and emotions and can move and act by themselves. The relationship between them and their pilots is like that between humans and horses. In the opening sequence of this piece, we see a series of symbols and architectures from different religions and civilisations: pyramid and sphinx, a Shinto shrine, archetypal Asian landscape and various Oriental architectures, strewn with naked women, who are major characters in this work. It is vain to criticise *Brain-Powered* simply on the grounds of sexism because the articulation of women and machines in Japanimation is so highly contextual, complicated and general that even mere otaku geeks unconsciously understand the problem of the cyborg in quasi-feminist discourse. *Brain-Powered* allows us to note some coincidences between Japanimation and rave or club culture. First, the characters dress in Asian and sometimes specifically club or rave party styles and combine traditional Oriental science with high technology: for example, cauterising wounds with the moxa herb. Second, the main technology in this story, the 'organic engine', is associated with psychedelic, 'trippy' colours. Elements of techno-designs, narrative, mysticism, and so on, continue to be common in both rave and Japanimation cultures several years after I first presented the term 'techno-orientalism' in the context of Japanese animation.

Both psychedelic trance and Japanimation are hybrid cultural moments in several senses. They are not based purely on postmodern eclecticism but also on *tactical syncretism*, which can be distinguished from pastiche or mere eclecticism that always presupposes the notion of purity, even in sophisticated cultural critiques. But there is no pure or authentic travelling culture. Syncretism then not only implies cut 'n' mix and sampling as pastiche, but also pinpoints a more subjective and tactical consciousness guiding radical appropriations. Hence syncretism requires the active involvement of the subject of appropriation, expressed as respect for other cultures quoted in the formation of hybrid cultural moments. The necessarily subjective discursive formation that organises party decoration out of Oriental imagery and goods, from feng shui to Hinduism, is subject to a tacit rule of rave cultures to avoid postmodern eclecticism and random juxtaposition of objects from different contexts. Despite their relative ignorance of the background of various cultures, the tactical syncretism of ravers and organisers leads them always to try to learn and respect their specificity. In this context, I distinguish between moments and elements. According to Laclau and Mouffe, moments consist of the articulation of discourse while elements do not possess discursively articulated structure. I wish to apply this distinction to the process of subcultural cut 'n' mix. Cultural themes juxtaposed in mere pastiche are only cultural elements. Such elements can become moments only

when they are articulated by discursive practices. Tactical appropriations of cut 'n' mix can be invented only in the context of constant
transition from elements to moments in a given culture, even
though this transition is always already incomplete.[10]

Respect for the feelings of the other and its cultures among urban
or media tribes is a form of care for eventual solidarity (coexistence)
with other tribes. As I argued above, one can travel from one tribe
to another: in the age of media tribalism, interactions and exchange
of tastes and styles between tribes are far from rare. One and the
same person can be a crazy fan of Japanimation and at the same
time deeply involved with psychedelic trance. For instance, some of
my students involved in rave culture have told me that Japanimation's design and colour sense reminds them of psychedelics.
Likewise, I have often heard of the impression that the tribal
atmosphere of open-air rave parties resembles scenes in Japanimation science fiction. Even at the narrative level, in many
Japanimations featuring robots or powersuits the pilots are doped
with injected drugs either for aggression or to provide altered states
of mind encouraging adaptation to the machines (rather like
computer or videogame freaks' use of magic mushrooms or other
drugs to heighten their experience).

Let me turn to some similarities and transversal issues in Japanimation and trance cultures at theoretical and ideological levels.
First, in both cultures, one can see competitive mimesis or mimetic
antagonism. Both cultures are deeply based on mimesis, imitation
and mimicry but at the same time, the mimesis in both shows some
conflictual and antagonistic moments. Readers will know that much
Japanimation depends on images of war and conflict: for example,
the image of 'pinpoint bombing' that has become a cliché since the
Gulf War. Ironically, even though Japan possesses a 'peace constitution' and people do not like to speak about political and
conflictual issues in everyday life, in popular fictions and expressive
cultures, people are almost preoccupied with the concept of
antagonism as the basis of sociality. At first glance, rave cultures
seem to have nothing to do with conflict or war. During the early
1990s ethnic war in the former Yugoslavia, rave parties often contributed to the anti-war movement, and the peaceful, harmonious
atmosphere of the rave scene is famous. But even in rave culture,
careful attention can reveal competitive and antagonistic factors at
play. Friction inevitably arises between ravers or DJs, but it is
typically resolved by non-violent negotiations and transformed into

tribal solidarity. Here the culture realises dance as politics, for dancing can supply the occasion to assume and undo a certain displacement and disorganisation of subjectivity. Through mimetic antagonism or competitive mimesis, dance can afford communal solidarity. In so far as politics consists in imitating and interiorising ethics and social discipline in the body, dancing invents and opens up the interactive community and communicative space for mimesis. In rave, mimesis functions without a model. Psychedelic trance in particular is beginning to articulate cultural and political effects and affects through dance in a proto-politics in which people are enabled to identify with the invisible (or coming) community.[11] This identification and solidarity derived from the mimetic character of spontaneous dancing, unlike traditional politics, tends towards pluralism, towards membership of several communities. Rave can provide a Deleuzean 'body without organs', constituted by 'a particular mind/body/spirit/technology assemblage' geared towards an alternative experience of self.[12] In this politics of dancing, the role of DJs is crucial. Already sociologists like Georgina Gore compare the position of the DJ in rave with the shaman of archaic societies.[13] The mimetic antagonism of ravers can only be resolved around the DJ as mediator and techno-shaman.

Second, in both Japanimation and trance, the position of women is very significant and one frequently encounters the merging of women into the machine and technology. Many Japanimations feature female protagonists frequently with super powers and even more commonly endowed with special relationships with technology. Interestingly they are often ethnically coded, despite the relative indifference to 'race' or ethnicity prevailing in Japanese society. Actually, the naked woman as cyborg and hybrid images of women and machines are clichés of Japanimation. These commonly embody themes of the loss of individuality to the wider body of technology. Major characters are always highly gendered even when they are technological entities rather than human. Similarly, in psychedelic trance the position of women is crucial. Unlike previous disco cultures, women are no longer treated as the target of sexual pick-ups, which tend to be taboo in Goa trance even though some romantic encounters do take place. Men also are encouraged to abandon overtly masculine behaviour. From time to time ravers in the trance scene talk about the unification of the self with nature, the universe and the others. Through various technologies – sound system, rhythm machines, decoration, videos and computer graphics, drugs and dance – ravers can invent an extended artificial body or collective identity. Crucially, ravers are quite aware that the 'nature' with which they feel unified is thoroughly artificial and technological.

Some scholars and researchers insist that women in rave culture are much more conscious and sensitive about this point than men, suggesting 'a positive female engagement with technology'.[14] Terms like 'cyborg subjectivity', which supplements some lack and void in the self through media technology, or 'nomadic subjectivity' which is constantly moving without fixed home, drawn respectively from the writings of Donna Haraway and Rosi Braidotti, may help connect these trends to issues in Japanimation. But rather than interpret and analyse raves in terms of these paradigms, what is at stake is finding out and reading the common discourse in the assemblage of the dancing body. Of course, it is not necessary to suppose some 'feminine principle' or fundamental 'eternal femininity'. This is the trap into which Japanimation frequently falls. Ravers in psychedelic trance culture, on the contrary, are aware of the danger of this trap and conscious of the illusory character of their own cultures. In this sense they are quite different from the sexism of psychedelic culture in the 1960s.

Third, both cultures can point towards future alternative politics. The hybridisation of body and technology in Japanimation explores the potential of cyberfeminism and cyborg politics. Rey Chow has defined the strategy of the cyborg *feministas* rejecting the binary opposition of masculine human subject vs. feminised automaton.[15] She argues that this strategy retains the notion of the automaton – the mechanical doll or cyborg – but changes its fate by giving it another life; this is the task of the cyborg as transgressive half machine, half animal. Conversely, when a subject takes up the tactics of transgression, it unconsciously becomes like a cyborg. For the cyborg feminist, this strategy should be extended further than 'animating the oppressed minority'. Cyborg feminists have to make the automatised and animated situation of their own voices the conscious point of departure in their intervention. In a very unexpected way, I think, Japanimation is providing the arena of such politics and interventions.

Throughout the world the Left has failed either to understand the meaning of rave or to take a tactical relationship between rave culture and politics; and it has overlooked the emergence of similar alternative politics in psychedelic trance culture. Historically speaking, rave has been closely connected to the Green and other new social movements resisting global capitalism; it is more concerned with the constitution of a singular mind/body/spirit/ technology assemblage for alternative politics of the self and community. The growing interest in shamanism, spiritualism and mysticism since the 1980s, and their putative connection with the ecology movement, needs to be recontextualised and even radically criticised in the so-called 'New Age' cultures (one thinks here of the case of the Aum religious cult in Japan as an extreme example), although their role should not be overestimated. Spiritual concerns are interwoven not only with technology and the discourses on drugs and electronic media in their junctures with literature and the arts, but also lived and practised in each concrete situation of everyday life. As a temporary conclusion, at least, it could be said that techno-oriental subcultures, including Japanimation and trance music, like the gestures of a lot of urban and media tribes, could be an ideological apparatus or trap, but at the same time tactical consumption is already an option for everyone. The aim of my analysis lies in providing some platforms for critical views on globalisation and its empowerment rather than a simple celebration. Of course, that critique will continue in the cultures of Japanimation and trance themselves.

NOTES

1. Maffesoli, Michel, *The Time of the Tribes*, London, Sage, 1966; Baumann, Zygmunt, *Life in Fragments*, Oxford, Blackwell, 1995 and *Postmodernity and its Discontents*, Oxford, Blackwell, 1997; Hetherington, Kevin, *Expression of Identity: Space, Performance, Politics*, London, Sage, 1998.
2. In *Speed Tribes*, New York, Harper Perennial, 1994, Karl Taro Greenfield analyses Japanese youth and its cultures from *Boso-zoku* to *Otaku-zoku*.
3. Concerning the notion of techno-orientalism, see Morley, David and Robins, Kevin, *The Space of Identity: Global Media, Electronic Landscapes and Cultural Boundaries*, London, Routledge, 1995.
4. Harvey, David, *The Condition of Postmodernity*, Oxford, Blackwell, 1989, pp. 308–11.
5. Levi, Antonia, *Samurai from Outer Space: Understanding Japanese Animation*, Illinois, Open Court, 1996.
6. Gill, Tom, 'Transformational magic: some Japanese superheroes and monsters' in Martinez, Dolores P (ed.) *The Worlds of Japanese Popular Culture*, Cambridge, Cambridge University Press, 1996.
7. Concerning the relationship between diaspora and globalisation in the age of cyberculture, see Cubitt, Sean, *Digital Aesthetics*, London, Sage, 1998, pp. 143–5.

8. I borrow this term from De Landa, Manuel, 'Virtual environment and the emergence of synthetic reason' in Dery, Mark (ed.) *Flame Wars: The Discourse of Cyberculture*, Durham, Duke University Press, 1993.

9. Gilroy, Paul, 'Route Work: the Black Atlantic and Politics of Exile' in Chambers, Iain and Curti, Lidia (eds) *The Postcolonial Question*, London, Routledge, 1996, p. 22.

10. Laclau, Ernesto and Mouffe, Chantal, *Hegemony and Socialist Strategy*, London, Verso, 1985, pp. 103, 113.

11. On dancing as proto-politics and mimesis, see Miklitsch, Robert, *From Hegel to Madonna: Towards a General Economy of Commodity Fetishism*, Albany, State University of New York Press, 1998.

12. Pini, Maria, 'Cyborgs, Nomads and Raving Feminine' in Thomas, Helen (ed.) *Dance in the City*, London, Macmillan, 1997, p. 118.

13. Gore, Georgina, 'The Beat Goes On: Trance, Dance Tribalism in Rave Culture' in Thomas, *Dance in the City*, p. 62.

14. Pini, 'Cyborgs, Nomads and Raving Feminine', p. 125.

15. Chow, Rey, *Writing Diaspora: Tactics of Intervention in Contemporary Cultural Studies*, Bloomington, Indiana University Press, 1993.

6 Wicked Cities: The Other in Hong Kong Science Fiction

Gregory B Lee and Sunny S K Lam

I think that identity is a product of the will. Not something given by nature or history. What prevents us, in this voluntary identity, from encompassing several identities? I do it. To be Arab, Lebanese, Palestinian, and Jewish, is possible. When I was young, that was my world. We travelled ignorant of borders between Egypt, Palestine, and Lebanon. At school there were Italians, Jews, Spaniards or Egyptians, Armenians, it was normal. I am with all my force opposed to this idea of separation, of national homo geneity. Why not open our spirits to others? Now there's a real project for you.

Edward W Said[1]

Battery operated space vehicle from China.
Takes 2 'C' size batteries.
Bump and go action
Floating Ball from blowing Air
Blinking Lights
ITEM#: SV-ME-102–98 PRICE: $20.00 + p/h[2]

Science fiction, like its more recent progeny, cyberpunk, has rarely been thought of as anything other than an American and European genre. Asia's, and in particular Hong Kong's, and later, China's role has been that of the producer of the plastic and tin sci-fi space toys rather than that of high-tech, glossy media producer. Indeed, it has only been with the advent of the Japanese *manga* and *anime* that there has been an awareness of non-'Western' futuristic fantasy. But in fact the genre of science fiction in this part of Asia has some celebrated antecedents. In the pre-republican era of the late Qing dynasty there were already utopian narratives articulating fantasies based on the imagined possibilities of Western science. After the 1911 Revolution, science and modernisation became increasingly seen as a means for China to reassert its national identity and to combat colonialism. Later, the 1919 May Fourth intellectual revolution started with the trope of 'Mr Science and Mr Democracy' inscribed on the banners of Peking's student demonstrators protesting against the unfairness of the 1919 Versailles Peace Treaty that transferred German colonies to a modernised, technologically advanced Japan.

A more ambivalent vision of science and its Western manipulators was produced by the modern Chinese novelist Lao She (1898–1966), better known for his novel the *Rickshaw Boy*, in his 1930s sci-fi novel entitled *Maochengji* (literally, 'the tale of cat city') in which a Chinese space traveller visits Mars where he discovers its cat-like inhabitants fighting amongst themselves and ultimately being defeated by an invading enemy; an allegory of Chinese helplessness in the face of Western and Japanese modernity and colonialism:

> Our goal had been Mars. According to my late friend's calculations, we were already in the Martian atmospheric envelope before the accident occurred ... The soul of my dead friend ought to be at rest, for to be the first Chinese on Mars was really something worth dying for![3]

Towards the end of the novel, the visiting alien space adventurer witnesses the advance of the cat-people's enemy, imperialist invaders (who seem to resemble China's Japanese aggressors) who take advantage of the cat-people's weaknesses:

> This was the first time I had seen the enemy army. In stature, most of them were a bit shorter than the cat-people ... When all of the cat-people were kneeling, at a signal from one of the short enemy who was obviously an officer, a row of soldiers sprang forward ... They tapped the cat-leaders on their heads with their short clubs. The latter immediately lowered their heads, shivered, and then collapsed lifeless on the ground. Were the clubs electrified? I couldn't tell.[4]

But even in the face of total destruction, the cat-people are incapable of unity and collective resistance:

> Towards the end, I actually saw a few cat-people try to resist, but even then they could only manage to band together in groups of

three to five at the most. On the very brink of death they still didn't understand the need for co-operation. Later on, on a small mountain I ran into ten or so cat-people who had escaped ... Before the enemy troops had arrived in the area, the group was down to two ... Rather than killing them, the enemy soldiers locked them in a large wooden cage where they continued to struggle until they had bitten each other to death.[5]

A pessimistic ending to this allegorical tale laying the ultimate responsibility for defeat at China's own door rather than that of the coloniser, and a charge similar to that of Lao She's contemporary Lu Xun, who claimed that the still feudal-minded China was a self-consuming 'cannibalistic society'.

Such works were not only attempts to critique Western domination and China's seeming helplessness. They were also attempts to negotiate the realities of modernity. While condemning Western, and Japanese, imperialist strategies, at the same time China's writers and filmmakers in the 1920s and 1930s saw in modernity the possibility of overturning feudalism and patriarchy, and constructing in their stead a modern nation state. Since then many parts of Asia have seen revolution and counter-revolution, but increasingly over the past 20 years they have experienced urban modernity, even hyper-modernity. At least one generation has grown up in Hong Kong entirely alienated from the rural, and only experiencing this hyper-modern post-industrial society and its cultural formations; mainland China has also produced its first generation of city-dwellers who have little knowledge of China's countryside's reality nor of China's premodern practices.[6]

Hong Kong, however, remains China's most modern city, and has represented itself in many ways as the model for China's capitalist development, but as Richard Rogers has recently shown a faithful mimicry of Western capitalist urban modernity will ultimately prove disastrous for China's people. Unless Chinese regnant authority commits to 'planning for sustainable cities, it will soon be faced with massive congestion, pollution and social dissatisfaction on an even larger scale than is endemic to the cities it is using as role models'.[7]

The questions addressed by Rogers are practical and materially real. The French writer and critic Serge Latouche is also concerned with the non-material condition of the non-West. However, in his discussion of what non-Western societies have lost, 'the loss of sense that afflicts them and gnaws at them like a cancer', there seems to be a nostalgia for an imagined past 'authentic'. For Latouche the non-Western world is underdeveloped, exploited, marginalised, left behind. It is not, however, that Latouche does not take account of Japanese, South-East Asian and increasingly Chinese modernisation, but that there is an erasure of the modern realities of Japan, Hong Kong, parts of South-East Asia and of China in which modernisation is seen entirely negatively, in terms of cultural loss, a nostalgia for some authentic local, without any place given to renewal, redeployment and the ingenuity of human creativity that can be forged of hybridity.[8] Even there, one might argue, there is loss, loss of 'cultural identity'. But in such arguments there is always the whiff of the orientalising tendency to valorise the East in terms of its past greatness.

The historical reality at the beginning of the twenty-first century is that many parts of Asia are constituent agents, not simply exploited objects, of modernity. Let us take for example the Chinese authorities' avid encouragement of the use and production of new technologies, in particular in the field of communication. As early as 1993 there were 460,000 mobile telephone subscribers and 6 million radio pager users in mainland China.[9] Six years later there were already 60 million mobile telephones in use, a figure expected to double by 2001; the pager or 'beeper' (*bipiji*) being already obsolete.[10] In mid-2000 the Finnish mobile telecommunications giant Nokia and China's Fujian Mobile Communications Corporation launched the 'world's first fully standards compliant commercial GPRS network', a technology permitting continuous connectivity to the Internet and opening up a range of services to mobile users via a WAP (wireless application protocol) portal.[11] Thus, the expansion of mobile telephone possession will have consequences going far beyond more convenient voice communication. While for reasons of cost and of lack of availability of standard telephone lines, the number of home computers linked to the Internet still lags behind consumer desire for access to the world wide web, the new WAP technology permitting connection to the Internet over a portable telephone will result in an ever more enormous increase in Chinese Internet traffic; even without WAP technology, the number of Chinese households connected to the Internet had reached 9 million at the end of 1999 and 17 million by August 2000, with the number of Chinese internauts doubling every six months.[12] The prediction of foreign telecommunications companies is that by 2004 there will be 250 million portable telephones in China equipped with WAP technology yielding an equal number of potential Internet users.[13]

At the same time, the economic expansion-minded Chinese state seems to have set itself the ambitious and somewhat contradictory targets of both monitoring 'dissident' use of new technologies, and of encouraging the massive expansion in production, consumption and distribution of new forms of telecommunications.

China's modernity, then, is scored by the claws of colonialism, left full of contradictions, of half-finished processes, of confusions, of hybridities and liminalities. But is that so different from the rest of the modern world where women and working classes form the domestic colonised? In Asia these contradictions and consequences of capitalist development have simply been magnified and accelerated, giving rise to a concomitant magnification of the human dilemmas and suffering involved in capitalist urban industrialisation in general.

But if there is a 'loss of sense' in the modern world, a sentiment of alienation, then its transcendence, its overcoming, the process of de-alienation will not be simplistically achieved by a return to 'nativist' traditions of 'the East' any more than it will be by a 'return' to Morris dancing in England. Like Said, we would advocate not a pseudo-universality, nor a slight-of-hand multiculturalism (that is not the hybridity we intend), but rather the encouragement of new and composite identities based on new material realities that give rise to new imaginaries. In his recent book, Ziauddin Sardar represents postmodernism as but a more subtle agent of Western cultural imperialism continuing and even expanding the dominance of the ideologies and projects of colonialism and modernity in which other cultures 'are simply being taken from one domain of oppression into another'.[14] His condemnation of the cynicism of postmodernism and his arguments for 'non-Western cultural resistance *to* postmodernism' are compelling, but the appeal to tradition as the instrument of transformation of non-Western societies into 'cultures *of* resistance' raises certain concerns for us.[15] For while, understandably, Sardar is at pains to distance his conception of the 'authentic' tradition from that of 'traditionalism', there still seems to a longing for a 'lost' cultural authenticity. But we would ask: whence is this authenticity to be resurrected or reinvented, and would such a reinvention even be desirable? While Sardar sees the representation of tradition in pre-modern Islamic and Chinese painting as a 'dynamic force ready to confront the problems of modernity and the nihilism of postmodernism', can we forget the economic and technological modes in which premodern Chinese painting was embedded, and the oppressions upon which the livelihood of its practitioners and appreciators depended? While we would not oppose the recuperation of premodern painting and other forms of cultural production from the often conservative grip of the orientalists and sinologists, we should nevertheless be concerned at the prospect of privileging a supposedly cultural authenticity in the name of respecting 'traditional physical, intellectual and spiritual environments'.

Again, in the instance of Hong Kong, our central question would be: where is this authentic to be found or rather how is it to be invented in the real local context? The fact that Hong Kong has been 'returned' to China does not facilitate the recuperation of 'tradition', especially now that mainland Chinese traditions, where they exist, are now constructed and re-invented so as to sustain nationalism and centralist state market capitalism. Moreover, the old, feudal China is, happily, no more; its cultural texts and practices are now merely redeployed in the construction of an officially coddled national imaginary. And if not from the array of official nationalised and centralised 'traditions', from which part of the complex of cultural practices should these 'traditions' be re-imported or re-invented, and from when? So then where, when and what would constitute 'tradition' for Hong Kong? Hong Kong is an immigrant metropolis peopled by Chinese from every part of China, not just Cantonese-speaking Guangdong but also from Shanghai and Fujian, and Tanka boat-people, the Hakka (or 'Guest People') and by those whose ancestors came from even further afield, such as the now Cantonese-speaking third and fourth generation Indians. As for Chinese traditions in Hong Kong, these were invented or their invention nurtured by the post-1950s late colonialism of a British authority representing the interests of post-Second World War neo-colonialism in Asia. That authority was anxious to construct an alternative Chineseness that separated Hong Kong from both mainland communist and Taiwan nationalist appeals to the patriotic anti-colonialist imaginary. But in negotiation with that official and imposed alternative Chinese identity, or Hong Kongness, other colonised-produced identities have been constructed and imagined. There are even minority cultural formations which have resisted both colonialist and national-patriotic constructed identities.

However, none of the resultant cultural spaces and practices can be described as clear, or pure, or authentic. They represent groups and classes that are found in all modernised industrial societies. That is not to say that the various levels and enclaves of Hong Kong society have not developed peculiarities or that there are not traces of a premodern Chinese collective imaginaries, but the concerns of the majority of Hong Kong people today – the working class who are represented as, and intended to imagine themselves as, middle-class – are those of any urbanised, industrial society subject to the inevitable (as the financial events of the last few months of 1997 have once again clearly demonstrated) crises of capitalism. Worries about the implications for Hong Kong's autonomy or rather its multiple and multileveled identities were to the fore in the panoply of people's concerns, as the film that we shall discuss below, *The Wicked City*, clearly shows, but the major event of 1997 for most Hong Kong people was constituted by the material economic reality brought about by the stock market crash. Concerns over unemployment and economic survival in a market driven yet heavily state interventionist, non-welfare state now dominate over concerns with local identity. The politics of local identity, or identities, can no longer be used simply to exercise the neuroses of postmodern alienation. If such identities are to be useful they must be deployed in a meta-politics that must now engage in a process of de-alienation that will imply challenging and transforming both the oppressions of colonialism and of the dominant economic system.

While agreeing with the need to encourage and bring about the de-alienation of modernity or 'post'modernity and to combat the oppressions of colonialism, we would also emphasise the importance of recognising historical realities that have produced 'non-authentic', hybrid lived realities. Over the past 150 years social and cultural forces not only in Hong Kong but in China as a whole have been obliged to negotiate the realities of colonialism, semi-colonialism and neo-colonialism. New forms and practices have been produced; new identities have been invented or imposed. Emancipatory change, we believe, will not necessarily imply an *épuration*, or cleansing, of the non-authentic, but a redeployment and *détournement* of hybridised and local practices with the aim of imagining that future.

Hong Kong, a late capitalist and uniquely a late colonialist metropolis entered its new era of neo-colonialism after its 'handover' from the colonial authority of Britain to the sovereignty of the People's Republic of China, under the regnant, yet vassal, authority of the government Hong Kong Special Administrative Region (SAR). However, structurally no great changes have occurred. The metropolis is still dominated by ideologies falling within the logic of capitalism and culturally relies, to an incalculable extent, on the formula of mechanical reproduction in all sorts of productions.

Despite the success of claims by the new postmodern ideology that history, ideology and modernity are all dead, ideologies interpreted in terms of metanarratives of binary opposition (communism and capitalism, modernism and postmodernism, realism and surrealism) are still central to popular imaginaries. Yet, emphatic dichotomies leave unaddressed all sorts of meanings of ideologies within our communities. The politics of capitalism occlude unspoken, marginal cultures from the silent majorities to mask reality. Ideologies of minorities are thoroughly suppressed in Hong Kong. Thus, the Hong Kong imaginary tends to be constituted by the practices, beliefs and dominant ideology which uphold the regnant authority. So the emulation and redeployment of the decentring manifested in the literature and media productions such as science fiction novels, comics and films in 'postmodern' America and Japan has been useful in the elaboration of a wide range of alternative ideologies. This process has been negotiated by the Hong Kong media and culture industry itself constituted by ideologically distinct and competing ambitions unified, apart from economic interest, by its apparent distance from official and elite culture. The industry has nevertheless been capable of contesting and reconfiguring the Hong Kong collective imaginary or imaginaries. Science fiction-inspired technoculture filmic production in particular has been of central importance in this process.

Facilitated by technological advances, particularly the development of computer technology, techno-culture has become a central constituent of literature and media productions, and science-fiction films have recently dominated the box offices in both Hollywood and Hong Kong. However, their cultural impact on the production rather than consumption in Hong Kong is minor when compared to the United States. Certainly, imitation of Hollywood science fiction movies is not facilitated by the high production costs required by special effects which are unaffordable to local filmmakers. If anything, local media producers are affected by the cultural imaginaries in these movies that are a function of science fiction novels and comics.

Emerging in unison with the new imaginary of cyberspace is the term 'cyberpunk' employed to indicate a genre of science fiction novels in the mould of William Gibson's 1984 science fiction novel

Neuromancer which projects the disembodied consciousness of human beings into the matrix of consensual hallucination. Despite fears of a new kind of computer-generated alienation linked to an already existent human technophobia, the 1990s have witnessed an increasing propagation of the ideology if not the materiality of the virtual reality of postmodern computer-dominated environment. Gibson 'cyberspace' is now a commonly accepted figure within the spectacle of post-industrial societies.[16] All participants in virtual reality (cyberspace) become members of the electronic virtual communities who live in the borderlands of both physical and virtual culture.[17] Like Benedict Anderson's imagined communities, the members of virtual communities will never know all of their fellow-members of the same or similar field of interest.[18]

However, a cyberspace such as the Internet still manages to represent itself as a friendly, open community, while non partici-pants see it as anarchic, in a negative sense, and in need of regulation.[19] The concept of 'nationality' is irrelevant to the identities of virtual communities. But virtual communities also seem transgressive of other cultural and canonical borders, the boundaries between genres, between media, between 'high' and 'low' and between major and minor cultures being no longer applicable. Thus we see the development of terminal identity, an unmistakably doubled articulation in which we find both the end of the subject and a new subjectivity constructed at the human-computer interface. It pervades all areas of cultural production, such as visual genres like comics and cinema, as well as the electronic: video, computer graphics and computer games.[20] It should not be forgotten, however, that economics and ideology still largely dictate the possibilities of participation in virtual communities. Certainly, large enterprises which produce the games and graphics still control the reproduction of ideology in society. Moreover, for several years now critics have been pointing to the possible sinister deployment of the Internet and other technocultural media:

> As the standing ruins of the Alfred Murrah Federal Building in Oklahoma City are being razed to ground, the American public is being warned that the extreme right had begun to infiltrate the Internet. In Japan, it has now been revealed that the Aum Shrinrikyo cult, accused of the Sarin gas attack upon a crowded subway train during the morning rush hour in Tokyo, appropri-

ated themes and imagery derived from popular manga and anime series in developing their paranoid visions of the forthcoming apocalypse.[21]

The ultimate emancipatory potential of such technologies and the new communities they have made possible may be in doubt, but these new media as well as the means of media production have indeed gradually become more open to wider social use in industrialised and industrialising societies both because of the user-friendly multimedia tools such as personal computers, and higher standards of cultural as well as technological education. An index of the emancipatory possibilities of new information technologies is provided by the negative reaction of the Chinese state in the face of the 'disorderliness' of cyberspace. The state's anxiety over the borderlessness of Internet traffic doubtless accounts for its harsh treatment of dissident webmasters, its attempts to control the consultation of foreign websites; recently, 525 of Shanghai's 1,000 or so cybercafés were condemned to closure for encouraging the youth of the city to play 'morally corrupting' computer games.[22]

While it may prove to be yet another temporary moment of technological promise whose democratic and de-alienatory possibilities were missed, we can imagine this decentred and boundless cyberspace as similar to the virtual space, the 'raptor vacuum', created by the monsters of the film *The Wicked City*. Cyberpunk culture constitutes a warning system, a set of cautionary moral tales, alerting us to the dangers of future developments in technology. Therefore, like the theory and culture of postmodernism, cyberpunk may be seen as a response rather than a resolutory strategy to the explosive proliferation of modern technology and implosive collapse of cultural boundaries. Cyberpunk culture, however, is not anti-technology, rather it maps out a matrix of the potential, negative and positive, of technology and the technological future. It constitutes a vision that is neither technophobic nor technophilic.[23] Moreover, we should add that, whatever the validity for East Asia of the criticisms of cyberpunk culture that have been made in the United States and Europe in terms of recuperation and commodification, the criticism of cyberpunk as 'the vanguard white male art of the age' ('Neuromanticism'), made by Istvan Csicsery-Ronay, would be incommensurate either with Japanese or Hong Kong readings and practices of cyberpunk culture.

Although techno-cultures comprised of computer hardware and software, Internet online services, and so on, are unavoidably commodified in capitalist metropolises like Hong Kong, cyberpunk culture which embraces technology may serve to awaken the consciousness of its participants within commodified cyberspace and open up a channel through which the technological politics of the regnant class may be discerned. It may seem to offer to cybernauts a way to confirm the existence of individual identities within social groups or virtual communities in the process of techno-cultural development. Cyberpunk culture stands as a reminder to discern all the harmful and beneficial effects of technology on our cultural development, and not to delve into cyberspace so as to be once again dominated and colonised. *The Wicked City*, a film replete with an array of lavish and exquisitely produced special effects, self-referentially foregrounds the illusions producible by cyberculture, and the likelihood of its recuperation by capitalism and militarism.

The Wicked City, *Yaoshou dushi* in Chinese (literally 'demon beast metropolis'), is a cinematic transcription of a Japanese comic of the same title (itself based on a novel by Hideyuki Kikuchi) transliterated in Japanese as *Yoju toshi*, and sometimes billed as *Supernatural Beast City*. The film differs considerably from the 1989 Japanese *anime* film of the same title. The 1992 Hong Kong-produced *The Wicked City* was directed by Peter Mak (Mak Tai Kit) and produced by Tsui Hark. It starred Leon Lai, Tatsuya Nakadai and the Hong Kong megastar Jacky Cheung. *The Wicked City* is a futuristic science fiction film set, however, in Hong Kong's immediate pre-handover moment. Humans are combating the 'raptors' a race of demons with a variety of supernatural powers that include the ability to conjure up illusory representations of reality, powers of elastic and liquid metamorphosis, and the capacity to transform themselves into human form. The aliens or demons (there is no indication that they are extraterrestrial) also enjoy the benefit of longevity; the 'good' demon played by Tatsuya Nakadai, is 150 years old, which in 1997 would make himself exactly as old as the colony of Hong Kong itself. The film is shot in both Tokyo and Hong Kong, but Hong Kong's ultramodern skyscape, in particular the futuristic Bank of China building, constitutes not only the central physical setting but also a major character.

Some of the demon-monsters, or raptors, have taken the road of legitimacy, and attempt to dominate human society via economics. For instance the character played by Tatsuya Nakadai, Yuan Daizong

(identified in the English subtitles as Daishu, using Japanese translit-
eration, as are several major characters) is represented as attempting
to play the role of a respectable businessman. Others, like the son
and would-be usurper of Daishu, are attempting to take over by
means of violence and addiction; the highly addictive and fatal drug
'happiness' is being imported and administered to all humans. All
raptors are suspect and hunted by the humans' special police. Jacky
Cheung plays a police agent, Ken/A Ying, who is half-human and
half-raptor. His superior officer constantly suspects him of betrayal
and cannot accommodate the possibility of positive raptor qualities
or the impurity of the hybrid. At the end of the film as Ken lies
dying, the superior officer's reconciliation comes in the form of an
ideologically conservative affirmation that Ken is human after all.
There is ultimately no acceptance of his raptor qualities, Ken's
goodness must be entirely due to his 'humanity'. In contrast, and in
line with the unusual polyphonically rich dialogue of this film,
Daishu, representing the raptor wisdom, has already declared: 'Being
different isn't the same as betrayal.'

The film is very much concerned with identity, multiple identities
and confused identities. Several characters, bother raptor and police,
have retained their Japaneseness from the comic book origins of the
filmic production. This is indicated not simply by the English
subtitles' usage of Japanese names, but also by the use of several
Japanese actors and the deployment of heavily Japanese-accented
Cantonese by characters like the police inspector. And yet this is very
consciously a film about Hong Kong. But even Hong Kong is represented as multiply valenced. Hong Kong is Hong Kong as
foregrounded by the references to 1997, as when the police inspector
states that the handover year presents the raptors with an opportunity to take over. But Hong Kong is also metonymically elsewhere
the ultra-modern metropolis of late capitalism. Unlike the average
Hong Kong film, Hong Kong's economism is critiqued throughout
The Wicked City. The peaceful raptors takeover plan is based on
'money ... man's greatest weakness', and noble raptor Daishu
proclaims early in the film: 'Our influence has penetrated their
economic system. Economics is humankind's weakness.' Even the
police inspector joins in the collective critique: 'When influenced
by money we all become short-sighted.' Daishu's final comment on
the economism of modernity is: 'Human beings place possessions
ahead of emotions.' In a lightly veiled allusion to Hong Kong triad
gangs and the complicity of venal Hong Kong police officers, one of

the human police officers in *The Wicked City*, Orchid, is corrupt and co-operates with the drug-trafficking raptors. Her justification, a direct allusion to the acceptable and respectable officially propagated Hong Kong capitalist ideology, is: 'I just want to make the most money in the shortest time.'

Time is not only a capitalist concern, time is typically a classic concern of the science fiction movie. *The Wicked City* meets that agenda. Part of the wicked raptor plan is to turn humans back into beasts by making human time go backwards. But the passage of time is seen in a more global sense, and several references to time can be read on the level of the plot, or at a metalevel in reference to capitalism's effects on the global environment: 'Since this planet's days are numbered our common enemy is time.' But time in the countdown to the handover of Hong Kong to the People's Republic of China has yet another level of meaning. Time is not just running out for humanity, the clocks are not just turning backwards in terms of global history, time in the film and in its context, the shadow of the handover has a very specific valence. Ken represents a common, everyday sentiment of the early 1990s, when he says curtly: 'Time is a real pain.'

The exhaustion of Hong Kong's time is also alluded to in the closing shots of the old raptor Daishu, as old as Hong Kong itself. His energies depleted after the struggle with his evil son, he rapidly starts to show his 150 years. It is left to him to complete the basic critique of late capitalism when, being driven out of Hong Kong along its ultra-modern highways, he says: 'This city is so lonely. I hope they'll never need the raptors' happiness.' Money, time and alienation. And even more urgently and specifically for Hong Kong in the 1990s, an uncertain future.

The Wicked City is an unusual Hong Kong film in the ways it re-uses and alters the cultural imaginaries of Hollywood movies, Japanese comics and Hong Kong's own ideology. Film and comics are generally considered to be straightforward entertainment in Hong Kong and thus ideology is rarely consciously foregrounded in local films and comics. In everyday life in Hong Kong, the unconscious ambition of the majority is the avoidance of official ideologies. With a view to escaping domination by the ideology of the regnant power, the hegemonic narrator, we must attempt to achieve a space for the survival of other narratives and ideologies in our cultural imaginaries. The imaginary of *The Wicked City*, Hong Kong, is an attempt to do that. Tetsuo Najita has noted that a culture controlled by technology does not merely remove the principles of certainty but will result in the possibility of mechanical reproduction, or the continuous reconstitution of things as they are, only more or less.[24] It reminds us that the hyper-modern condition, the condition of what is now commonly but often unthinkingly called 'postmodernity', may be a curse or a space of opportunity depending on our own navigation of it. While conceding the indispensable status of technology in modern society, we need to bear in mind the monolithic cultural domination by particular stereotypical interpretation of techno-culture.

While many may be willing to immerse themselves in cyberspace in order to achieve the terminal identity of virtual communities, it is important to remember that virtual communities originate in and must return to the physical.[25] The technology that plays a vital role in navigating cultural development in postmodern society results from the knowledge of historical traditions and cultures. In the acceptance of the techno-cultural changes in the process of modernisation, there is also room to redeploy the surplus values of traditions and cultures with a view to developing a new form of culture that may be defined temporarily as 'post-cyberpunk culture'. Cyberpunk culture reflects how technology can enhance human life and how it can also be a destructive force, but it does not address the current cultural needs of human beings and does not deal with such alienating social problems as poverty, racism, disintegration of families, addiction to drugs and sex, and so on.[26] Idealistically, the development of film culture would involve a historical review of human traditions and a forecast of our technological as well as cultural development in the future.

The cyberpunk Japanese comic and animation *Wicked City* were transposed to the film *The Wicked City* in Hong Kong. The monsters of both the manga and the film possess dual identities, which reveal the ambiguity of postmodern metropolises such as Tokyo and Hong Kong as well as that of their residents' identities. In local comics, dual identities are rare and most local comic characters are either Chinese kung-fu-fighting heroes whose social status and social roles are similar to those of American-style superheroes, or gangsters or anti-social heroes constructed as oppositional to the monolithic anti-social bureaucracy, and thus constituting a totally 'deviant' concept of heroism. These subjective identities result from the homogeneous ideologies of capitalism and are derived from the ideas of binary opposition in accordance with the concepts of commercialisation, the politics of subjectivity that determine the commercial nature of characters. Such stereotypical subjective identities are believed to guarantee commercial success.

On the contrary, this subjectivity that excludes the possibility of dual or multiple identities of characters in local media productions is detrimental to alternative procedures of socialisation and simply serves to ensure media and cultural development's investment in the reproduction of conservative stereotypes. Many Hong Kong films which feed into the narratives of local comics reproduce similar dominative identities. So genres of local film and comics are limited to irrational heroisms such as super-heroism, anti-social heroism, mock-heroism, and so on. Thus, the ideology transmitted to their consumers offers only escapism from reality and promulgates no strategy by which to resolve individual and social alienation. Thus the alternative cultural imaginaries to be found in foreign cyberpunk comics and films are rare and difficult to cultivate in Hong Kong.

The dual identities in cyberpunk comics and films are both windows and mirrors through which the ambiguities of our metropolises and the survival of marginalities are represented. Dual identities, of course, are actually existent in Hong Kong society, but the 'id' is highly suppressed and usually hidden. Many individuals are marginalised by the moralities of the dominant class. Thus in filmic production either the 'ego' or the 'id' is therefore expressed in terms of binary oppositional identities of characters in order to fulfil the desires of media producers and silent majorities. For instance, Jackie Chan acts as a rigid, patient, brave policeman, a superhero, in the film *Police Story*. He represents the 'ego' or the subject of the narrative, a moral hero, to portray a desired subjectivity of particular media producers and spectators. In John Wu's films such as *A Better Tomorrow*, *The Killer* and *Full Contact*, the anti-heroes are the 'ego' or the 'id' of human beings in society. They are inevitably killed or converted into moral subjects at the end of the films. Their identities may be transformed from the 'ego' to the 'id' or vice versa but hybrid coexistence is not permitted.

Thus, the dual identities of the monster special police represented in *The Wicked City* are extremely unusual in Hong Kong cinema. The marginal and marginalised identities of particular Hong Kong people such as gays and lesbians have little space in which to express themselves, and are almost literally forced to hide themselves from the mainstream on the limits of social life. Like Hollywood movies, many Hong Kong films are dreams for audiences that celebrate the successes of capitalism in the dominant culture, and marginal identities have no place in that narrative.

Japanese popular cultural production, on the other hand, in particular Japanese comics, abounds with characters representing or constituting alternative selves, 'alien identities'. As Susan Napier recently wrote:

> In other post-war media such as film or manga, the alien sometimes seems omnipresent, a staple of popular culture throughout the post-war period. One can trace a fascination with the alien back as early as 1953 to the scaly prehistoric monster in the movie *Godzilla*, which became first a domestic and then an international hit. In recent years perhaps the most striking rendition of the alien has been the aforementioned series of grotesque metamorphoses undergone by Tetsuo in the 1989 comic and animated film *Akira*.
>
> Thus, to discuss the alien in Japanese fantasy is to bring up issues of identity, desire and, also, ultimately of power. The alien is the Other in its most fundamental form, the outsider who simultaneously can be the insider, and it is this polysemic potential that is enthralling and disturbing to the reader. The alien threatens the collectivity more than any other presence.[27]

The alien identities in such texts are delineated through fantasy to reveal the variety of alternative selves that are useful to the processes of self-identification of their readers. The alien popularly presented in the fantastic in post-war, as well as more recent, 'postmodern' Japanese comics and animated films, is used not simply to shock readers, but to awaken them to the smug comfort of the mainstream capitalist spectacle. The fantastic in this variety of comics and animated films can be construed as constituting a subversion of modernity and so these genres of Japanese comics and animated films with a limited number of exceptions such as *Akira* are generally defined as deviant and occluded by the dominating mediators.

The unlimited cyberspace constructed as a utopian space supplying the opportunity to re-evaluate as well as reinvigorate cultures and cultural imaginaries is the space explored in cyberpunk films of which *The Wicked City* is a prime example. The virtual reality of the film foregrounds the alternative identities of the protagonists, in particular those of the monster special police, as well as the subjectivities of real Hong Kong people. In doing so it exposes the actual persona dilemmas and uncertainties of Hong Kong inhabitants like the inspector in the film who is reluctant to accept the possibility of dual identity in this neo-colonial period. Indeed, the inspector embodies the denial common to many Hong Kong people incapable or unwilling to locate their dual identity as the colonised of both the West (Britain) and of the People's Republic of China, but who willingly recognise the identity in the stereotype of global, yet local, capitalism.

While mechanical and electronic reproduction may convention-ally be seen as a curse of modernity facilitating the economic and cultural domination by capitalism through commodification, the space and time of 'hyperreality' may be perceived by elements within the new generations of urban, industrial modernity as a frame out of which to challenge the economic realities of capitalism, and to emancipate cultural development from the bind of a binary opposition no longer capable of making sense of a society in which the ideology and spectacle of modernity has been exposed as 'the visible *negation* of life, as a negation of life which *has become visible*'.[28] The trend of cyberpunk development in Hong Kong is similar to that of telecommunications in its early stage. We are assigned a number for identification, an e-mail address 'cybersun@hkstar.com' for approaching the cyberspace of Internet, a (or a number of) telephone/mobile phone number and/or a pager number for calling anybody or being called at home, at the office or at any location. In 1998–99, the University of Hong Kong plans to supply every student on campus with a notebook computer and saturate the physical campus with Internet/Intranet connection sockets. In this headlong rush to place Hong Kong at the forefront of IT literacy and func-tionality, the worst problem is that many youngsters are duped by the commodified images such as the romantic heroes of advertise-ments, the wealthy businessmen, the superstars, and the top-dog gangsters of movies and comics whose mobile phones are symbolic of authority in the imaginary of the global capitalistic metropolis.

In the last decade of the twentieth century, while cyberspace gained ground, cyberpunk cultures and the seemingly unlimited fields of interests in cyberspace, ensured the possibility of different means and directions of identification and cultural development for those who had the necessary knowledge, desire and economic means to divert cyberspace and use it otherwise. The terms 'cyberpunk', 'cyberspace' and 'cybernetics' come from the Greek word *kybernetes* meaning 'pilot'; 'cyber' cultures hint at Greek traditions of autonomy

and agency foregrounded so eloquently by the late Cornelius Castoriadis in his rereading of pre-modern Greek democracy.

In *Wicked City*, the cyberspace, the virtual reality made by
monsters reminds audiences of the centrality of their original
physical state; the dual identity of the monster special police representing the marginality of Hong Kong people's cultural identity, an
angst not over the loss of nativist tradition, but rather over the fear
of the disappearance of a particular identititarian certainty in neo-
colonial Hong Kong. Japanese comic culture still has many
particular, alternative ideas created by its authors in terms of their
cultural tradition and globalised world vision that can enliven
cultural development for film and comic productions. Although
Hong Kong is also a hybrid metropolis like Tokyo, the spaces for the
development of alternative cultures are insufficient and the cultural
ecosystem is heavily commodified. Stereotyped Hollywood-style film
productions cannot change the hegemony of commodity culture but
favour its extension. Cultural imaginaries of cyberpunk films, comics
as well as novels in America and Japan have not, to the same extent,
developed in postmodern Hong Kong where people's thoughts are
highly depersonalised and stereotyped by commodity culture under
the logic of capitalism.

Like the virtual space and the dual identity of the monster special
police in the film *The Wicked City*, Japanese comic culture is highly
revelatory of the cultural imaginary of Hong Kong. The cyberspace
of the film that is full of ambiguous images and allegories reflects, to
a certain degree, the decadent atmosphere of the 'Judgement Day',
the return of Hong Kong to China in 1997, makes, in a particular
sense, a linkage with the cyberpunk culture of the Japanese manga
and certainly deconstructs a vital part of local cultural phenomenon
and dual identity. The signified of the Bank of China building as the
wicked headquarters and the duelling with the clock transformed by
the monster interprets common anxieties and fears of the Hong
Kong people concerning the return in 1997. The dual identity of the
monster special police agent as well as his marginality (he is
ostracised by both the monster community and human society)
parallels the identity and condition of Hong Kong people. However,
the film betrays a lack of intensive and sophisticated investigation
of the 'postmodern' as well as the neo-colonial Hong Kong cityscape.
Moreover, the film does not depart from the dominant masculinist
ideology common to most Hong Kong movies. Thus, the Lee Ka-yan
character, a 'good' female monster, is represented as a sex object

within the film, and in terms of power relations is treated as an appendix of man; one of the traits of dominant gender ideology being that a woman who is 'feminine' must be highly submissive while a man who is really 'masculine' must exercise a high degree of agency.[29] The ideologically emancipatory representations of many Japanese comics, especially girls' comics, that show men and women enjoying equal social status and agency, often integrated into an androgynous body have not yet been deployed by the Hong Kong filmmaker.

After Thatcher's visit to China in 1983 and again after the 1989 Tiananmen Square massacre, Hong Kong people felt compelled to define their own culture as a unique cultural entity. Hong Kong as a specific cultural identity was recognised, and lived, by many of the younger generation; nonetheless, this kind of hybrid identity has lacked an ideological sense of nationhood. So while, in the globalised information civilisation of the twenty-first century, cultural development may be more dynamic, complex and diversified, in the local context of Hong Kong specific hybrid cultural identities, especially alternative identities, have been deformed or totally repressed in most local film productions.[30] With the exception of *The Wicked City* and the films we shall mention below, cultural identity has been expressed monovocally and new Hong Kong generations have been unable to locate representations of their multiple identities in the mass media.

Just before the 'return' or the 'handover' of Hong Kong to the People's Republic of China in 1997, a time to which the film *The Wicked City* alludes, the hybridity of now neo-colonial and late capitalist Hong Kong was both real and potentially recuperable to the cultural reimagining of new generations. In the project of maximising the surplus-value of hybrid cultures, which now surround us everywhere, the utopian and dystopian spaces constructed in cyberpunk science fiction films, comics and novels may prove a useful catalyst for the reimagining of urban cultures, but in the few years since the 'handover' Hong Kong society has shown little evidence of any such mutation. Today, in terms of cultural identity, we can perhaps identify three categories of imaginary in post-British Hong Kong. The first would comprise those who regard themselves as Chinese, support the PRC's regnant authority but nevertheless object to new legal immigration from mainland China and revere Western language and technology; the second would regard themselves as 'Hong Kong Chinese' with an identity distinct from that of the mainland Chinese; and the third constituted mainly by the younger generation of Hong Kong people who cannot find any identity for themselves and refuse to accept the predetermined set definition of cultural identity established by the regnant authority. In other words, they have no sense of 'permanent' identity.

While there have been no film productions in Hong Kong since 1997 which could be regarded as cyberpunk sci-fi movies, a few locally made human-drama films have sought to challenge the social vision constructed by the techno-colonial power dominating the neo-colonial Hong Kong of the early twenty-first century. Two exceptional films that have attempted to deal with questions of cultural, social and sexual identity are Lawrence Lau Kwok Cheong's *Spacked Out* (2000) and Wong Kar-wai's cinematographic collaborator Chris Doyle's *Away With Words* (*Sam Tiao Yan*). The latter is shot in a sleazy, smoky downtown bar and tells the story of three young marginalised characters, Asano (Tadanobu Asano), an autistic Japanese recently arrived in Hong Kong who speaks nothing but Japanese, a gay Englishman, Kevin (Kevin Sherlock), and a Chinese woman, Susie (Mavis Xu). The three overcome all their differences to become a powerful trio linked by a close camaraderie. While doubtless more pressing social problems might have been found in the public housing estates of Hong Kong, the film can be read as an allegory for the kinds of alliances that are possible and fruitful in the lived reality of postcolonial late capitalism. *Spacked Out* (*Mo Yan Ga Sai*, literally 'No One Driving'), made by the relatively new film company Milkway Productions, addresses not so much hybrid identities, but the identity crises of four rebellious high school students who have grown up on the outlying working-class district of Tuen Mun. Thirteen-year-old Cookie is pregnant, but her boyfriend has disappeared to Mongkok to sell pirated VCDs. From a broken home Cookie can only rely on her friends Sissy, Banana and Bean Curd, all seeking to overcome their alienation in sentimental and sexual adventures. Banana finds excitement in short-lived romance, while Bean Curd and Sissy are lesbians. The film thus represents a reality far removed from the neo-Confucian conformism of obedient patriarchal family life promoted by the authorities.

We started this chapter with a discussion of recent theses on post-modernity and the Other. We noted Latouche's concerns and his doubts about the 'pseudo-universality' of Western late modernity. There is no doubting Latouche's historical revulsion with the savagery of modernity and 'postmodernity'. But in Latouche's vision there seems to be an over-valorisation of difference as a positive force. While he condemns the 'nostalgia for the universal', there is the suspicion that he opposes it with a hidden nostalgia for the lost difference of the Other. But there can be no de-reification. The desire to live differently is legitimate, the ambition to unveil the dupery of progress is similarly understandable, but while there may be a re-deployment and recuperation of past elements, there can be no material return to the past. Only the future can offer hope, even if from our current perspective that future seems all too bright for technological capitalism, yet sadly dim for humanity. But there is no going back. For Hong Kong, a real, temporal 'return' to China would entail regression to a moment of Chinese imperial feudalism and despotism of 150 years ago. Such a return would require a realisation of the raptor plot to turn back humanity's clock; a possibility that thankfully is still in the space and time of fantasy.

In the concluding sentence of Lao She's *Maochengji*, whose doleful allegory of China's incapacity to adapt to the modern world we related at the beginning of this chapter, the Chinese space traveller also dreams of a 'return' to an ideal future/past. Whether he would have rejoiced at the reality that has developed during the 70 earth years elapsed since his departure it is perhaps too early, or too late, to tell:

> After living on Mars for another half year, I encountered a French exploration craft and thus was able to return alive to my own great, glorious, and free China.[31]

For sure, China has hitched a ride on the meta-machine of Western consumerist techno-capitalism (and is paying the price in terms of the globalisation of its inhabitants' everyday practices and worsening environmental pollution), but in terms of human emancipation the journey is far from over.

NOTES

1. 'Ne renonçons pas à la coexistence avec les Juifs', interview in the *Nouvel Observateur*, 16 January 1997 [translation: GBL].
2. http://sci-fi-toys.com/space_v.htm
3. Lao She, *Maochengji*, translated by William A Lyell, Jr as *Cat Country*, Ohio State University Press, 1970, p. 3.
4. Ibid., p. 290.
5. Ibid., pp. 293–4.
6. Commenting recently on the fact that Beijing now 'boasts' more than 30 McDonald's restaurants and on the past 30 years of Americanisation,

which we now call 'globalisation', of the world's eating habits, especially the conversion of non-milk-consuming societies to the consumption of dairy products, Gregory Lee had some difficulty in persuading a 20-year-old student from Beijing that milk products (milk-shakes, cheese, and so on) were not a 'traditional' part of the Chinese diet. In other words, McDonald's and Chinese domestic milk producers have succeeded in naturalising 'alien' lacteal fast-food products in traditionally non-milk-consuming socio-economies. As a result, in China millions now suffer from illnesses and diseases associated with milk fat and from an incapacity to digest milk products.

7. Rogers, Richard, *Cities for a Small Planet*, London, Faber and Faber, 1997, p. 53.
8. Latouche, Serge, *L'Occidentalisation du monde*, Paris, La Découverte, 1992, p. 69 [translation: GBL].
9. UPI, 6 November 1993.
10. CND, 18 May 2000.
11. http://asia.internet.com/wireless/2000/8/0831-mcon.html; report posted 31 August 2000.
12. CND, 29 September 2000.
13. Ibid., 18 May 2000.
14. Sardar, Ziauddin, *Postmodernism and the Other: The New Imperialism of Western Culture*, London, Pluto Press, 1998.
15. Ibid., p. 273.
16. William Gibson, *Neuromancer*, New York, Berkley Publishing Group, 1984, p. 5.
17. Benedict, Michael, *Cyberspace: First Steps*, London, MIT Press, 1991, p. 112.
18. Anderson, Benedict, *Imagined Communities: Reflections on the Origin and Spread of Nationalism*, London and New York, Verso, 1991, p. 6.
19. Pike, Mary Ann, *Special Edition: Using the Internet*, 2nd edition, USA, Que Corporation, 1995, p. 17.
20. Bukatman, Scott, *Terminal Identity: The Virtual Subject in Postmodern Science Fiction*, Durham NC, Duke University Press, 1993, p. 9.
21. Hollings, Ken, 'Tokyo Must Be Destroyed: Dreams of Tall Buildings and Monsters: Images of Cities and Monuments' in *CTheory* [online] (1995) http://www.ctheory.com/a27-destroy_tokyo.html (accessed 28 February 1998).
22. CND, 8 August 2000; 29 September 2000.
23. Kellner, Douglas, *Media Culture: Cultural Studies, Identity and Politics between the Modern and the Postmodern*, London and New York, Routledge, 1995, pp. 302–3.
24. Miyoshi, Masao and Harootunian, H D (eds) *Postmodernism and Japan*, Durham NC, Duke University Press, 1989, p. xiv.
25. Benedict, *Cyberspace*, p. 113.
26. Kellner, *Media Culture*, pp. 325–6.
27. Napier, Susan J, *The Fantastic in Modern Japanese Literature: The Subversion of Modernity*, London, Routledge, 1996, pp. 91–102.
28. Debord, Guy, *Society of the Spectacle*, Detroit, Black and Red, 1983; *La Societé du spectacle*, Paris, Buchet-Chastel, 1967, p. 10.

29. Loeb Adler, Leonore and Denmark, Florence L (eds) *Violence and the Prevention of Violence*, London, Praeger Publishers, 1995, pp. 151–2.
30. McCaffery, *Storming the Reality Studio*, Durham NC, Duke University Press, 1992, p. 246.
31. Lao She, *Cat Country*, p. 294.

7 Saying 'Yours' and 'Mine' in *Deep Space Nine*

Kirk W Junker and Robert Duffy

As the story goes, René Descartes began a meditation (which ultimately brought him to believe in his own existence through doubt) by wondering how he could know that everyone else was real. How could he know that they were all not just part of his world only, like in a dream, a fictional world that ended when he woke? Generally, of course, we live our lives without asking this question. And even when we do, we live as though we do not know the answer. More intriguingly, when we do ask the question and for lack of an answer just leave the question bracketed and go on, we do not always go on as though we are convinced of the realness of others. Instead we do so *as though* others only do matter insofar as they are related to our own world. We behave *as if* everyone else is just a part of our own world, as for instance Saleem Sinai does in Salman Rushdie's *Midnight's Children*.[1] Sinai was born at the precise moment of the independence of India, and imagines not only destiny, but a causal link as well.

When we encounter resistance to this way of behaving, when unpredicted events occur, or people behave in unanticipated ways, we awaken to identifying and naming 'them' or 'they', and through identifying and naming, we characterise their behaviour: 'They said it would rain today' (but it did not); 'They always park their cars in front of my house and prevent me from parking there'; 'They say it always rains for a funeral'; 'They are dirty thieves'; 'They are not trustworthy'; 'They don't know any better.' Thus we anchor our sense of our own real existence in distinguishing ourselves from others – if we did not, we might still be living the dream which Descartes pondered. This highlights the root of our concern in this chapter – the ways in which word and image facilitate the creation and maintenance of them, of they, of yours; in summary, of the 'Other'.

CREATING THE OTHER THROUGH LANGUAGE

Having said this, we are nevertheless mindful that Descartes was not the first metaphysician to ponder this question. Aware as always when discussing the cultural construct of the West that '"A" is for Aristotle',[2] we first look to his *Metaphysics*. There he points us to the process of the creation of otherness; a process that begins in the nature of being contrary. He calls the nature of being contrary 'contrariety', and says that 'contrariety is a kind of difference, and difference is a kind of otherness'.[3]

Literary critic and language scholar Kenneth Burke goes further with the creation of otherness and casts it as a language concept, which we should probably not interpret as being necessarily opposed to casting it as a metaphysical concept, since Burke maintained that he was most uncomfortable when he disagreed with Aristotle. Burke's complete definition of the 'human' is 'the symbol-using animal, inventor of the negative, separated from his natural condition by instruments of his own making, goaded by the spirit of hierarchy, and rotten with perfection'.[4] The three elements of this definition that we are most interested in are the symbolicity, the separation and the hierarchy.

Despite the kinship which Burke may have felt for Aristotle, in moving from metaphysics to symbolicity, Burke left Aristotle's *Metaphysics* and *Rhetoric* and adopted what has been named the 'new rhetoric'. Aristotle, in his 'old' *Rhetoric*, defined rhetoric as the faculty of observing in any given case the available means of persuasion'.[5] Here is where Burke and others break with Aristotle's idea of symbol use and state that a better attitude toward contemporary persuasion (the new rhetoric) understands persuasion not as an explicit or overt act, but rather through the process of identification. Hence we have an explanation offered for the popular movement in so many circles towards identity politics. This brings us closer to understanding the symbolic nature of persuasion that occurs in so many non-suspect places, without the overt use of coaxing, chiding or goading. Far more subtle is the unannounced presentation of difference, and the resulting otherness that Aristotle spoke of in his *Metaphysics*. Seen this way, the metaphysics of persuasion works as a two-step process: distinction of A from B, and then identification with A or B. In observable practices, we can see this in operation through symbol use.

This two-step symbol process – separation of the other from the self, and the identification of phenomena with the self – is further refined by Burke in his distinction of dialectical from positive terms.

In this connection, we might note a distinction between positive and dialectical terms – the former being terms that do not require an opposite to define them, the latter being terms that do require an opposite. 'Apple', for instance, is a positive term, in that we do not require, to understand it, the concept of a 'counter-apple'. But a term like 'freedom' is dialectical, in that we cannot locate its meaning without reference to the concepts of either 'feudalism' or 'socialism'.[6]

In anticipation of criticisms leading to nihilism, Burke cautions us by noting that:

However, the statement that a term is 'dialectical', in that it derives its meaning from an opposite term, and that the opposite term may be different at different historical periods, does not at all imply that such terms are 'meaningless'. All we need to do is to decide what they are *against* at a given period ... Much of the cruder linguistic analysis done by the debunko-semanticist school ... involves the simple fallacy of failing to note the distinction between positive and dialectical terms, whereby, in applying to *dialectical* terms the instruments of analysis proper to *positive* terms, they can persuade themselves that the terms are meaningless.[7]

Among other types of dialectic which Burke discusses, the notions of merger and division, mind-body and being-nothing are most relevant for us here. Burke begins his discussion of dialectic as merger and definition by referring to Plato's *Phaedrus*, wherein Socrates 'describes the principle of merger as "the comprehension of scattered particulars in one idea"'. Regarding division, Socrates 'says that the dialectician must learn to carve an idea at the joints, "not breaking any part as a bad carver might"'.[8] Burke notes that one may find the dialectical principles of merger and division in any systems of classification, whether it is a formal science or poetry.[9] Although he does not refer to it, this notion of merger and division looks very much like Aristotle's prolegomena to the above-discussed concept of contrariety leading to otherness. There, Aristotle works through the notion of unity and plurality as being opposites. Burke states that 'the merger-division shift draws upon the fact that any *distinction* is liable to sharpening into a *contrast*, and any contrast may be attenuated into the form of distinction'.[10] This notion of dialectic is very much related to that of identification, and Burke emphasises identification as being the hallmark of new rhetoric.[11]

The second and third of the dialectical principles that are relevant to our present discussion are that of mind-body, being-nothing and action-passion. These principles are further refinements on merger and division, which itself is a refinement of the notion of dialectic. Although the principles of merger and division apply to all thought, the principles of mind-body and being-nothing, 'singly or in combination, variously overlapping, and variously manipulated, will be found to figure any statement which embodies the principles of merger and division specifically'.[12] Here it is very important to notice that Burke says that they will figure into any *statement*; that is, the linguistic enterprise by which we may ultimately create or maintain otherness.

According to Burke, the first major steps usually taken in the process of developing mind-body or being-nothing ideas are 'towards the localising of *identity*'.[13] The mind-body pair, without explicitly being named as such, is very similar to the Cartesian *res-cogitans/res-existensa* split, including all the dialectical considerations which critics and supporters of Descartes have exposited. By comparison, we find that the being-nothing pair has its most prevalent form in yet another dialectical pair, 'the essence-existence pair, with either member of the pair being capable of selection as the "reality"'.[14] Again, however, we are talking about what we feel is the essentially linguistic nature of this, not what might be called the psychological or ontological one which Sartre discusses in 'The Existence of Others'.[15] Thus we can see a bit of the linguistic way, the symbolic way, in which we create the other. In summary, the two-part process begins in naming the other with terms that would characterise the other – 'you', 'they' or 'them' for instance. Having begun this process of separation, we then assign all new acquaintances the property of being identified more as like the self, or more as like the other. This is the so-called 'new rhetoric', otherwise known as persuasion by identification. Once one has identified someone as being like himself, he is more easily persuaded that that person's additional attributes, identified and named, are 'good' ones, ones like his own – 'one of us, one of us, gabba, gabba, hey'.

And the corollary of course is that the attributes of the person identified and named as the other will not be accepted and be characterised as 'bad'. Hence we see the dialectical nature of the naming process, different from the naming process of positive terms which

Burke described. To what end does all of this bring us? For Burke, one of the important ends that this process leads us to is the recognition of how we have, with instruments of our own creation (in this case, the naming of 'us' and 'them'), separated ourselves from our natural condition. We may speculate that that natural condition might be more akin to unity than difference. But more importantly, this process also brings us to the recognition of the 'spirit of hierarchy'. According to Burke, once we begin distinguishing things such as 'yours' and 'mine' we necessarily create a hierarchy. This hierarchy creation is not a second-order moral glaze placed over the language of distinction, but is built into the language of distinction itself. But to see all of this linguistic process at work, and to highlight some of its ramifications, we had best call upon an example. Here, we turn for an extended example to the television show *Deep Space Nine*.

'YOURS' AND 'MINE' IN *DEEP SPACE NINE*

As Fiske notes, television's familiarity and its centrality to our culture is what makes it so important and so fascinating (but at the same time, so difficult to analyse).[16] Initially it seems strange that a show set in such an alien setting could strike such a resonant chord with a contemporary Western audience. Upon closer examination though, we see that the world of *Star Trek* is actually quite a familiar one. In the *Star Trek* universe the human-dominated Federation of United Planets explores a world inhabited by a variety of alien races. Earth leads the Federation, and the Earth of *Star Trek* is Earth from an American perspective – it is the American Earth that the founding fathers foresaw, a true Utopia founded upon the principles of equality, tolerance and democracy. In the original *Star Trek* series with Captain Kirk and his crew, we saw that the pioneer spirit which built America was alive and well in the Federation. To emphasise that point, Kirk's starship was called the *Enterprise*.

The world was a simpler place in the 1960s, and the original series of *Star Trek* reflected that. Captain Kirk's world was a world where the bad guys were easily recognisable, named and identified, both within the show and without. Once the viewer was led to identify with the positive image of the *Enterprise* crew, it became the task of the audience to complete dialectically its position by distinguishing itself from the others. The simplicity of the identification and distinctions were almost as blatant as old Hollywood westerns with good guys in white hats and bad guys in black. And in case you did not catch that, the others were conveniently named for you –

'aliens'. Everyone knew for instance that the Klingons were the real Russians on the show, not Ensign Chekov. Brutal and unrelenting, they lent a grim resonance to the show. With the Cold War casting a shadow over American life, it was comforting to see that same struggle replayed every week on TV with America always coming out on top, both morally and physically. *Star Trek* was essentially ideological reinforcement for the American dream, an endorsement that the American way of life was the most natural and human of ways to live. Ironically, the *Enterprise*'s one alien character, Mr Spock, fuelled much of the reflection on what his dream meant. An outsider, without emotion or ego, he provided a foil for the emotional Dr McCoy. Their verbal fencing highlighted the underlying tension between modern rationality and old-fashioned values that was beginning to be felt in the American society of the time. But the overall message was still an optimistic one. Both Spock and McCoy were on our side, one of our people. Even the emotionless Spock was half-human, and the viewer was always left with the sense that his stoic exterior was more facade than genuine character.

Deep Space Nine differs from other *Star Trek* series and the feature films in several respects. It is the darkest of all four television shows (*Star Trek*, *Star Trek: The Next Generation*, *Deep Space Nine* and *Voyager*), and it is the one in which confrontations with other species, other cultures and other religions are the most prevalent. The plot was engineered to set this atmosphere of distinction up from the start. Having slowly been weaned away from the familiarity of *Star Trek*'s white guy Captain James T Kirk, to *The Next Generation*'s white-guy-with-foreign-name, Captain Jean-Luc Picard, we arrived at black guy Captain Benjamin Sisko as the main protagonist in *Deep Space Nine*. (Thereafter, having presented the other with foreign name and then as black, otherness shifted its focus to gender with white woman Captain Catherine Janeway in *Voyager*.) Fiction provides us with the opportunity of identification in the way that we learn to see it, using such terms as 'protagonist' and 'antagonist' to identify the players, and thus tip our hands as audience about the person(s) with whom we identify. *Why* we identify with A rather than B is a point of tension to be negotiated between the author and the audience. *That* we do is a convention into which the rhetoric of identification allows us to willingly, even unconsciously, walk.

Sisko is a single parent who is assigned by the Federation of United Planets to run *Deep Space Nine* on behalf of the nearby planet of Bajor. His real job is to help persuade the Bajorans to join the

Federation, thereby becoming one of us, and to protect the Bajorans from the Cardassians (them), who up until recently occupied Bajor. They are like that – fascists, imperialists, colonisers. You know how they are. By the end of the pilot episode two new developments thicken the mix. Sisko discovers a wormhole, a gateway through space, which leads to a previously unexplored region of the galaxy. His discovery of this wormhole makes him a major figure in the Bajoran religion, which of course forces him to confront the spiritual beliefs of the people he is supposed to convert to Federation ideology. Thus the beings set up for the audience as the Other subvert the wishes of dominant us by making us one of them instead of them one of us.

Throughout the series, all these factors often conspire to put Sisko's Federation ideals under the microscope. Although he is not the only Federation officer on the station, Sisko serves primarily as an icon for the Federation, an embodiment of its ideology. His determination that Federation ideals are the best ideals to live by is continually tested, both by his enemies and his friends. The cast of *Deep Space Nine* contains more aliens than any other *Star Trek* show. Just as Sisko functions as an icon for his species and its ideology, so too do most of these characters.

African-American actor Avery Brooks plays Sisko. With Brooks in the role of the commander, we begin to see some problems with the simple identification and distinction of the Other, which had previously seemed to be so easy. For instance, Sisko is meant to represent the Federation, which as we have seen is a representation of America. He is African-American; a member of a subculture of American society, and a 'minority' by legal definition in that country. This of course makes it more difficult for viewers who are not a member of that subculture to identify with Sisko as representing them. In short, some Americans' first reaction is to identify Sisko as being the Other. The same sort of comfortable differences that did not lead to Otherness with Chekov and Spock in the first series are present in the characters of Chief Miles O'Brien (Irish) and Doctor Bashir (British of Indian descent). These characters' origins in the British Isles are very much a part of their characters. They hang out together in Quark's, drink 'pints', play darts; in short they conform to the American view of how someone from the British Isles behave. This tactic works well for these sort of characters. But the show's lead character is meant to represent the Federation as a whole, and so should therefore be accessible to all viewers. The main strategy for overcoming this problem is not to overtly portray Sisko as being African-American. One of his main passions is baseball, a game with which an American audience would identify. His position as station commander further displaces him from a typical black character. In the vast majority of cases, black characters on television are portrayed as having lower status than the white characters around them.[17]

Traditionally, it would be necessary to know who the audience is before a character can be positioned in such a way that the audience will be expected to identify with him or her. Likewise, the audience would need to be known before a character can be positioned as the other. In this line of thinking, the audience should not be positioned to identify with the other, lest it become alienated from the protagonist, and consequently, from the show itself. But who is the other in *Deep Space Nine*? In the *Star Trek* of Captain Kirk's day the significance of these ideologies would have been easy to read. In the first series, every major alien species had a direct socio-cultural correspondence with a culture foreign to the United States here on Earth: the Klingons were the Russians, the Romulans were the Chinese (it is arguable that the Vulcans were the English), and so on. This is still true to a certain extent of course. New villains, the Borg, have been identified as bearing more than a passing resemblance to the stereotypical Japanese, from the American perspective, with their rigid, hi-tech society. The Klingons still resemble the American perspective of the Russians to some extent, especially in their uneasy status as sometimes friends, sometimes foes. Unlike *Star Trek*, however, *Deep Space Nine* no longer assigns an alien species a clear-cut resemblance to a foreign race or culture here on present-day Earth. The others in *Deep Space Nine* today are more sophisticated affairs. They are used to explore cultural and ideological themes. Therefore while Klingons may still resemble the Russians from the American perspective, they are now used more generally as a representation of warrior culture. The Federation itself could be seen as an exploration of a possible evolution of American society. Now that this technique has been expanded to other alien species though, it goes some way towards correcting a previous ideological deficit.

Previously the Federation had represented an idealised version of American society, with its virtues magnified and all its flaws erased. The representation of other societies, such as the Klingon portrayal of the Soviet Union, tended to present an extremely critical view of those societies. All that American society perceived to be negative of the other societies was magnified and used as the primary characteristics in the portrayal of those species. In *Deep Space Nine*, this is no longer true to the same extent. When an alien species is used to represent a foreign, contemporary race or culture, care is now taken to present a more balanced view of them. However, these societies are not simply presented on their own merits, but are compared and contrasted with the Federation. The Federation way of life functions as a sort of baseline, a yardstick against which all other cultures are measured, making identification of the self and other in this barnyard of relative species an obvious task that an audience is positioned to accept effortlessly. The Federation rarely comes off badly in comparison. An alien species, whether representing an existing race on Earth or not, almost never gains the same status as the Federation. The de-coupling of the alien species from exclusive use as metaphors for a contemporary foreign race or culture has two causes. Today's America no longer has a single clear-cut enemy to fight. Even more telling however, America no longer has the sense of moral superiority it had at the height of the Cold War. Thus in films and television, the Other is now often found within American culture – in the government, the military commerce or even the home. For shows like *Star Trek* or *Deep Space Nine*, which are already set in a place somewhere out there, how to portray this presents a serious dilemma. *Star Trek* is built upon the premise that the Federation is a Utopia. To back away from this too much would be to change the show's premise too much. One of the attractions of *Star Trek* is that it embodies an ideal that we all know we are not living. So how can the show both embody that ideal and still present stories of relevance to today's society? *Deep Space Nine* adopted a twofold solution to this problem. The first element is its versatility in the use of aliens. Their second tactic further capitalises on this versatility by falling back upon a variation of one of its original plot devices, the alien character.

A character who is generally regarded as having attained some popularity is an alien named Quark. Quark runs Quark's Place, the station's lone bar and social centre. He is a member of a species, the Ferengi, who are characterised by extreme capitalistic beliefs, in particular some of the most negative aspects associated with capitalism. Nothing is more important to a Ferengi than profit. We routinely see Quark and his brother Rom betray each other for money. At one point Rom plots to have Quark killed in order to gain ownership of Quark's Place. When Quark finds out, he is not angry, but rather so impressed by Rom's initiative that he promotes him to assistant manager of the bar. Ferengi morality seems impenetrable to an outsider. Greed really is good to them, and legality is a secondary consideration. Quark himself is a notorious criminal and smuggler, the central figure in the station's underworld. Yet as he tells one Federation character, 'No one involved in extra-legal activities thinks of himself as nefarious.'[18]

Quark's status on the station is that of a tolerated nuisance, an unpleasant fact of life. Sisko's relationship with him is especially conflicted. On the one hand Sisko clearly appreciates Quark's value. In the series' pilot episode Sisko persuades Quark to stay on the station, giving as his reason that *Deep Space Nine* needs the sense of community and stability that Quark's Place provides. Sisko tolerates even his criminal activities on the grounds that whoever will replace him could be worse. Sisko says of him, 'Quark has his own rules, which he does follow. Once you understand the rules, you understand Quark.'[19] On the other hand, Quark is clearly a thorn in Sisko's side. He instructs his security chief to keep a close eye on him at all times. He shows great initial reluctance to his son becoming friends with Quark's nephew. Above all, he seeks to avoid Quark's presence at every opportunity.

Despite this though, Sisko often finds a use for Quark. When dealing with the Dominion, the latest and most menacing of *Star Trek* villains, the Federation decides to open trade relations as a means of encouraging contact. Later on, when tensions between the two powers increase, it becomes necessary to use those trade links to exert pressure on the Dominion, and Sisko chooses Quark to handle this task. Although a supporter of this tactic, and present when it is being used, Sisko's choice of Quark as financial enforcer allows him to maintain a moral distance from the act.

The moral unease this generates is exemplified in Sisko's relationship with Quark. Although many of his crew frequent Quark's Place, Sisko rarely does. He never gambles there, significantly avoiding any associations with such frivolous financial pastimes. Sisko's fellow officers, all of whom frequent the bar, do not follow Sisko's example. One of them even beats Quark at gambling. Not all of the Federation share Sisko's moral aversion to the place, but Sisko's behaviour again allows the Federation a token distance from the moral implications of gambling and drinking at the bar of a known criminal. Most tellingly, Sisko finds Quark's presence distasteful. Whenever the two speak, it invariably involves Quark making some sort of financially motivated appeal to Sisko. Their relationship is defined by Sisko's unease at Quark's greed. If Quark makes Sisko uneasy, then the rest of his race are treated with outright disgust, none more so than the leader of the Ferengi, the Grand Nagus. The Nagus is depicted as gross and decrepit. Outfitted in garish and vulgar, but obviously expensive, clothing, the Nagus is portrayed as having no control over his more base appetites. He is lecherous and chauvinistic. Sisko cannot stand him. The reason for this is obvious – the Nagus is a reminder of all the worst qualities of greed and avarice; qualities that Sisko would like to pretend he and the Federation do not have. Indeed, Quark once openly accuses Sisko of feeling this way.

In one episode he explodes at Sisko's treatment of him and accuses him of being racist. He points out that in Earth's past, humans were much like the Ferengi and then goes on to list human excess throughout history, from concentration camps to slavery (the only word in the list to get a reaction from African-American Sisko). There is nothing in Ferengi history, he assures Sisko, that could compare with this list. 'We're not worse than you, we're better.'[20] Perhaps what Sisko really hates about the Ferengi is that they remind him of who his people used to be (that is, us). But Sisko does need the Ferengi and their commerce. By using Quark only when he needs to engage in such activities he manages to give the impression of some distance from that philosophy, but it is ultimately not a convincing tactic. Such a relationship between Federation and alien species has become a common feature in *Deep Space Nine*, and it would not be possible without a character such as Quark. The Ferengi race as a whole may represent the Other. It is greedy, loathsome, and patriarchal. Quark himself though is not portrayed as negatively as this. His loyalties are not as simple as the rest of his race, and he is often seen to act in a non-Ferengi manner. His countrymen often accuse him of having been corrupted by his contact with humankind. Throughout the series practically every alien member of a *Star Trek* crew, even default members like Quark, have had this accusation levelled at them. A comment made by Quark to another 'friendly' alien, the Cardassian Garak, neatly explains the situation.[21] The two are discussing root beer, a typical Federation (and typically American) drink. Both find it to be too sweet, 'insipid' even. Yet Quark notes that if you drink enough of it you get to like it. 'Just like the Federation', Garak notes. The implication is that both Garak and Quark have found themselves 'corrupted' by their contact with he Federation. They have assumed some human characteristics. As such they are no longer completely the Other, yet they are also not one of 'us'. They serve as a bridge between their cultures and the culture of the Federation – ambassadors of identification between us and them. Such bridging characters allow *Deep Space Nine* to connect the Federation, an icon for all the virtues of America, to the show's many alien races, which serve as representations for some of the more questionable characteristics of the American audience. Ultimately, the bridging characters must be assimilated, however.

One such character is Worf. Commander Worf is a Klingon, a race that embodies the warrior ethic. They consider honour, courage, passion and loyalty to be the chief virtues. Worf was raised by humans though, and as such is caught in the middle of two cultures. Because of the demanding nature of Klingon culture and its turbulent relationship with the Federation Worf serves, this is often a difficult place to be. His struggle to manage is often used to show how tolerance is required to deal with other cultures, but it also provides a comment on the value of the Klingon character. Klingons in *Deep Space Nine* are usually portrayed much as a sidekick character is in many cop shows – well meaning and honourable, but ultimately just a little bit slow. When the Klingons open hostilities with the Federation, Worf sides against his species. Although he believes in all the Klingon virtues, he believes in the Federation values of reason, justice and equality more.

A bridging character can be more useful when the species in question is less similar to the dominant culture. One such case is that of the Cardassians. The Cardassians are fascists, having a militaristic society that exhibits racist characteristics. The Cardassian role in the occupation of the planet Bajor echoes the actions of Nazi Germany, and Gul Dukat, one of the main Cardassian characters and former commander of *Deep Space Nine* during the occupation, shows many similarities with Hitler. Gul Dukat has been used as a bridging character, but the Cardassian character of choice for this role is Garak, currently a tailor on *Deep Space Nine*. Garak is a mysterious and somewhat sinister character. He is a former member of the Obsidian Order, the Cardassian secret police. His position in the organisation, which is said to be the most ruthless and oppressive of its kind in the galaxy, is not known for sure, but he is known to have acted as an assassin on occasion. Garak values strength, guile and deception. On one occasion he is told the story of the little boy who cried wolf. When asked if he understood the moral of the story he replies that he does. 'Never tell the same lie twice.'[22]

Garak is often used when the Federation must confront the Cardassian empire, or the Dominion, which in latter episodes annexes Cardassia. He is often used to provide an insight or perform an action that would be unseemly coming from a Federation character. For example, in the episode 'Rocks and Shoals'[23] the crew find themselves faced with the choice of either dying or winning a battle by helping the morally repulsive enemy commander betray the honourable soldiers in his unit. Garak is the one who argues in favour of the latter option. He brushes aside any objection that such an action is 'against the rules'. 'Humans have rules ... which tend to make achieving victory a little too hard in my estimation.' The crew in the end does help the enemy commander betray his crew, but even Garak seems to find it distasteful. Although Cardassian morality does not condemn this action as human morality does, Garak still display some traces of human empathy and guilt. This makes him as not being completely Cardassian in character. Like Quark, he is an honorary human or 'our Cardassian' as he is sometimes referred to on the Internet. He connects Cardassian ruthlessness to human morality.

Another episode shows a reverse bridging (assimilation in the reverse direction) relationship at work.[24] In the episode, the Federation is at war with the Dominion, which is using annexed Cardassia as a base. With the war going badly Sisko asks Garak for help. He has reasoned that the only hope for success lies in bringing the Romulans into the war on the Federation side. The Romulans have up to this point been neutral. Sisko wants Garak to help him obtain proof from Cardassia that once the Federation falls the Romulan empire will be next. Garak quickly convinces Sisko of the impossibility of obtaining legitimate proof and convinces Sisko to let him forge proof. Spurred on by reports of Federation casualties, Sisko agrees. That decision marks a moral descent for Sisko. He agrees to sell biochemical weapons to obtain the materials to make the forgery. He also has to bribe Quark to cover up the crimes of the forger they have hired. Quark happily agrees to the bribe, and at its conclusion thanks Sisko for reminding him that 'everyone has his price'. Quark has juxtaposed his negotiations for profit with Sisko's negotiations for his countrymen's life, and in so doing has thrown their moral validity in doubt.

The climax comes when Garak assassinates a Romulan senator, placing the forgery, which has turned out to be imperfect, on the scene of the crime. When the Romulans find the body they assume that any imperfections in the forgery are the result of the blast that killed their senator. Assuming that the Dominion killed him to prevent the forgery reaching their government, the Romulans declare war on the Dominion. Sisko is furious, but when he confronts Garak he is quickly pulled up short. He is forced to admit the tactical validity of Garak's move. He is also forced to admit that his conscience is not worth the lives that would have been lost had the Romulans not been persuaded to help the Federation. In the end he decides to live with what has happened. Sisko, a paragon of Federation virtue, has been forced to accept his role as an accomplice in a completely morally reprehensible act. Moreover, it has been accomplished in such a way that the viewer can identify with his decision. Assassination was formerly seen as a Cardassian tactic. The Cardassians were the amoral Other, the strangers who do not possess our appreciation of human rights. Now their position has become our own. The relationship between Sisko and Garak has allowed this connection. As Garak says to Sisko, 'You came to me because you knew I could do all those things you could not.' That distinction is now much harder to make.

CONCLUSION

More than 100 years ago Oscar Wilde already pointed out that 'most people are other people'. In a Kiplingesque world of fixed meanings on East and West, on the self and the other, such a pronouncement would likely have been received as a gnomic *bon mot*. This one-time *bon mot* has now become institutionalised, however, and in its institutionalisation, has become a 'postmodern twist'. While discussing the Disney film *Pocahontas*, Ziauddin Sardar notes that the settlers sing, 'Savages, savages, barely even human ... not like you and me, which means they must be evil.' The native Americans sing in response, 'The Paleface is a demon. Beneath that milky hide there's emptiness inside ... Savages, savages different from us, which means they can't be trusted.' According to Sardar, 'Here we have the essential postmodern twist on history – we are all Others now and all concepts of others are pretty much the same.'[25] Having created this otherness through the dialectal naming of 'mine' and 'yours', we have set ourselves up for battles of hierarchy. What may be new under the sun, however, is that since we may all be others, what was 'yours' could now be called 'mine', and what was 'mine' might now be called 'yours'. This can scramble a hierarchy of even Federation proportions.

NOTES

1. Rushdie, Salman, *Midnight's Children*, London, Jonathan Cape Ltd, 1981.
2. By this we mean that accounts of Western cultural history treat Greek classicism as the beginning of Western culture. That is of course very debatable, but the important thing for us is that the story is told as though this is the way it is.
3. Aristotle, *Metaphysics*, Book IV, 2, p. 1004a.
4. Burke, Kenneth, *Language as Symbolic Action*, Berkeley, University of California Press, 1966, p. 328.
5. Aristotle, *Rhetoric*; Book I, 2, p. 1355b.
6. Burke, Kenneth, *Philosophy of Literary Form: Studies in Symbolic Action*, 2nd edn, Baton Rouge, Louisiana State University Press, 1967, pp. 109–11, fn. 26.
7. Ibid.
8. Burke, Kenneth, *A Grammar of Motives*, Berkeley, University of California Press, 1962, p. 403.
9. Ibid., p. 417.
10. Ibid., p. 418.
11. Burke, Kenneth, 'Rhetoric – Old and New', *Journal of General Education*, 5, 1951, pp. 202–9. Identification is also discussed throughout Burke's *Rhetoric of Motives*, Berkeley, University of California Press, 1962.
12. Burke, *Grammar*, pp. 418–19.
13. Ibid., p. 418 (emphasis added).
14. Ibid., p. 419.
15. Sartre, Jean-Paul, 'The Existence of Others', in *Being and Nothingness: A Phenomenological Essay on Ontology*, trans. Hazel E Barnes, London: Washington Square Press, 1956, pp. 301–15.
16. Fiske, J and Hartley, R, *Reading Television*, London and New York, Routledge, 1994, p. 20.
17. Ibid.
18. 'The Sound of Her Voice', *Deep Space Nine*, 6 June 1998, Paramount, Los Angeles.
19. 'Hippocratic Oath', *Deep Space Nine*, 14 October 1995, Paramount, Los Angeles.
20. 'The Jem'Hadar', *Deep Space Nine*, 11 June 1994, Paramount, Los Angeles.
21. 'Way of the Warrior [2]', *Deep Space Nine*, 30 September 1995, Paramount, Los Angeles.
22. 'Improbable Cause', *Deep Space Nine*, 22 April 1995, Paramount, Los Angeles.
23. 'Rocks and Shoals', *Deep Space Nine*, 4 October 1997, Paramount, Los Angeles.
24. 'In the Pale Moonlight', *Deep Space Nine*, 15 April 1998, Paramount, Los Angeles.
25. Sardar, Ziauddin, *Postmodernism and the Other: The New Imperialism of Western Culture*, London, Pluto Press, 1998, p. 90.

8 False and Double Consciousness: Race, Virtual Reality and the Assimilation of Hong Kong Action Cinema in *The Matrix*

Peter X Feng

In a seminal 1975 essay, Jean-Louis Baudry interrogated the power of the reality effect of cinema on the spectator, or more precisely upon what he called 'le ciné-sujet', the subject as constituted by cinema (p. 62).[1] Baudry draws an analogy between cinema and Plato's cave, from which the philosopher emerges (temporarily blinded by the light of day) to report of prisoners who are captivated by representations of reality. Noting that the prisoners would not leave the cave even if their chains were broken, Baudry asks why the cine-subject finds the cinema so appealing, and he turns to Freudian psychoanalysis for an answer. 'Cave, grotto, "sort of a cavernous underground", people have not failed to see in it a representation of the maternal womb, of the matrix into which we are supposed to wish to return' (p. 767).[2] Unable to return to the womb, we instead enter the movie theatre's matrix: if someone were to refuse ever to leave the theatre, we would consider her/him to be mentally ill, but we would understand the impulse.

Larry and Andy Wachowski's *The Matrix* (1999) offers a parable of the cinematic apparatus. Laurence Fishburne's Morpheus has emerged from the cave and seeks to liberate the prisoners, but he does not realise that Joe Pantoliano's Cypher resents being unchained and wants to return to the bliss of the cave. Morpheus pins his hopes on Keanu Reeves's Neo, and he sets about reprogramming him: as in the 1995 film adaptation of William Gibson's *Johnny Mnemonic*, Reeves' passivity and wooden demeanour make him the über-cyber-movie hero.[3] Reeves' charisma emerges precisely from his lack of presence, a quality that Gus Van Sant found enigmatic in *My Own Private Idaho* (1991) and that Jan DeBont found heroic in *Speed* (1994). As Bey Logan observed, *The Matrix* cannily draws on both sides of Reeves' coin: '*The Matrix* seems to redefine the two sides of his nature. It's too out there for Hollywood, too expensive to be a true independent.'[4] If *The Matrix* is Reeves' vehicle, then Reeves is *The Matrix*'s vessel: his star persona (what Logan might call his hybrid indie-Hollywood appeal) is uniquely suited for a story in which characters' abilities change according to their surroundings, and in this we come back to Baudry's cine-subject: spectators imbue their favourite stars with their own personalities and thereby endow themselves with cinematic qualities. In short, while Reeves' Neo jacks into the Matrix, spectators of *The Matrix* are jacking into Reeves.[5]

In this essay, I offer a series of allegorical readings of *The Matrix*, situating the film in relation to cyberpunk and related fantasies of swapping one's consciousness from body to body, discussing the film's casting, and musing on its production by the new transnational Hollywood. Each reading could also be described as an attempt to explain how characters pass from one level of consciousness to another, through a series of nested diegeses within the film. By nested diegeses, I mean the worlds within worlds in the film's narrative: 'the Matrix' is a virtual reality simulation that resembles a North American city in 1999, a world within a world. Within the Matrix, Neo is the hacker alter-ego of Thomas Anderson, a white-collar drone. When he meets Morpheus, Neo discovers that humanity has been enslaved by machines following a war between humanity and Artificial Intelligence (AI): the machines created the Matrix to occupy and pacify human minds while they harvest the energy produced by their bodies. Human resistance fighters hack into the Matrix, where they are able to perform superhuman feats since they possess awareness of their potential to transcend physical laws that are, after all, only simulated. Morpheus has been searching for a human with the potential to defeat the Agents (sentient programs who appear in the Matrix as men-in-black), and Neo turns out to be 'the One'.

The resistance operate in submarine-like hovercraft such as Morpheus' ship, the *Nebuchadnezzar*. The *Nebuchadnezzar* is thus the film's 'reality', or its primary diegesis. The Matrix itself is a virtual world built by the machines: insofar as it is another reality within the film, it is a diegetic world nested within the film's primary diegesis, a diegesis that I will name Inner Diegesis$_1$. There is another virtual space built by the resistance, where the humans plug in so they can train, debrief, and arm themselves: the Construct (Inner Diegesis$_2$) is of a lower order than the Matrix, since as a training ground there are no real consequences (demonstrated when Neo falls off a skyscraper and bounces off the ground). In the Matrix, however, if your virtual body is killed you die. And in the primary diegesis, if your body is disconnected from the Matrix while your consciousness is inside it, both you and your virtual body die.

The Matrix (Inner Diegesis$_1$) is populated by prisoners whom the resistance fighters contemptuously call 'copper-tops', mere batteries unaware of their enslavement. From the resistance perspective, copper-tops are trapped in false consciousness while the resistance fighters possess double consciousness. I am borrowing the term 'false consciousness' from Marxism, where it describes 'those who live their relation to economic life exclusively within its categories of thought and experience':[6] copper-tops misunderstand the nature of their relationships with each other and to the Matrix.[7] 'Double consciousness' is of course W E B Du Bois' famous formulation, the phenomenon of the racialised subject's awareness of both how he sees himself and how he is seen by others.[8] While racialised ideologies often cast double consciousness as a tragic handicap,[9] we might also conceive of double consciousness as a potential advantage in negotiating complicated hegemonic formations with their competing interpellations. Here I am suggesting that the source of Neo and of the other resistance fighters' agility when jacked into the Matrix comes from their awareness of themselves as existing simultaneously in two worlds.

I began this chapter by suggesting that Keanu Reeves' blank visage allows spectators to jack into him. Surely a great deal of the appeal of *The Matrix* for audiences is attributable to spectatorial fantasies of being able to execute the superhuman martial arts moves of Neo (and the fact that Neo was able to learn those moves effortlessly marks it as doubly fantastic). Like Baudry, Christian Metz argues that spectatorial involvement arises from the way that cinema turns the spectator into a subject who exists to see and perceive, and that this is accomplished through identification with the camera (pp. 803–4).[10] The celebrated visual effects of *The Matrix* do not just engage with the spectator's passion for perceiving (as when the camera swoops around the action, which Metz would note marks the spectator's identification with the camera as 'a transcendental, not an empirical subject' [p. 804]): the slow-motion effects allow the spectator to perceive the Matrix as Neo does. Visual effects sell us (consumers) on *The Matrix*, but they do not merely bring us into the theatres but indeed encourage us to enter the Matrix itself. Let us take a moment and contemplate the visual effects of *The Matrix*, for it is through analysis of this mode of perception that I find my own points of entry into the film.

Banal irony: this film that supposedly celebrates the human spirit's triumph over machines could not have been achieved without computer technology. For example, in the film's advanced form of Flow-Motion dubbed 'bullet time', the effect of a moving camera shooting up to 12,000 frames per second is simulated. This effect was achieved with an array of still cameras with 1/1000th-of-a-second shutters, whose placement was determined after a computer graphic (CG) 'visualisation' plotted the exact position of each camera;[11] each camera was then aligned using a laser-guided tracking system (p. 72). In short, a computer model determined the contours of the profilmic space. A computer program then created images to fill 'in between' the still shots: this process of creating images attributable to virtual cameras is called interpolation (and here I might note that *interpellation* is what happens when a computer visualisation tells you where to stand, *interpolation* is what happens when a computer extrapolates and simulates bodily movements that the cameras were unable to capture or that you were unable to perform). The backgrounds were rendered using a virtual cinematographic process that converted as few as a dozen stills of the set into a 3D environment: lighting levels were adjusted so that the background matched the foreground.

This irony of computer-constructed film sequences that are supposed to depict humanity's ability to transcend AI is, as I noted, somewhat obvious. I mention it because I want to take an almost incidental technical aside as my way into the film, jacking into *The Matrix* through an unguarded backdoor, as it were. Bullet time technician[12] Dan Piponi explained that the still cameras in the rig were not perfectly aligned and captured images with slight but noticeable variations in exposure: in his words, 'We had to bring that pixel into alignment, plus create software needed to color-correct the still images so they could be blended together' (p. 72). Transcendent 'humanity' is only visualisable in a world in which representations of humans are carefully manipulated via colour correction.[13] *The Matrix* depends on the elision of racial difference.

RACIAL DRAG IN VIRTUAL REALITY

When Morpheus is captured by the Agents, he is told that the Matrix was originally a Utopic virtual reality that wasn't convincing enough to keep humanity enslaved. (If the first version of the Matrix were a diegesis, then it would fit Comolli and Narboni's category 5, a narrative seemingly fully within the dominant ideology but cracking apart at its seams.[14]) The Matrix version 2.0 is more convincing because it is less perfect – as such, it is better able to suspend humans in 'false consciousness'. One example of *The Matrix*'s imperfection is its reliance on stale racial archetypes. The leader of the resistance cell is Morpheus, equal parts spiritual guide and rebellious slave – of course Morpheus is black, and the camera lingers on his tortured body. The Oracle is a folksy black earth-mother who runs a virtual daycare centre populated with precocious children. In the Matrix, race functions as a narrative shorthand, not surprising given that the machines desire human consciousness and virtual performance to be strictly correlated – a textbook definition of essentialism.

The resistance fighters strut through the Matrix secure in their beautiful bodies, manifestations of their idealised self-images.[15] Their ability to perform incredible feats of martial arts prowess reminds me of nothing so much as Nintendo's *Street Fighter II*, a video game in which players choose to manipulate racially marked characters such as the Japanese Ryu, the Chinese Chun Li and the Indian Dhalsim.[16] In his essay 'cyborg identity/metamorphosis/skin', Quentin Lee connects *Street Fighter II* with Michael Jackson's bodily transformations through plastic surgery and *Thriller*'s lycanthropy: Jackson's body is a conflicted, contradictory and contested terrain of racial and sexual discourses. Lee compares desire for Michael Jackson with choosing (to be? to control?) a character in *Street Fighter II*. The link between desire for and identification with a screen character is at the centre of theories of cinematic spectatorship.[17] 'A Child is Being Beaten' is a useful touchstone for such investigations since Freud attempts to account for how children shift from observer to participant as they narrate scenes of punishment. Fantasies of bodily transformation thus go hand in hand with spectacles of physical violence.[18]

The Internet and the cinematic cyberpunk narratives it has inspired offer a space in which users can perform racial drag, suggesting that jacking into virtual spaces occasions fantasies of passing (in terms of race, gender, age, and so on). The game *Street Fighter II* permits racial drag only within the highly circumscribed limits of its narrative setting, but the Internet theoretically allows users to inhabit gendered and raced profiles indefinitely, limited only by the user's successful deployment of textual signifiers of identity. The narrative of *The Matrix* is structured by the consequences of failed passing: if a hacker unplugs from the Matrix, his/her body dies and his/her virtual persona disintegrates. In specifying that hackers cannot transcend their bodies upon pain of death, *The Matrix* insists on the coherent materiality of the bodies that inhabit its primary diegesis. *The Matrix* thus rejects a narrative resolution common to cyberpunk, wherein consciousness separates from the body and lives on in cyberspace,[19] instead evincing Judith Butler's distinction between performance and performativity, wherein 'performance' describes Internet users in drag while 'performativity' describes the process of citation wherein the body's materiality is continually re-inscribed. This is a welcome corrective to Baudrillard's celebration of cyberpunk as a means to transcend bodily materiality and deny mortality, a desire that Vivian Sobchack scathingly labels 'beating the meat' (with deliberate masturbatory connotations: auto-erotic orgasm as transcendence). Sobchack observes, 'The increasing transparency of one's lived-flesh enabled by new technologies ... leads to euphoria and a sense of the limitless extension of being beyond its materiality and mortality. This, however, is "false" consciousness – for it has "lost touch" with the very material and mortal body that grounds its imagination and imagery of transcendence.'[20] The imagery of the Matrix – its deployment of racial archetypes of blackness and men-in-blackness (which is to say, Will Smith notwithstanding, whiteness) – is reliant on the world we live in: *The Matrix* is thoroughly implicated in our bodily materiality.[21]

TYPECASTING AND MULTIRACIAL ACTORS

Earlier I read an intimation of race in an apparently innocent reference to 'colour correction'. I now want to return to that quotation to highlight another racial intimation: 'We had to ... create software ... to colour-correct the still images so they could be blended together.' Colour-correction is the means, blending is the eventual goal. To be precise, racial difference is not elided, but put in service of a miscegenated aesthetic.

Tank is the name of a crucial member of Morpheus' resistance cell. Born in the space of the primary diegesis, Tank has never entered virtual reality himself: instead, he runs the *Nebuchadnezzar*'s computers and hacks into the Matrix. Shot by Cypher, Tank survives the blast and kills Cypher before he can unplug Neo, permitting him to return to the primary diegesis where he comes to comprehend the Oracle's prophesy. In a sense, Tank rises from the dead before Neo does, establishing a narrative structure in which resurrection of the material body in the film's primary diegesis allows Neo to make the quantum leaps in consciousness that attend his transitions in and out of the Matrix. By operating the machinery that permits the resistance fighters to hack into the Matrix, and by embodying the hope for a future humanity born and not harvested by the machines, Tank crosses the borders that define humanity and shows the way to the future. This transitional figure is portrayed by Marcus Chong, an actor of mixed African and Chinese ancestry.[22]

The multiracial typecasting does not end with Marcus Chong. As many Asian Pacific filmgoers know, Keanu Reeves has an English mother and a Chinese-Hawaiian father. While Reeves reportedly describes himself as white, Asian American spectators frequently label Reeves as Asian Pacific passing as white. Neo's passing from one diegesis to another occasions leaps in consciousness; Reeves' passing for white implies the heightened awareness of double consciousness.

The term 'passing' is highly problematic: I want to embrace its complexities and ambivalences, its complicity and duplicity, in the context of performance and spectatorship, for passing is not necessarily an act but may be a spectatorial perception. Following Ari Rosner, Teresa Kay Williams draws a distinction between active and passive passing, implying that passing is not necessarily something that Reeves does but rather a way that he is read. Williams asks rhetorically, 'Can a multiracial individual pass for what he or she is *not*? Can a multiracial individual pass for what he or she is? Does passing for what you are count as really passing?'[23] To judge a multiracial individual for 'passive passing' is to assume that the individual has control over how he/she is read or misread.

I attribute the problematic of passing to Asian American spectators to emphasise that passing is a triangular narrative structure: it requires not just the purportedly passing figure, but a dupe who does not recognise the pass and an insider who registers that the dupe has failed to read the passer 'correctly'. Reeves can only be passing if an audience of insiders judges that another audience (presumably white) has been duped; the insiders believe that there is a true (Asian Pacific) identity behind the appearance. (Ironically, the insiders might be presuming that the duped audience is unproblematically white.)[24] Elaine K Ginsberg notes that 'One of the assumed effects of a racist society is the internalization, by members of the oppressed race, of the dominant culture's definitions and characterizations. This is the context in which the literature of race passing has most often been read'.[25] In this context, people of colour temper their impulse to judge putative passers with their sympathy for the complicated manner in which the passer negotiates a racist society: Ginsberg quotes Nella Larsen's *Passing*, in which a character observes, 'We disapprove of it and at the same time condone it.'[26]

If we conceive of Reeves' passing for white not as something that he does, but as something that others perceive, then passing may involve Reeves' awareness of how he is seen by others; passing is therefore double consciousness turned upside down, for the mainstream sees the multiracial movie star not as different, but as white. Reeves' ancestry usually escapes commentary in the mainstream press: in researching *The Matrix*, I found only one magazine article that made note of Reeves' multiracial ancestry: the UK-based action movie magazine, *Impact*, floridly remarks, 'What Chinese blood flows in the veins of Keanu Reeves must have sung as he finally found a role that played to his mixed ancestry.'[27] Reeves' Chinese blood (and Canadian nationality) is shared with Chong, and black/Asian Tank links Asian/white Neo to black Morpheus, perhaps via an intertextual allusion to Melvin and Mario van Peebles' *Panther* (1995), in which Chong played Huey Newton.[28]

INDUSTRIAL ASSIMILATION

The 1997 Hong Kong handover precipitated an exodus of the island's action filmmakers. *The Matrix*'s directors Larry and Andy Wachowski tapped the director and fight choreographer of *Fist of Legend* (1994), Yuen Wo Ping, to train the actors, stage their scenes and oversee the wire work. The absorption of Hong Kong style into Hollywood's melting pot was noted by many commentators, for example, Rynning's observation that the film introduces 'the Asian cinematic technique of wire-fighting into an American action film'.[29] Multiracial Keanu Reeves becomes the primary conduit for *The Matrix*'s assimilation of Hong Kong action film-making.

I see a metaphor for the assimilation of Hong Kong action cinema in the film's nested diegeses. The film's primary diegesis is a science fiction world, but one in which humans have soft bodies, flabby from underuse: the fantasy of this diegesis is that the knowledge necessary to overthrow the machines can be downloaded instantaneously, and that bodies can be reconstructed using high-tech acupuncture. Similarly, Hollywood film-making turns to Hong Kong to recondition actor's bodies and to train them in the physical and mental skills of martial arts film-making. (One wonders if the AI machines should have constructed the Matrix to resemble North America before the 1997 handover, thereby forestalling the introduction of martial arts know-how into the programming.)

Neo trains in the Construct, a.k.a. Inner Diegesis$_2$. The poses that Keanu Reeves adopts throughout the dojo sequence are patterned on the style of Jet Li, whose *Black Mask* (1996) was Yuen Wo Ping's last film in Hong Kong.[30] In the Construct, everyone knows kung fu – like *Street Fighter II*, the Construct is a fantasy world in which flabby-bodied users jack into idealised bodies. (Like a video game, the Construct is deployed as a series of 'levels' through which the user advances.)

Between these two poles – a diegesis of flabby bodies and a diegesis of superhuman bodies – lies the Matrix, a.k.a. Inner Diegesis$_1$. In the Matrix, the majority of the inhabitants do not know kung fu, only a select few can perform superhuman feats. The superiority of our protagonists can best be displayed within the Matrix, which lies between the Hollywood world of the *Nebuchadnezzar* and the Hong Kong world of the Construct. Inner Diegesis$_1$ represents Hong Kong action cinema assimilated into Hollywood. Neo, the chosen One, prevails by grace of his double consciousness, his awareness of his existence in the film's primary diegesis and in Inner Diegesis$_2$. The successful postmodern subject is an Asian passing for white, a resistance fighter passing as a drone, a martial artist hiding not behind Jet Li's black mask but behind Keanu Reeves' blank mask.

When initial plans to shoot *The Matrix* in Chicago and LA were scrapped in favour of an Australian location with a favourable exchange rate, the Wachowskis modified the Matrix into a nondescript American city, permitting Sydney to be used for select exterior shots.[31] If the imperatives of transnational capital compelled the producers to relocate to Sydney, the location of Rupert Murdoch's Fox Studios marks Hollywood's foray into the Pacific Rim.[32]

'A WORLD WITHOUT RULES AND CONTROLS, WITHOUT BORDERS OR BOUNDARIES'

Late capitalism's shift into a transnational phase makes it more difficult but more imperative to update Marx's theories of culture and ideology. What is the relationship between the superstructure of cinematic fantasy and the base of transnational capitalism? What is the nature of false consciousness in a global economy? Reading *The Matrix* as an allegory of transnational capitalism suggests that false consciousness consists of thinking locally and not globally (in Hall's terms, functioning with only the local as 'category of thought and experience'[33]). For the copper-tops in the Matrix, false consciousness consists of not being aware of their actual function in the AI economy. The flow of transnational capital is in the process of restructuring local and global economies: Rupert Murdoch's media empire provides the circuit for Hollywood to exploit Australia's film industry[34] and Hong Kong cinema expertise.

In his book *Asian/American: Historical Crossings of a Racial Frontier*, David Palumbo-Liu argues that the US's vision of its role in the global system 'is inseparable from historical occasions of real contact between and interpenetration of Asia and America, in and across the Pacific Ocean. The defining mythos of America, its "manifest destiny", was, after all, to form a bridge westward from the Old World, *not just* to the western coast of the North American content, but from there to the trans-Pacific regions of Asia.'[35] Palumbo-Liu shows that for most of the twentieth century, American modernity was marked by its efforts to modify Asian bodies and psyches to serve the US. As the Pacific century dawns, American anxieties about Asian investment in Monterey Park, California (birthplace of the English-Only movement), and other west coast sites reveal a fear that Asians are superior transnational subjects.[36] The arrival of Asian money, characterised as neo-Confucian, forces the US to adapt somatically and psychically.

In the words of *The Matrix*'s visual effects supervisor, John Gaeta, I found a startling echo of David Palumbo-Liu's thesis. In referring to 'bullet time' and other visual effects, Gaeta observed, 'All of these techniques and alterations in time created new physiological and psychological moments for the audience.'[37] While American business fears neo-Confucianism, Hollywood is engaged in assimilating Neo's martial arts.

NOTES

1. Quotations in French are taken from Baudry, Jean-Louis, 'Le dispositif: approches métapsychologiques de l'impression de réalité', *Communications*, 23, 1975, pp. 56–72. Quotations in English are taken from Jean Andrews and Bernard Augst's translation, originally published in *Camera Obscura*, 1, and oft-reprinted.

2. 'La caverne, la grotte, "sorte de demeure souterraine", on n'a pas manqué d'y voir une représentation du ventre maternel, de la matrice dans laquelle nous aspirerions à retourner' (p. 62).

3. Keanu and Neo almost rhyme. Thanks to Anne Friedberg and Sheila Murphy for pointing out that Reeves is the ultimate cyberhero.

4. Logan, Bey, 'The Light Fantastic', *Impact*, 90, June 1999, p. 19.

5. This is of course attributable in part to Neo's function in the narrative: since we learn about the Matrix as he does, he is our touchstone, just as we cling to Alice when we follow her into the rabbit hole. Here I might observe that the rabbit hole is a subterranean space perhaps analogous to Baudry's and Plato's caves.

6. Hall, Stuart, 'The Problem of Ideology: Marxism Without Guarantees', in *Stuart Hall: Critical Dialogues in Cultural Studies*, Morley, David and Chen, Kuan-Hsing (eds) London, Routledge, 1996, p. 36.

7. I draw this formulation of false consciousness from Stuart Hall's 1983 discussion in 'The Problem of Ideology'. Hall attempts to recuperate the term, since 'false' suggests that the philosopher has a 'true' consciousness and that people living within a distorted ideology have a 'false' or incorrect understanding of their situation. Hall suggests that those who live within capitalist ideology do not have a false or distorted understanding, but a partial and inadequate one (pp. 36–7). The question of 'false consciousness' is crucial in understanding ideology: if consciousness were merely 'false', then education should lead to revolution; instead, efforts should be focused on understanding people's investment (in multiple senses) in the system that exploits them.

8. I use the male pronoun because Du Bois does, as a reminder that Du Bois is specifically describing Negro men in the US. However, I would argue that Du Bois allows us to extend the concept to all racialised subjects and to women as well. While he seems at first to distinguish the Negro from six other races, he attributes the gift of double consciousness not to essence but to location, to being a minority, to 'being a problem': 'After the Egyptian and Indian, the Greek and Roman, the Teuton and Mongolian, the Negro is a sort of seventh son, born with a veil, and gifted with second-sight *in this American world* – a world which yields him no true self-consciousness, but only lets him see himself through the revelation of the other world. It is a peculiar sensation, this double consciousness, this sense of always looking at one's self through the eyes of others ... One ever feels his twoness ...' (p. 45, emphasis added).

9. Palumbo-Liu, David, *Asian/American: Historical Crossings of a Racial Frontier*, Stanford, Stanford University Press, 1999. David Palumbo-Liu argues that assimilationist discourse employs the metaphor of schizophrenia to describe the minority subject's inability to accede fully to the nation's 'invented hegemonic memory' (p. 12) – a failure to link one's present self to the sanctioned version of the past — thereby pathologising Du Bois' 'double consciousness' by casting 'the psychic instability of the subject [as] a product of his or her own inability to make cultural choices' (p. 300).

10. Relevant passages from Christian Metz's *The Imaginary Signifier* are collected in Baudry, Leo and Cohen, Marshall (eds) *Film Theory and*

Criticism: Introductory Readings, 5th edition, New York, Oxford University Press, 1999, to which these page numbers refer.

11. Martin, Kevin H, 'Jacking into the Matrix', *Cinefex*, 79, October 1999, p. 70. See also Magid, Ron, 'Techno Babel', American Cinematographer, 80:4, April 1999, pp. 46–55; Massa, Maria, '(Un)real, Dude', *SFX*, 52, June 1999, pp. 66–71; Probst, Christopher, 'Welcome to the Machine', *American Cinematographer*, 80:4, April 1999, pp. 32–44; Winstanley, Cam, 'Reality Inc.', *Total Film*, 30, July 1999, pp. 60–5.

12. Piponi's official title is science officer with Manex Special Effects.

13. This pun was inspired by the example of Marlon Riggs' *Color Adjustment* (1991).

14. Comolli, Jean-Luc and Narboni, Jean, 'Cinema/Ideology/Criticism', in Baudry and Cohen (eds) *Film Theory and Criticism: Introductory Readings*, p. 757.

15. Morpheus terms appearance within the Matrix or the Construct as 'residual self-image', but he does not explain where this residue originated. Insofar as these idealised representations cannot be located in material experience, they might be attributed to the Lacanian Imaginary. However, the gendered and racial specificity of these representations suggests that self-image emerges from the Symbolic: if these representations do not correspond with awareness of real bodies, then physical appearance in the Matrix and the Construct is determined by consciousness. Rather than bodily materiality shaping consciousness, we have the reverse (see Butler, Judith, *Bodies that Matter*, New York, Routledge, 1993), indicative of *The Matrix*'s foundering on the shoals of essentialised identities.

16. Lee, Quentin, 'cyborg identity/metamorphosis/skin', *Critical Mass*, 1:2, spring 1994, p. 114.

17. See Mayne, Judith, *Cinema and Spectatorship*, London Routledge, 1993, for a deft survey of theories of spectatorship.

18. Freud, Sigmund, '"A Child is Being Beaten": A Contribution to the Study of the Origin of Sexual Perversions,' *The Standard Edition of the Complete Psychological Works of Sigmund Freud*, Vol. 17, edited and translated by James Strachey, London, Hogarth Press, 1955, pp. 179–204. *Street Fighter* was adapted into a 1994 movie with a racially diverse cast including Jean-Claude Van Damme, Raul Julia, Ming-Na Wen, Kylie Minogue, Roshan Seth and Wes Studi; however its narrative was firmly set within one diegesis, which is to say that the film took the characters for granted and did not narrativise their deployment by players or spectators. Likewise, the 1995 film of *Mortal Kombat* (whose cast included prominent white and Asian characters, but no black faces), the 1995–96 TV show *Mortal Kombat: The Animated Series*, the theatrical sequel *Mortal Kombat: Annihilation* (1997), and the 1998–99 syndicated TV show *Mortal Kombat: Conquest*, did not acknowledge their genesis as a videogame within their narrative diegeses, even as these diegeses necessarily differed in detail between incarnations. The racially diverse casts of these movies and shows thus does not invoke the possibility of cross-racial identification so much as it does the hyper-pluralism of the martial tournament genre, a genre whose cinematic touchstone remains *Enter the Dragon*

(1973) and continues through *The Quest* (1996) and *Space Jam* (1996). The last, in which NBA players team with animated characters, reveals that the inspiration behind the diverse casts is not a vision of interracial unity so much as the synergy of cross-market platforming of 'properties' owned by various entertainment conglomerates; Michael Jordan's recent announcement that he is giving up endorsements suggests that he has realised that his pay cheque does not compensate him adequately for becoming corporate property.

19. See the 'Terminal Flesh' chapter of Scott Bukatman's *Terminal Identity*, Durham, Duke University Press, 1993.

20. Sobchack, Vivian, 'Beating the Meat/Surviving the Text, or How to Get Out of This Century Alive' in *The Visible Woman: Imaging Technologies, Gender and Science*, Treichler, Paula A, Cartwright, Lisa and Penley, Constance (eds) New York, New York University Press, 1998, p. 317. Sobchack's argument develops from Baudrillard's reading of the erotics of cyborg prosthetics in J G Ballard's *Crash*; along the way she critiques readers of 'Cyborg Manifesto' who miss Donna Haraway's irony (p. 314). Greta Niu offers an interpretation of the manifesto that examines Haraway's deployment of Asian women as cyborgs; Niu, Greta Ai-Yu, *People of the Pagus: Orientalized Bodies and Migration in an Asian Pacific Rim*, Diss. Duke University, 1998; Ann Arbor: UMI, 1998; AAT 9829659 (pp. 27–31).

21. By contrast *The Thirteenth Floor* (released almost simultaneously with *The Matrix*) reveals even uglier implications. In that film, based on Daniel Galouye's *Simulacron-3* (New York, Bantam, 1964), a world which looks like ours has built a simulation of 1937 Los Angeles. Users jack into characters who are modelled after their physical appearance, temporarily displacing the character's constructed personality. If a character is killed while a user is jacked in, the user's consciousness is terminated and the user's body awakens with the consciousness of the simulation's character. *The Thirteenth Floor* thus posits mortality as the limit of the simulation, but supposes that simulated consciousness can be downloaded into a user's body. The turning point for the film is the revelation that 1999 is itself a simulation created in the twenty-first century; thus *The Thirteenth Floor* goes *The Matrix* one better by nesting a diegesis within a diegesis within a diegesis. The final plot twist implies that the twenty-first-century character played by Gretchen Mol has manipulated her husband into jacking into the 1999 simulation so that he can be killed; she can return to her world with a husband with a personality upgrade. The sunshine and sea breeze at the film's end cannot fully dispel the image of Mol as femme fatale.

22. Some sources state that Marcus Chong is Tommy Chong's son, some his godson or nephew, which would make him Rae Dawn Chong's brother, half-brother, or cousin.

23. Williams, Teresa Kay, 'Race-ing and Being Raced: The Critical Interrogation of "Passing"', *Amerasia Journal*, 23:1, 1997, pp. 62–3.

24. See Kawash, Samira, *Dislocating the Color Line: Identity, Hybridity, and Singularity in African-American Literature*, Stanford, Stanford University Press, 1997. Samira Kawash discusses the triangular structure of passing (p. 234,

n. 39) with reference to Amy Robinson's 'drama of the pass': 'It Takes One to Know One: Passing and Communities of Common Interest', *Critical Inquiry*, 20:4, 1994, pp. 715–36.

25. Ginsberg, Elaine K, 'Introduction: The Politics of Passing', *Passing and the Fictions of Identity*, Durham, Duke University Press, 1996, p. 9.

26. *Quicksand* and *Passing*, edited and introduction by Deborah McDowell, New Brunswick, Rutgers University Press, 1986, pp. 185–6, cited in Ginsberg, *Passing and the Fictions of Identity*.

27. Logan, Bey, 'The Light Fantastic, *Impact*, 90, June 1999, p. 18. In evaluating this magazine's fetishes, consider that the same issue includes an article on Thailand as 'another bastion of Asian action cinema' alongside the third instalment in an assessment of Rambo as 'the century's most misunderstood movie hero' (p. 3).

28. Chong also portrayed Amerasian gang-leader Fu Qua Johnson in the *Vanishing Son* television movies (1994).
    Nishime reads Neo as multiracial child fathered by Morpheus and reanimated by Trinity. She also points out that his removal from the Matrix mimics birth: he emerges from an amniotic sac, umbilical chords detach, and he travels down a birth canal. Recall that Baudry compared the cinema and the cave to the womb. See Nishime, LeiLani, 'Is Keanu Reeves a Cyborg?: APAs in Science Fiction', Conference Presentation, *Association for Asian American Studies*, Scottsdale, Arizona, 25 May 2000.

29. Rynning, Roald, 'Magic' Trix', *Film Review*, 583, July 1999, p. 54.

30. Arakawa points out that Reeves also performs one of Bruce Lee's signature moves, flicking his own nose with his thumb. See Arakawa, Suzanne K, 'To Whit, (Still) Too White?: How Millennium-End Sci-Fi Films Use "Asian-ness" in the Struggle to Imagine and Reconfigure Race Relations in the U.S.', Conference presentation, *Society for Cinema Studies*, Chicago, 11 March 2000.

31. Fischer, Dennis, '*Matrix* star Keanu Reeves battles the evils of cyberspace slavery', *Cinefantastique*, 31:4, April 1999, p. 20.

32. Gerald L Houseman defines the Pacific Rim in terms of US interests in economy, security, and diplomacy (*American and the Pacific Rim: Coming to Terms with New Realities*, Lanham, MD, Rowman and Littlefield Publishers, 1995, p. 3, cited in Niu, *People of the Pagus*, p. 10).

33. Hall, 'The Problem of Ideology', p. 36.

34. Actor Hugo Weaving expresses his misgivings about the future of Australian national cinema in the shadow of Hollywood in Fischer, '*Matrix* star Keanu Reeves' (p. 20). Meaghan Morris discusses the economic context for Australian film production in the 1980s in her prescient essay 'Tooth and Claw: Tales of Survival, and *Crocodile Dundee*', collected in *The Pirate's Fiancée*, London, Verso, 1988.

35. Palumbo-Liu, *Asian/American*, p. 2.

36. In his closing chapters, Palumbo-Liu analyses how anxieties about Asian economic power are manifested in science fiction by Philip K Dick and William Gibson. Space precludes me from exploring in detail why Neal Stephenson should be added to this list, but I will make a few suggestive comments. The hacker protagonist of *Snow Crash* (New York, Bantam, 1992) is the multiracial offspring of a Korean woman and an African

American soldier who met while he was stationed in Japan. *The Diamond Age* (New York, Bantam, 1996) updates the yellow peril horde by imagining an army of Chinese girls abandoned by parents desperate for sons. *Cryptonomicon* (New York, Avon, 1999) links Second World War genocide to a 'data haven' created in South-East Asia in the present. Asians are the future and the past, saviours and threats – Asians are economic creatures.

37. Martin, 'Jacking into the Matrix', p. 69.

9 Global Visions and European Perspectives

Dimitris Eleftheriotis

Current discourses define 'Europe' primarily as an 'idea' or a 'culture', shaped by historical processes and events and imagining itself in terms of certain 'emblems that constitute the time and space of the Europeans'.[1] At the same time they acknowledge and celebrate the existence of a diversity of cultures. Recent publications of pan-European organisations (such as the Council of Europe or the European Union) debating and determining European cultural policy are very anxious to offer definitions invested with intellectual and political legitimacy. It is important to note the overwhelmingly anxious tone of these reports, as they try to reconcile the desire to discover unifying concepts with the need to avoid essentialism, which appear to be fundamental conditions in claiming the right to make policy in the name of Europe. The 1997 report *In From the Margins: A contribution to the debate on culture and development in Europe*, for example, declares that 'there are many Europes, whether viewed from a historical perspective or in terms of contemporary practicalities'; it duly proceeds, however, to discover Europe's unity in the realm of ideas:

> As well as ideas of Europe, there is too a Europe of ideas, transcending geography. From its Graeco-Judaic origins, transmitted through the Roman Empire it persisted in the Renaissance of the fifteenth and sixteenth centuries. It was accompanied by revolutionary technological advances, among them the invention of the compass and the printing machine. In the age of Reason during the eighteenth century, this culminated in a set of scientific and philosophical concepts (democracy, a progressive theory of history, human rights) and methods (rational enquiry, the industrial revolution). Although Europe has its roots in Christendom, its modern characteristics are predominantly pragmatic, materialist and secular.[2]

Here a selective reading of the history of the last 2,500 years is used in the definitions of the origins and essence of Europe. The historical events, periods and processes privileged are the Greek and Roman antiquity, the Renaissance, the Enlightenment, the French Revolution, the Industrial Revolution and, one can add (as the report does later on), realism and modernism as the aesthetic expressions of the European experience of the last two centuries.

The European identity that emerges through this eclectic (and overwhelmingly hegemonic) re-working of history is celebrated in the humanist rhetoric of the *European Declaration on Cultural Objectives*, which affirms that:

> The main aim of our societies is to enable everyone to achieve personal fulfilment, in an atmosphere of freedom and respect for human rights; such fulfilment is linked to culture which, together with other social, technological and economic influences, is an essential factor in the harmonious development of society; human resources – spiritual, intellectual and physical – provide both the object and the mainspring of development; these resources take the form of aspirations and values, of ways of thinking, being and acting, and they represent the fruits of historical experience and the seeds of the future.[3]

Sceptics like Sven Papcke, on the other hand, question the necessity and political desirability of European identity. Papcke, while hostile to the project of discovering a unified essence of Europe, is still able to assert:

> The individual and his or her free will is a European discovery – if not a European invention, like the notion of political liberty. From it grew a *civil society* in Europe. Nowhere else have been the ideas of personality, democracy, social justice, liberty, human rights and so on defined.[4]

The key question that needs to be addressed here is the practical and political usefulness of such descriptions of European-ness. Agnes Heller is one of the critics rejecting the possibility of pinning down a meaning to the word, even if this is guided by the will to deconstruct it:

Modernity cannot be buried for it never died; rather, it simply worked out its own determinations. Europe, European culture, the European tradition and the like cannot be buried because they were never in existence. Mythological heroes and demi-gods are not buried.[5]

The resistance to pinning down a meaning for Europe is, nevertheless, enhancing its God-like ability to be 'present everywhere and yet invisible'.[6] Offering a definition based on the reading of modern history as discussed earlier has certain advantages. It makes obvious the fact that this understanding of Europe occupies a hegemonic position in national, transnational and pan-European political and cultural discourses and policies. It also offers a point of reference for mapping difference and diversity within Europe and for exploring the numerous contradictions inherent in such definition. Finally, it represents a rallying point, something tangible that we can engage with and deconstruct. Importantly, this hegemonic definition of Europe has become the target of postcolonial criticism, whose critique of Eurocentricism[7] has provided extremely invigorating and ground-breaking theoretical work. To dissolve Europe into an incoherent multitude of diversities is to make it immune to such criticism.

It is indeed postcolonial criticism that has sharply brought to attention some important historical processes and events that hegemonic definitions of European-ness exclude:

- The so-called 'journeys of discovery' that led to the colonisation of the rest of the world and the crucial military role that 'cultural achievements' such as cartography played in the process.
- The ruthless exploitation of the human, natural, economic and cultural resources of the planet of which the slave trade represents the most obvious and shameful example.
- The various pseudo-scientific discourses of racism that were produced in the name of reason and objectivity in order to support European oppressive practices.
- The systematic destruction of the planet in the name of technological progress.
- The bloodbaths of the last two centuries that were carried out in the name of democracy and/or nationalism.

- The systematic dismissal of the cultural production of the rest of the world as inferior and insignificant.

These processes and events are clearly as exclusively European as the ones that the dominant definition foregrounds. Like the Freudian unconscious, they form an historical and cultural repressed in European identity, which surfaces again and again as a strong sentiment of collective guilt. Antoine Compagnon notes that European identity is founded on doubt:

> Not only Descartes' hyperbolic doubt, that is, the strength to make a *tabula rasa* of one's own reason, as has been achieved repeatedly in the history of Western thought and science, but also the doubt which I would call, with Hegel, the moment of 'unhappy consciousness'.[8]

It is indeed this 'unhappy consciousness', this collective guilt, usually disguised as philosophical doubt, intellectual liberalism or political self-criticism, that is expressed in Europe's commitment to cultural diversity under the banner of multiculturalism. Commonly, this usually takes the form of a re-working of European values in order to accommodate diversity and difference.[9] As a result, diversity in the form of multiculturalism is celebrated as an expression of cultural democracy, while difference is endorsed in terms of the fundamental human right to self-expression. The following passage from another Council of Europe resolution is revealing:

> Policy for society as a whole should have a cultural dimension stressing the development of human values, equality, democracy and the improvement of the human condition, in particular by guaranteeing freedom of expression and creating real possibilities for making use of this freedom ... Cultural policy can no longer limit itself exclusively to taking measures for the development, promotion and popularisation of the arts; an additional dimension is now needed which, by recognising the plurality of our societies, reinforces respect for individual dignity, spiritual values and the rights of minority groups and their cultural expressions. In such a cultural democracy, special efforts must be made on behalf of disadvantaged and hitherto unprivileged groups in society.[10]

Despite the humanist (and patronising) rhetoric, the contradiction between essential 'unifying concepts' and 'cultural diversity' is impossible to resolve in any meaningful way except ad hoc political pragmatism. European unity in the sphere of culture, then, becomes an ideal and not a given, and it is to be achieved through the measures and policies introduced.[11]

It is important to consider some of the other contradictions inherent in dominant definitions of Europe, the first of which revolves around the universal character of European values. Europe's privileged identity depends on an intellectual heritage that negates its geographical and cultural specificity (other than its claimed historical origin).[12] Because European values are transformed into 'universal principles', to be European means to be nothing in particular. In a different but highly pertinent context, Richard Dyer has noted that 'there is no more powerful position than that of being "just" human. The claim to power is the claim to speak for the communality of humanity.'[13] The ability of the European identity to dissolve itself as a particular position echoes Foucault's analysis of modern subjectivity as demonstrated within representation in Velasquez's *Las Meninas*.[14] The fact that the self-effacing subjectivity described there is defined as modern rather than European is not an analytical oversight but it reflects this constitutive aspect of European identity on the level of philosophical meta-language. The structural similarity and the conceptual overlap between European-ness, modern subjectivity and whiteness (as both Dyer and Foucault demonstrate) have powerful effects on discourse and politics. At a historical moment when all three categories are under attack, nevertheless, this powerful construction becomes an insurmountable weakness in attempts to answer questions about the specificity and distinctiveness of contemporary European identity.

Another aspect of the dissolution of European-ness into universality is the 'planetary consciousness' that characterises Europe's historical relationship with the rest of the world since the Renaissance.[15] This originates with the first perception of the world as a planet and the representational and political activities that accompanied it. Europe sees itself as part of a whole but from a privileged position and with a specific role to fulfil. In the course of history the role and the position may change (for instance, from exploring to exploiting to civilising to raising ecological awareness), but the perception, dictated by Europe's 'planetary consciousness', remains fundamentally the same. The disastrous results of centuries of

European interventions have led to the recent crisis around the impossibility to discover a meaningful role for Europe in the world that goes beyond simply expressing its 'guilty' or 'unhappy' consciousness. It is not paradoxical, then, that Europeans have intensified their efforts to reclaim a position and a role in the world waving the flag of enlightened multiculturalism and exploring their self-inflicted colonial 'traumas'.

I want to turn my attention now to a film directed by Wim Wenders (*Until the End of the World*, original title *Bis ans Ende der Welt*, Australia/Germany/France, 1991) which offers concrete manifestations of the European contradictions and attitudes discussed above.

UNTIL THE END OF THE WORLD

Until the End of the World tries hard to be a global film. It is an international co-production involving three countries and four production companies: Warner Bros, Argos Films, Village Roadshow Productions and Road Movies Filmproduktion. It was shot on location in many different countries (Australia, Italy, Japan, Portugal, Russia, the USA, France and Germany) and relied on local crews for much of the technical support. It boasts a cast of international stars: William Hurt, Sam Neill, Jeanne Moreau, Max von Sydow and Solveig Dommartin, among others. It is not only in terms of the production process that the film appears to be global, but also in terms of its thematic preoccupation with the future of the planet, its narrative mode (a chase around the world) and its potential global appeal (a film relevant to different people across the globe). The latter is a highly contentious issue, however, as the film was very much a failure in box office terms and not particularly popular with the critics. More importantly, I will argue that in its attempt to speculate about our global future the film mobilises distinctive and definitive European perspectives.

The film's imagining of the near future, as is usually the case with science fiction, focuses on technological development. To its credit, *Until the End of the World* avoids naive technological determinist views of the future, making clear links between the past, the present and the future and exploring the social and cultural dimensions of technology. The film is particularly preoccupied with the future of 'technologies of vision', the techno-scientific and artistic ways through which we represent the world around us.

These technologies of vision are contrasted to more traditional processes of storytelling. I will examine the narrative structure of the film with particular emphasis on the position and the function ascribed to the narrator. The discursive origins of technologies of vision and the film's critique of them do not occupy antithetical positions, but belong to a singular historical process, sharing a common 'destiny' and coming from the same perception of the world. In other words, the film's indictment of technologies of vision offers a futuristic vision of the world that is nothing else but a Euro-vision.

This vision is particularly significant as the film can be also seen as a contradictory, confused but very powerful statement on the future of cinema in Europe. This is further underlined by the fact that the film is directed by Wenders who

> ... has committed himself to promoting European film through his chairmanship of the European Film Academy [while] he also warns of the supreme importance of retaining a specifically European cinema, since without its own images Europe will lose its identity.[16]

Interestingly, as Stan Jones argues, Wenders perceived his film-making as part of a 'European way of seeing'[17] which he contrasted to the American view of the world. *Until the End of the World* is particularly important as it can be read not only as an allegorical manifesto on the future of cinema but also as a fiction about the future of technologies of vision and vision itself.

Technologies of vision are systems of organising and ordering our visual perception of the world. This usually involves sophisticated technology (as in digital imaging, television, cinematography, photography, cartography and map-making, X-rays), but it can also be accomplished by simple applications of scientific principles (as in perspectival systems of representation, the camera obscura, shadow theatre and optical toys) and even very 'low-tech' embodiments of practical knowledge (as in the structure of lecture theatres, hospitals and prisons, or in the 'packaging' of nature as a set of landscapes, panoramas and vistas).

Until the End of the World presents us with a vast array of such technologies ranging from digital cameras, camcorders, computer graphics and videophones to futuristic apparatuses such as machines that enable blind people to see and equipment that records the unconscious process of dreaming. Significantly these technologies are also shown as key communication instruments: the technologies of vision of our past, present and future also define the possibilities and modes of human communication.

Indeed, a way of understanding both communication processes and technologies of vision is in terms of their belonging to the same project of conquering time and space distance – a process characteristic of European modernity. This is powerfully expressed in McLuhan's fantasy of the global village,[18] which connects technological 'progress' with an optimisation of communication opportunities and democracy.

In his book *The Condition of Postmodernity*, David Harvey examines time–space articulations in European systems of representation, scientific discourses and political processes, and proposes 'time–space compression' as one of the defining characteristics of modernity and postmodernity:

> I use the word 'compression' because a strong case can be made that the history of capitalism has been characterised by a speed-up in the pace of life, while so overcoming spatial barriers that the world sometimes seems to collapse inwards upon us ... As space appears to shrink to a 'global village' of telecommunications and a 'spaceship earth' of economic and ecological interdependencies – to use just two familiar and everyday images – and as time horizons shorten to the point where the present is all there is (the world of the schizophrenic), so we have to learn how to cope with an overwhelming sense of compression of our spatial and temporal worlds.[19]

Interestingly, in its very title *Until the End of the World* suggests a coming together of time and space. The 'end' of the world is both a moment (the destruction of the planet, the moment the Indian satellite gets shot down by the Americans) and a place (the antipodes, the final destination in the journey of the characters around the world).

The film launches a humanist critique of the myth of the 'shrinking world': far from bridging the distance between people, or between individuals and their dreams and desires, modern technologies of vision appear to be alienatory and destructive. The film very perceptively foregrounds some of the recurring themes of European modernity starting with the primacy accorded to sight. In a detailed analysis of the role of the senses in different cultures and historical periods, Constance Classen traces a long history of

European obsession with the visual, an obsession that intensifies with modernity.[20] As Classen argues, this preoccupation with vision stretches across a wide field of disciplines, sciences, artistic practices, everyday life[21] and public imagination. *Until the End of the World* equates indirectly but clearly blindness with death as the restoration of Edith Farber's (Jeanne Moreau) vision becomes a life-absorbing quest for her son Sam (William Hurt) and her husband Henry (Max von Sydow).

Equally significant is the fact that the importance of vision is defined negatively, in terms of the tragic consequences of its loss. This kind of negativity is also encountered in the perception of time and space (and even of the world itself), as they can only be perceived at the moment and place of their 'end'. According to Michel Foucault, this is a major (and tragic) paradox of modern European definitions of life. The emergence of secularism and scientific rationalism liberates human beings from the restraints of theology, while at the same time it leaves them unprotected from mortality.[22] Life, Foucault argues, is only understood within the modern discursive regime as non-death – this principle underlies the foundation of the human sciences and conventional medicine[23] and epitomised by anatomy which seeks to discover the secrets of life in the examination of dead bodies.

Henry and Sam try to define the meaning and purpose of their own lives in a similar fashion in terms of a negativity (in fact a double negativity): the removal of blindness. It is worth noting at this point that Max von Sydow's most memorable role is that of the Knight in Ingmar Bergman's *The Seventh Seal* (Sweden, 1956), where he engages Death in a game of chess with his life as the stake. The Knight comes close to defeating Death but he loses in the end, a striking similarity to Henry's ultimately unsuccessful struggle to defeat blindness in *Until the End of the World*.

Henry's scientific project is criticised by the film as a rational but ultimately inadequate way of perceiving life that reduces experience to a series of visual and neurological data. *Until the End of the World* employs a number of strategies to this effect: fragments of dialogue ('the eye does not see the same as the heart'), narrative incidents (Sam losing his sight in the process of recording 'the biochemical event of seeing', Claire's (Solveig Dommartin) addiction to the 'dream-recording machine'), but most powerfully around the character of Edith.

Her relationship to the new technology that will deliver her from blindness is ambiguous. While curious and excited about the possibility of 'seeing again' she also seems to be stoically resigned to the role of the victim assigned to her by her husband. In a highly emotional sequence she rediscovers vision as her brain replays Claire's and Sam's recordings of messages from her relatives. The sadness of the experience outweighs the fascination of seeing people again.

The visual contact with the image of her daughter (the first person she sees) is marked by sentiments of distance, separation and loss, rather than the pleasures of a reunion. The sequence opens with numerous shots of the hectic preparations for the experiment. This immediately attracts attention to the technological apparatus and the processes of control rather than the emotional implications of the event. Furthermore, the actual experience initiates with Edith's oral description of the material components of the image ('Colours. Blue. Yellow. Red. A person sitting by a window. Blue hairband. Yellow dress. She's sitting hands folded'), which is followed by a rather ambiguous moment of recognition ('Can this be our daughter Henry?'). This drives a wedge in the assumed natural, transparent and self-affirming link between the signifier and the signified of the image, and it foregrounds the basic inadequacy and impossibility of the project: capturing the signifier does not entail the reproduction of the experience.

Furthermore, the overwhelmingly sad mood of the sequence can be understood in terms of Roland Barthes' well-known argument that the photographic image is marked by a sense of loss or death, as the presence of the photograph is the ultimate proof of the absence of the person depicted.[24] In this instance, the splitting of the signifier and the signified is caused by the overwhelming reality of life as a continuum and the impossibility to bridge the gap between past and present – in Edith's experience the referent returns with a vengeance. This is further emphasised by the nature of the recorded messages addressed to Edith: they celebrate the technological miracle of the restoration of her vision but they also lament the lack of direct contact with her and emphasise the time that has lapsed; for example, 'This is your granddaughter. You went away before she was born' or 'I wish Sam had found me home in Lisbon – with the kids.'

The voice-over confirms the sadness of the experience: 'Edith Eisner had been eight years old when she lost her sight. The experience of seeing the world again was exhilarating but it was also confusing and disorientating and unpredictably sad. Her childhood friends aged fifty years in a minute; the world they moved in was darker and uglier than she could possibly have imagined. It would have been ungracious for her to mention these things. Her grief was there for those with eyes to see it.'

To the complete incomprehension of her husband, Edith chooses to die rather than live in a world that has now become meaningless to her. Here again we see the equation of sight with life (formulated negatively): as she is not able to choose blindness, she chooses death.

Until the End of the World proceeds to criticise the implications of the obsession with the image and technologies of vision: Henry develops an electronic system of recording and playing back dreams. The Mbantua people abandon the camp and Henry, who is now obsessed with success and fame, continues to work alone until US agents arrest him. Claire and Sam become dream addicts wandering in the narcissistic labyrinth of their own unconscious and lose interest in each other and any desire to live outside the world of images.

At this point the film offers an alternative to the destructive addictiveness of the culture of the simulacrum.[25] Both Sam and Claire are cured, the former through the rituals of the Mbantua people and the latter through reading Gene's story which is at the same time the narrative of the film.

The importance of narrative in a postmodern world obsessed with the image and the visual has been emphasised by cultural theorists and critics. Fredric Jameson's pessimistic diagnosis of a contemporary culture immersed in a perpetual present describes it (in terms that echo the film's critique) as schizophrenic. The term implies the breaking down of the signifying chain and the dislocation of the relationship between signifier and signified which results in a loss of meaning – the dissolution of a continuous temporal structure (a sentence or a story for example) into numerous fragmented instances in which the 'present' emerges 'overwhelmingly vivid and material'. This form of temporality leads, according to Jameson, to an inability to articulate a coherent historical perspective and to temporally arrange lived experience or social life.[26]

Eugene Fitzpatrick, the narrator of the film, expresses a similar conviction in the film as his voice-over explains: 'I didn't know the cure for the disease of images. All I knew was how to write. But I believed in the magic and healing power of words and of stories.' The film clearly implies that Claire is cured precisely because she reads the narrative that Gene has written, a chronicle of Claire's adventures that helps her to get her life in perspective and make sense of it.

Until the End of the World explores the act of storytelling in a variety of ways. It foregrounds the complexity surrounding the role of the enunciator of the story. The narrator is defined as being a character in the story (Eugene Fitzpatrick, the novelist), as performing a function (telling the story of the film) and as a position (from which we make sense of the diegesis). Furthermore, the film problematises the relationship between enunciation and enunciated. When Claire tells Gene that she plans to go to Berlin to look for Sam, her utterance 'I'm going to Berlin' appears on the screen of his voice-sensitive computer. In this way a tension is created and playfully exploited between the moment of action and the moment of narrating the action, between enunciation and enunciated. Later, the collapse of Gene's computer leads to a return to the beginning of the story: 'I'd been trying to write a novel that wouldn't come right ... so as we run before the fatal winds I began again ... I wrote: "1999 was the year the Indian nuclear satellite went out of control ... ."' Finally, *Until the End of the World* introduces a model of 'depth' (again reminiscent of Jameson's critique of postmodernity) whereby storytelling is shown as closer to capturing the richness and complexity of lived experience than the superficial reproduction of the visual data of this experience through technologies of vision.

On the other hand, the nature of Sam's cure from his image addiction relates to Jean-François Lyotard's reappraisal of the function of narrative in postmodern societies.[27] The kind of knowledge that the Mbantua people mobilise in order to cure Sam is described by Lyotard as 'narrative', a term that emphasises the fact that this type of knowledge circulates within society almost exclusively by means of storytelling. Significantly, Lyotard suggests that such knowledge has the effect of maintaining the cohesion of society and it is in this respect radically different from scientific knowledge that develops in relative independence and with little feedback from society.

Until the End of the World, then, offers a comprehensive survey of the role and function of narrative in contemporary culture. At the same time, the film criticises our society's obsession with the visual. This appears to be a paradox, as cinema depends on a combination of the two, on the inter-relationship between audio-visual and narrative modes of representation. Furthermore, it can be argued that the appeal of *Until the End of the World* lies primarily with the audio-visual: not only in terms of the exotic locations, the impressive photography and the beauty of the dream sequences, but also in terms of the carefully selected non-diegetic music (for many the most appealing aspect of the film). It seems that Wenders is trapped within a binarism (surface/depth, image/narrative) that the film fails to resolve. This is not the only binarism that the film relies upon: the old dichotomies mind/body, instinct/science, male/female are all informing the stereotypical technophobia of the film.

EURO-VISIONS

Martin Heidegger and Michel Foucault have identified as a defining characteristic of technologies of vision the unbreakable link between techno-scientific representations of the world and the political project that they help to realise. Heidegger explains how the development of perspectival representation is closely related to a will to objectify and master the world. Heidegger understands the latter as both the 'world around us' and the world in the political and economic sense (the planet and its resources).[28] Foucault, on the other hand, makes specific connections between scientific discourses, technological applications and political practices in his analysis of technologies of vision as systems of maintaining social order and control.[29] Furthermore, as postcolonial criticism has demonstrated, these systems of control are closely connected to the European scientific, political and cultural domination of the world.

Until the End of the World's critique of technologies of vision is restricted to a purely individualistic dimension, as the obsession with the image is blamed for the destruction of European sensitivity. It is only in a humorous and rather tokenistic fashion that the film refers to political implications and possible action – in the final sequence of the film Claire is shown orbiting the planet in a 'Greenspace' satellite 'watching the planet for pollution crimes'.

The film represents the world as a set of attractive and exotic locations that provide a commercially appealing and visually stunning background to the action. The engagement with 'other' cultures is completely superficial as they are often reduced to orientalist stereotypes. While 'depth' is required to re-capture Europe's 'soul', 'surface' is rendered adequate for the representation of Russia, Siberia, China and Japan as the worn out visual clichés demonstrate. Aboriginal and Japanese 'traditional' methods are employed in order to cure the effects of Western technology – yet another binarism that the film mobilises.

The critique of technology offered is not new or original. The film's humanism falls well within the Romantic tradition of European modernity. From Mary Shelley's *Frankenstein* to Fritz Lang's *Metropolis*, and from Daniel Defoe's *Robinson Crusoe* to Sigmund Freud's reading of the Promethean myth,[30] what we witness again and again is Europe's anxiety with technology. This is often represented as human-made technology out of control, threatening the very existence of humans and throwing Renaissance and Enlightenment definitions identity into deep crisis, and is undoubtedly symptomatic of Europe's 'unhappy consciousness', discussed earlier. Importantly, this anxiety (as is clearly the case in *Until the End of the World*) is expressed in an insular, soul-searching manner, without awareness of its own historical perspective and with no will to address its political implications. The film's critique of technologies of vision is structured around sensibilities treated as universal and eternal instead of arising within the specific context of the crisis of European identity and culture.

The anxiety around the power of images is currently particularly intense in Europe. Characteristic of this tendency is the fact that the two most influential critics of the culture of the simulacrum, Jean Baudrillard and Umberto Eco, not only locate this culture outside Europe, but also assume a European position of distance and superiority. 'American intellectuals envy us', claims Baudrillard,[31] while Eco asserts, 'When I am in France or Germany I am not conscious of being European. When I am in the United States I am.'[32]

While Wenders does not seem to make such a blatant statement in *Until the End of the World*, he clearly employs an 'us' and 'them' binarism, which places Europeans in situations where they learn from other cultures in order to cure themselves. The film is about Europeans discovering the cure for the 'disease of the images' and, if we unravel the metaphor, about the future of European cinema. This is particularly significant, because as already discussed, Wim Wenders is an influential personality whose vision of the future of the European film industry is often evoked in debates around cultural policy.[33] If *Until the End of the World* is a model for the European film of the future, a clear 'recipe' emerges – a self-reflexive narrative, supported by impressive photography, a marketable soundtrack and international stars – which offers a balanced combination between anxious European soul-searching and a reaffirming demonstration of global sensitivity.

The suggested remedy nevertheless is vague and contradictory. The rediscovery of the art of storytelling and the respect for other cultures is a banal and empty suggestion which echoes the equally vague analysis of the policy-maker who in a manner reminiscent of *Until the End of the World*, urges the

> ... artist to consider Europe, the necessity for it to protect itself, to be a presence and to have a perception of other cultures which are infinitely richer, but which are denied costly technological means so that other cultures, other stories do not disappear with it.[34]

Ironically, the film's commitment to storytelling is undermined by the fact that the pleasures that it offers have very little to do with the circular and contrived narrative but mainly with the attraction of the images and sounds. The dream sequences, a mixture of film, video and digital technology, are the most memorable and engaging of the whole film. The soundtrack proved to be more successful commercially than the film itself.

Despite its rhetoric then, *Until the End of the World* imagines (and offers a comprehensive example of) a future in which cinema's specificity is lost within a general audio-visual sector of convergent media. Remarkably, this is identical to the view of the (not so distant) future expressed by European policy-making bodies: not only in many recent debates and documents does the term 'audio-visual' replace specific references to cinema but the audio-visual itself becomes part of a broader framework as blueprints for an 'information society'[35] emerge.

NOTES

1. Compagnon, Antoine, 'Mapping the European Mind', in Petrie, Duncan (ed.) *Screening Europe*, London, BFI, 1992, p. 109.
2. Council of Europe, *In from the Margins: A contribution to the debate on culture and development in Europe*, Strasbourg, Council of Europe Publishing, 1997.
3. *European Declaration on Cultural Objectives*. Appendix to Resolution no. 2 of the 4th Conference of European Ministers responsible for Cultural Affairs, Berlin, 23–25 May 1984.
4. Papcke, Sven, 'Who Needs European Identity and What Could It Be?' in Nelson, Brian *et al.* (eds) *The Idea of Europe: Problems of national and transnational identity* New York and Oxford, Berg, 1992, p. 72.
5. Heller, Agnes, 'Europe: An Epilogue?', in Nelson *et al.*, *The Idea of Europe*, p. 23.
6. Compagnon, 'Mapping the European Mind', p. 106.

7. For example, Sohat, Ella and Stam, Robert, *Unthinking Eurocentrism: Multiculturalism and the Media*, London and New York, Routledge, 1994.
8. Compagnon, 'Mapping the European Mind', pp. 110–11.
9. For a distinction between cultural diversity and difference see Bhabha, Homi K, *The Location of Culture*, London and New York, Routledge, 1994.
10. Resolution no. 1 'On the Challenge to Cultural Policy in Our Changing Society', 1st Conference of European Ministers responsible for Cultural Affairs, Oslo, 17 June 1974, as quoted in *40 Years of Cultural Co-Operation: 1954–1994*, Strasbourg, Council of Europe Publishing, 1997.
11. Ibid., pp. 125–38.
12. For a discussion of some of the problems arising see *Specificities and Universality: Problems of Identities*, Strasbourg, Council of Europe Press, 1995.
13. Dyer, Richard, *White*, London and New York, Routledge, 1997.
14. Foucault, Michel, *The Order of Things*, London, Tavistock, 1970, pp. 3–16.
15. See for example Rabasa, Jose, 'Allegories of Atlas', in *Inventing A-M-E-R-I-C-A: Spanish historiography and the formation of Eurocentricism*, Norman and London, University of Oklahoma Press, 1993.
16. Jones, Stan, 'Wenders' *Paris, Texas* and the "European way of seeing"', in Everett, Wendy (ed.) *European Identity in Cinema*, Exeter, Intellect, 1996, pp. 45–52.
17. Ibid.
18. McLuhan, Marshall, *Understanding Media: the extensions of man*, London and New York, Ark Paperworks, 1987.
19. Harvey, David, *The Condition of Postmodernity: An enquiry into the origins of cultural change*, Oxford, Blackwell, 1990, p. 240.
20. Classen, Constance, *Worlds of Sense: Exploring the senses in history and across cultures*, London, Routledge, 1993.
21. For example see Classen's discussion of the changing perception of the role of the rose in the garden, *Worlds of Sense*, pp. 15–36.
22. Foucault, *The Order of Things*.
23. Foucault, *The Order of Things*, and Foucault, Michel, *The Birth of the Clinic*, London, Tavistock, 1973.
24. Barthes, Roland, *Camera Lucida*, London, Flamingo, 1984.
25. Baudrillard, Jean, *Simulations*, New York, Semiotext(e), 1983, and *America*, London, Verso, 1988; see also Eco, Umberto, *Travels in Hyperreality*, London, Pelican, 1987.
26. Jameson, Fredric, 'Postmodernism or the Cultural Logic of Late Capitalism', *New Left Review*, no. 146.
27. Lyotard, Jean-François, *The Postmodern Condition: A report on knowledge*, Manchester, Manchester University Press, 1984.
28. Heidegger, Martin, *The Question Concerning Technology*, New York, Harper and Row, 1977.
29. Foucault, Michel, *Discipline and Punish*, London, Penguin, 1977.
30. Freud, Sigmund, 'The Acquisition and Control of Fire' in *The Origins of Religion*, London, Pelican, 1985.
31. Baudrillard, *America*, p. 79.
32. Eco, Umberto, 'All for One, One for All', *Guardian*, 11 September 1992.
33. Finney, Angus, *The State of European Cinema: A new dose of reality*, London, Cassell, 1996.

34. Carrière, Jean-Claude in *Conflict or Cooperation in European Film and Television*, Manchester, European Institute for the Media, 1992, p. 25.
35. See for instance *European Community Audiovisual Policy*, Luxembourg, Office for Official Publications of the European Communities, 1992; also the *White Paper on Growth, Competitiveness, and Employment*, Brussels, December 1993, and *Europe's Way to the Information Society: An Action Plan*, Brussels, July 1994.

Notes on Contributors

Sean Cubitt is Professor of Screen and Media at the University of Waikato, New Zealand. A well-known art critic and specialist on digital media, he is on the editorial board of *Screen* and *Third Text*. His most recent books are *Digital Aesthetics* (Sage, 1998) and *Simulation and Social Theory* (Sage, 2000).

Robert Duffy is a PhD student and research assistant in Science Communication at Dublin City University. He teaches Computer Science and is a member of the European Network of Science Communication Teachers.

Dimitris Eleftheriotis is Lecturer in Film and Television Studies at the University of Glasgow. A regular contributor to *Screen*, he is currently completing a book entitled *The Popular Cinemas of Europe*.

Peter X Feng is Assistant Professor of English and Women's Studies at the University of Delaware. He has published articles in *Cinema Journal*, *Cineaste*, *Amerasia Journal*, *Jump Cut*, and elsewhere. He is presently completing *Identities in Motion: Asian American Film and Video* and editing an anthology entitled *Screening Asian Americans*.

Kirk W Junker is a Lecturer in Science Communication jointly appointed by The Queen's University of Belfast and Dublin City University. A litigation attorney with the Pennsylvania Department of Environmental Protection, he moved to England to teach at The Open University in Milton Keynes, UK. He is a member of the European Network of Science Communication Teachers and a regular contributor to the journals *Futures* and *Social Epistemology*. His publications include *Science and the Public* (editor, Open University Press, 1998) and *Communicating Science: Professional Contexts* (co-editor, Routledge, 1999).

Sunny Sui-kwong Lam, an expert on intertextual relations between Hong Kong cinema and Japanese comics, has done extensive research on digital design and cinema, and the global development of techno-colonialism. He is currently working on cultural development projects in Hong Kong.

Gregory B Lee is Professor of Chinese at the University of Lyon, France. He formerly taught at the University of Hong Kong. His most recent book is *Chinas Unlimited: Making the Imaginaries of China and Chineseness* (Curzon Press, 2001). He is currently working on the redeployment of Taoist philosophy as a response to postmodernism and globalisation.

Jan Mair was an early member of the Institute of Popular Culture at Manchester Metropolitan University. After a decade of lecturing on Cultural Studies in the Department of Communication and Media Studies at Edge Hill University College, Lancashire, she now divides her time between writing and tutoring, raising her children and running a home for orphan cats.

Nickianne Moody is a principal lecturer in Media and Cultural Studies at Liverpool John Moores University. She is convenor for the Association for Research in Popular Fictions and editor of the ARPF journal *Diegesis*. Her research examines narrative across popular media, representations of plague in recent fiction, and a cultural history of animal welfare in Britain. She has edited collections on Medical Fictions, Consuming for Pleasure and Gendering Library History.

Ziauddin Sardar, writer, cultural critic and broadcaster is Visiting Professor of Postcolonial Studies, Department of Arts Policy and Management, the City University, editor of *Futures* and co-editor of *Third Text*. His most recent books include *Postmodernism and the Other* (Pluto Press, 1998), *Orientalism* (Open University Press, 1999) and *The Consumption of Kuala Lumpur* (Reaktion Books, 2000). A regular contributor to the *New Statesman*, he has also written a number of books in the best-selling *Introducing* series.

Toshiya Ueno is Associate Professor in the Department of Expressive Cultures, Wako University, Tokyo. A well-known critic and media theoretician, he has been involved with the free radio movement in Tokyo since the 1980s and is a sought after DJ of Psychedelic Trance techno music. He is the author of *Situation: The Politics of Rock and Pop* (1996), *The Artificial Nature* (1996), *Thinking Diaspora* (1999) and *Introduction to Cultural Studies* (2000) – all in Japanese.

Christine Wertheim teaches Critical Studies at Goldsmiths College and the Slade School of Fine Art. She is currently working on a book on the function of art in the twenty-first century, entitled *Smeared with an Obscene Vitality: Too Much of Not Enough.*

Index

Adams, Percy 9
Akira 126
Alien 40–1
Allen, Woody 36
Anderson, Benedict 119
Andrews, Major Michael 62
Andromeda 13
anime 94–110
Aristotle 135–6
Away With Words (Sam Tiao Yan) 130

Babylon 5 53, 54
Bacon, Sir Francis 11
Baker, Josephine 44
Bambaata, Africa 99
Barrow, General Robert 61
Barthes, Roland 173
Bataille, Georges 78, 79
Baudrillard, Jean 154, 177
Baudry, Jean-Louis 149–51
Baumann, Zygmunt 94
Bazin, André 27–8
Besson, Luc 12, 18, 19
Better Tomorrow, A 125
Blackadder Goes Forth 29
Black Mask 157
Blade Runner (Ridley Scott) 14, 22, 64, 97
Blavatsky, Madame 18
Bosch, Hieronymous 78, 90
Braidotti, Rosi 108
Brain-Powered 104
Brazil 31
Brooks, Avery 140–1
Book of Wonders, The 8
Boot, Das 56
Borg 74–93
Burke, Kenneth 135–8
Bush, George 46
Butler, Judith 154

Carné, Marcel 30
Caro, Marc 12, 18–33
Casablanca 30
Castoriadis, Cornelius 128
Chan, Jackie 125
Chardin, Pierre Teilhard de 28
Charlemagne 6–9
Cheong, Lawrence Lau Kwok 130
Cheung, Jacky 121, 122
Chomsky, Noam 38
Chong, Marcus 155
Chow, Rey 108
Citizen Kane 23

City of Lost Children 21
Classen, Constance 171–2
Clinton, Bill 34, 37, 38, 45
Clockwork Orange, A (Stanley Kubrick) 88
Cold War 10, 37, 38
Comolli, Jean-Louis and Pierre Narboni
    153
Compagnon, Antoine 167
Council of Europe 164, 167
Courage Under Fire 51, 71
Creed, Barbara 41
Criminal Justice Act 99
Csicsery-Ronay, Istvan 120
Cubitt, Sean 12

Daniken, Erich von 12
Dark City 22
Darwin, Charles 24
Day the Earth Stood Still, The 11–12
DeBont, Jan 149
Deleuze, Gilles and Felix Guattari 107
Delicatessen 18–33
Descartes, René 134, 167
Desert Storm 35, 46
Du Bois, W E B 102, 151
Duffy, Robert 15
Dyer, Richard 168

Eco, Umberto 177
Eleftheriotis, Dimitris 16
Elshtain, Jean Bethke 63
European Union 164

Fatal Attraction 87
Faustus 4
Feng, Peter X 15
Few Good Men, A 51
Fierstein, Harvey 44
Fifth Element, The 14, 19–20
Fiske, John 138
Fist of Legend 156
Flash Gordon 10
Foot, Paul 38
Foucault, Michel 168, 172, 176
Fox Studios 157
    see also Twentieth Century Fox
Fox, Vivica A 43–4
Frankenstein (Mary Shelley) 3, 4, 177
Frazer, J G 19
Freud, Sigmund 24, 78, 91–2, 149, 153,
    167, 177
Full Contact 125
Full Metal Jacket 56

Gaeta, John 158
Gasaraki 104
General's Daughter, The 51, 52
Gibbon, Edward 7
Gibson, William 118–19, 149
Giger, H R 40–1
GI Jane 51, 71
Gill, Tom 99
Gilliam, Terry 31
Gilroy, Paul 102
Ginsberg, Elaine K 156
Goa 100, 103
Godzilla (1953) 126
Goethe 4
Goldblum, Jeff 42
Goldsmith, Oliver 11
Good Will Hunting 29
Gulf War 106

Habermas, Jürgen 26–7
Hall, Stuart 158
Handmaid's Tale, The (Margaret Atwood) 57
Haraway, Donna 108
Hark, Tsui 121
Harvey, David 171
Hayward, Susan 35
Hegel, G W F 101, 167
Heidegger, Martin 176
Heinlein, Robert 70
Heller, Agnes 165–6
Hetherington, Kevin 95
Hitchhiker's Guide to the Galaxy, The 90
Hussein, Saddam 37, 45

Independence Day 11, 16, 34 50
Indiana Jones and the Last Crusade 18
Invaders from Mars 11, 34
Invasion of the Body Snatchers 10, 11, 34
Ishihara, Shintaro 96

Jackson, Michael 153
Jackson, Rosemary 79
Jameson, Fredric 24, 174, 175
Japanimation 94–110
Jeunet, Jean-Pierre 12, 18–33
John of Damascus 8
Johnny Mnemonic 149
Johnson, Dr Samuel 23
Johnson, Paul 37
Jones, Stan 170
Jour se lève, Le 31
Junker, Kirk 15

Kant, Immanuel 20, 25
Kellner, Douglas 35
Keynes, John Maynard 24

Killer, The (John Wu) 125
Kipling, Rudyard 147
Kraftwerk 99
Kublai Khan 10

Lacan, Jacques 84
Laclau, Ernesto 105
Lam, Sunny 15
Lao She 112–13, 131
Larsen, Nella 156
Last Battle, The 19
Latouche, Serge 113–14, 130–1
Lee, Gregory B 15
Lee, Ka-yan 128
Lee, Spike 43
Levi, Antonia 98–9
Li, Jet 157
Lock, Stock and Two Smoking Barrels 30
Logan, Bey 150
Lovelock, J E 20
Luhman, Niklas 26
Lu Xun 113
Lyotard, Jean-François 24, 175

Maffesoli, Michel 94
Mak Tai Kit (Peter Mak) 121
Mallarmé, Stéphane 28
Manderville, Travels of Sir John 8
Marco Polo 10
Marius 31
Marlowe, Christopher 4
Martel, Charles
Marx, Karl 2, 101, 151
M*A*S*H 29
Matrix, The 15, 23, 149–63
Maturana 26
McLuhan, Marshall 94, 171
Mead, Margaret 62
Meniñas, Las (Velasquez) 168
Meredith, George 24
Metropolis 177
Metz, Christian 151
Miami Vice 43
Midnight's Children 134
Millennium 54
Montesquieu 11
Moody, Nickianne 13
More, Sir Thomas 11, 12
Morgan, Glenn 54, 55
Mouffe, Chantal 105
Murdoch, Rupert 157–8
Murphy, Eddie 43
My Own Private Idaho 149

Najita, Tetsuo 123–4
Napier, Susan 126
Nietzsche, Friedrich 81, 90–1

1984 (Michael Radford) 32
Nutter, David 54, 56, 64

One Foot in the Grave 29
Outer Limits, The 1

Pagnol, Marcel 31
Palumbo-Liu, David 158
Panther 156
Papke, Sven 165
Paradise Lost (John Milton) 4
Passing 156
Pauw, Linda Grant de 70
Pearson, Keith Ansell 90–1
Phenomenon 29
Piercy, Marge 90
Piponi, Dan 152
Plato 136, 149
PLUR 103
Pocahontas 147
Police Story 125
Prisoner, The 53
Private Benjamin 71
Purple Rose of Cairo, The 36

Raging Bull 30
Reeves, Keanu 149, 150, 151, 155
Right Stuff, The 74
Robinson Crusoe 177
RoboCop 65
Rogers, Richard 113
Rosner, Ari 155
Roswell, New Mexico 47–8
Rushdie, Salman 134
Rutherford, John 35
Rynning, Roald 156

Sade, Marquis de 78, 79, 89–90
Said, Edward W 111, 115
Sardar, Ziauddin 36, 115, 147
Sartre, Jean-Paul 137
Schama, Simon 19
Seventh Seal, The 172
Shakespeare, William 23
Shane 11
Sievers, Wulfram 18
Smith, Will 42–3, 154
Sobchack, Vivian 63–4, 154
Socrates 136
Some Like It Hot 30
Song of Roland, The 7
Soylent Green 25
Space: Above and Beyond 1, 13, 51–73
Spacked Out (Mo Yan Ga Sai) 130
Speed 150
Spielberg, Steven 18
Stargate SG-1 59
Starship Troopers (Paul Verhoeven) 65–70

Star Trek 4, 9, 13, 52, 53, 54, 138–9
Star Trek: Deep Space Nine 83, 134–48
Star Trek: First Contact 14, 74–93
Star Trek: The Next Generation 89, 139
Star Trek: Voyager 14, 59, 76, 83
Star Wars 9, 16
Steiner, Rudolf 18
Street Fighter II 153, 157
Subway 19
Supernatural Beast City (The Wicked City) 121

Terminator, The 74
Thatcher, Margaret 76, 129
Thirteenth Floor, The 22
Thriller 153
Thomas, Dylan 46
Tiananmen Square massacre 129
Titanic 30
Top Gun 35, 56
Total Recall 14
Turner, Tina 44
Twentieth Century Fox 52
Twin Peaks 53

Ueno, Toshiya 14
Until the End of the World (Wenders) 16, 169–80
Usual Suspects, The 30
Utopia (More) 11

Van Sant, Gus 149
Varela 26
Voltaire 11

War of the Worlds (H G Wells) 47
War of the Worlds (George Pal) 34
Warhol, Andy 77
Waste Land, The 19
Weber, Max 2
Wells, H G 6
Wenders, Wim 16, 169–80
Wertheim, Christine 14
Weston, Jesse L 19
Wicked City, The (Supernatural Beast City) 121
Wilde, Oscar 147
Williams, Teresa K 155
Wong, James 54, 55
Wong Kar-wai 130
Wu, John 125

X Files 12, 47, 53

Yaeger, Chuck 74
Yellow Magic Orchestra 99
Yuen Wo Ping 156, 157